The Inequality Puzzle

Roland Berger · David Grusky · Tobias Raffel
Geoffrey Samuels · Christopher Wimer

The Inequality Puzzle

European and US Leaders Discuss Rising Income Inequality

Springer

Prof. Dr. Roland Berger
Roland Berger Strategy
Consultants GmbH
Mies-van-der-Rohe-Str. 6
80807 Munich
Germany
Roland_Berger@de.rolandberger.com

Prof. David Grusky
Stanford University
Sociology
Serra Mall 450
Stanford, CA 94305
USA
grusky@stanford.edu

Dr. Tobias Raffel
Roland Berger Foundation
Alt-Moabit 101b
10559 Berlin
Germany
Tobias_Raffel@de.rolandberger.com

Geoffrey Samuels
P.O. Box 188
Jamison, PA 18929
USA
gs@geoffreysamuels.com

Christopher Wimer
Stanford University
Institute for Research in the
Social Sciences
MC 2066
Stanford, CA 94305
USA
cwimer@stanford.edu

ISBN 978-3-642-42804-3 ISBN 978-3-642-15804-9 (eBook)
DOI 10.1007/978-3-642-15804-9
Springer Heidelberg Dordrecht London New York

Cover design: WMXDesign GmbH

Printed on acid-free paper

Springer is part of Springer Science+Business Media (www.springer.com)

Preface

Is there too much inequality? We are witnessing for the first time in many decades a vigorous public debate in the United States and many European countries as to whether income inequality is approaching unjustifiable levels. The financial crisis has drawn special attention to remuneration at financial firms, as well as other more broadly based increases in inequality, and the pendulum may well have swung back toward attitudes favoring strengthened regulations.

It is against this background of shifting public and political views about income inequality that the Roland Berger Foundation decided to solicit the opinions of U.S. and European political, business, and labor leaders by partnering with the Stanford Center for the Study of Poverty and Inequality. This initiative, led by a diverse team of five authors, sought to cast light on how prominent European and U.S. leaders are making sense of rising inequality. The objective was not to provide yet another scholarly tome on inequality, or another analysis of how the general public views inequality. We are already awash in such analyses. What we don't know, and what we have sought to offer, is a window into how senior leaders view this historic moment.

In the summer of 2009, we interviewed thirteen political, business, and labor leaders and presented these interviews in their original form. Ten years ago, we doubt that so many prominent leaders would have agreed to discuss issues of income inequality, and their willingness to do so now is an important signal that times have changed. This new orientation also suggests that issues of income inequality deserve a more prominent and constructive place on the contemporary public agenda.

We have framed the thirteen interviews with our own accompanying commentary to introduce the topic of inequality, summarize some of the themes in the interviews, and put forward various remedies. Because we come from different backgrounds, we do not always view the transcripts in the same light, and we have made no effort to paper over our different views. These differences, we believe, are far better exposed. Although we often have real differences of opinion, we also arrive at similar views in ways that may surprise some readers.

This book is no less distinctive in bringing together voices from both sides of the Atlantic. The United States and Europe have historically approached inequality from quite different positions, and it's instructive to learn how such differences play out within the worlds of business, politics, and labor.

We suspect that our readers will agree with us that the conventional wisdom on U.S.-European differences is unduly simple and is not mimicked by the positions of our contributors.

We would like to thank Roland Berger Strategy Consultants for providing the financial support to conduct personal one-hour interviews at locations in Europe and the United States. We would also like to thank the Roland Berger Foundation for initiating and supporting this project and the Stanford Center for the Study of Poverty and Inequality and the Elfenworks Foundation for providing additional support. We are grateful also to Alice Chou for her careful work soliciting some of the interviews, transcribing some of the texts, and assembling the manuscript.

Roland Berger
David B. Grusky
Tobias Raffel
Geoffrey Samuels
Christopher Wimer

July, 2010

Contents

Part 1: Introduction

Is There Too Much Inequality?

David B. Grusky and Christopher Wimer,
Stanford Center for the Study of Poverty and Inequality

Should we be troubled by the recent increase in income inequality? Throughout human history, even quite extreme levels of inequality have tended to be accepted as part of the natural order, indeed "just the way things are." This is not to imply that such acquiescence has ever been so complete as to eliminate *all* opposition. With the Enlightenment, a critical rhetoric of equality emerged in opposition to the civil and legal advantages of the aristocracy, a rhetoric that ultimately provided the intellectual underpinnings of socialism. This egalitarian rhetoric was of course the implicit narrative behind some of the world's most famous revolutions (e.g., the French Revolution, the Russian Revolution). However, such revolutions are rare events that stand out precisely because the larger and dominant tendency is to accept the current regime, even a highly unequal one, as legitimate. The contemporary world is no exception to this general pattern of acquiescence. Although public opinion polls have registered *some* dissatisfaction with the amount of inequality, this dissatisfaction is usually quite muted and, at most, registers as a worry or complaint in conversations with friends, family, or pollsters rather than spontaneous protests in the streets or more organized anti-inequality political movements.

The tendency to accept and even embrace inequality underlies the extraordinary stability of contemporary capitalism. But recent events, most obviously the financial crisis and recession, may bring about a refashioning of the long-standing "social compact" that to date has convinced vast swaths of the population to regard inequality as quite acceptable. This compact, as it is usually understood, holds that high levels of inequality are justified and unproblematic as long as (a) those who come out ahead do so by winning a fair and open competition, and (b) the rest of the population, although by no means rich, can expect to enjoy a comfortable and decent lifestyle as long as they work hard and play by the rules. In all market economies, this type of compact enjoys considerable support, although it is certainly more deeply institutionalized in Anglo-American societies than Continental or Nordic ones.

The question then becomes whether the financial crisis and subsequent recession will make some people less willing to accept or justify inequality

R. Berger et al., *The Inequality Puzzle: European and US Leaders Discuss Rising Income Inequality*, DOI 10.1007/978-3-642-15804-9_1, © Springer-Verlag Berlin Heidelberg 2010

as the outcome of hard work and talent. This typical justification, which is the heart of the social compact, might be undermined in two ways. First and most obviously, insofar as a great many talented and hard-working workers remain unemployed or underemployed during a prolonged recession, it becomes more difficult for them (and perhaps others) to embrace the simple premise that hard work and talent straightforwardly make for success. Second, such widespread duress at the bottom of the class structure, in itself challenging to the compact, has developed amidst highly public revelations that at least some top executives have reaped extraordinary riches despite their firm's poor performance. The presumption that merit earns rewards may therefore come under challenge in light of concerns that neither the unemployed poor or amply compensated rich fully deserve their fate. It may not help in this regard that precisely those who reaped riches at the top are regarded by many as responsible for the economic crisis and the economic difficulties it caused for the less fortunate.

We don't yet know how, if at all, these various developments will affect public views about inequality. It is altogether possible that the vast middle class, or at least that portion of the middle class that feels secure about its economic future, will remain untroubled by these developments. At this very early juncture, it does nevertheless appear that the recession and financial crisis have triggered some public awareness of rising income and wealth inequality, and even outright anger that workers at the top, particularly in the financial and banking sectors, were permitted to reap rewards that may be in excess of what their performance merited. We have accordingly witnessed increasingly strident calls to restrict executive compensation, to tie it more directly to merit or firm performance, and to overhaul tax regimes. In late 2009, when the BBC World Service completed a global poll on a range of economic and inequality topics, approximately 41% of U.S. respondents and 67% of U.K. respondents were in favor of government "doing more to distribute wealth more evenly."[1] It is striking that such strong support could appear in countries that so famously support deregulated capitalism and competitive markets. When the same question was asked in Germany, France, and Italy, the percent of the population favoring more active redistribution was significantly higher (77%, 87%, and 89%, respectively). It also bears noting that some concerns about rising inequality predated the full-blown financial crisis. According to a 2008 FT/Harris poll, three-quarters of adults in the five largest European coun-

---

[1] See http://www.bbc.co.uk/pressoffice/pressreleases/stories/2009/11_november/09/poll.shtml for more details on the survey.

tries and the United States not only regarded the gap between rich and poor as excessive, but additionally expected it to widen over the next five years.[2]

Because we know even less about the views of political, economic, and labor elites, it would be helpful to examine how they have come to understand inequality and what, if anything, should be done to reduce it. Do elites think that the post-war social compact may be weakening and that high levels of inequality will accordingly be regarded as less defensible? Do they view the takeoff in executive compensation as a violation of the social compact? Are they interested in reigning in such compensation? Do they also worry about the growing gap between highly educated and less-educated workers? Is poverty a matter of concern? The purpose of this book is to address such fundamental questions by interviewing a cross-section of some of the world's most powerful business, political, and labor leaders. We wish to open a window into how elites assess inequality in these extraordinary times.

We are not just interested in how elites understand rising inequality but also how, if at all, they propose to reduce it. We have asked them whether there is a role for government in combating possibly excessive levels of inequality, whether some of the more commonly advanced solutions might do more harm than good, and whether new and creative solutions to excessive inequality can be offered. The resulting in-depth interviews provide a platform for those who witnessed firsthand the takeoff in inequality to reflect candidly on where we are and what is to be done. This format makes it possible for them to go beyond the occasional media sound bite and engage instead in more sustained reflections about one of the most prominent developments of our time.

The backdrop to the economic crisis is, of course, an ongoing increase in income inequality in most, but not all, rich countries. Because our contributors make frequent reference to these trends, it is useful to conclude this introductory chapter with a brief summary of the current state of evidence on inequality. We rely on the definitive report *Growing Unequal?* recently published by the Organization for Economic Cooperation and Development (OECD).

---

2 Financial Times/Harris Poll, 2008 (May). "Monthly Opinions of Adults from Five European Countries, China, Japan, and the U.S." http://www.harrisinteractive.com/news/FTHarrisPoll/HI_FinancialTimes_HarrisPoll_May2008.pdf.

We begin, then, by examining the overall level of income inequality within 30 OECD countries. As shown in Figure 1, there's substantial variability across these countries in the extent of income inequality, with of course the Nordic countries, especially Denmark and Sweden, registering the lowest levels of inequality. The middling ranks include such countries as France, Germany, Austria, Canada, and Japan, while the most extreme inequality appears in such countries as Italy, the United States, Turkey, and Mexico. The Gini coefficient, a commonly used indicator of inequality, has been applied in Figure 1,[3] but much the same conclusions would be reached with other measures.

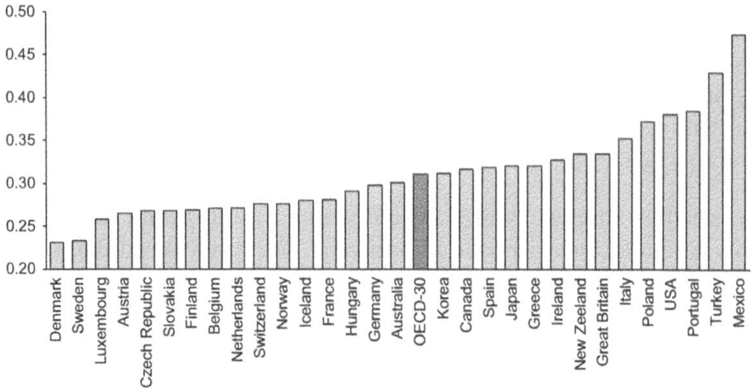

Figure 1: Gini coefficients of income inequality in OECD countries, mid-2000s (Source: OECD income distribution questionnaire)

What about trends in income inequality? In the same report, the OECD observed that income inequality rose at a "moderate but significant" pace, with the data suggesting an average increase across countries of approximately two Gini points in the last 20 years (see Figure 2). Likewise, data from the Luxembourg Income Study,[4] perhaps the best comparative resource on income and inequality in rich countries, show that most countries have experienced at least a modest rise in income inequality at some

---

[3] The Gini coefficient for income measures the dispersion or spread of income across a society. It equals one if a single person holds all of a society's income and equals zero if everyone holds exactly the same amount of income.

[4] The Luxembourg Income Study is a cross-national data archive including income and wealth microdata from a large number of countries at multiple points in time. For further information, see http://www.lisproject.org/.

point since the 1980s, although there are of course important differences across countries in the timing and extent of such change.[5]

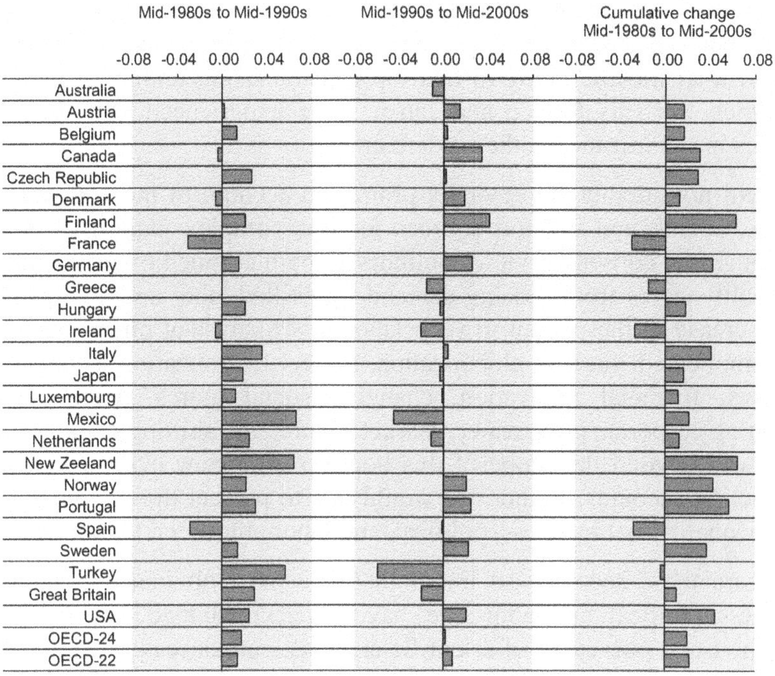

Figure 2: Trends in income inequality: Point changes in the Gini coefficient over different time periods (Source: Computations from OECD income distribution questionnaire)

These overall inequality trends cannot tell us whether certain sectors of the income distribution account for most of the changes when inequality rises or falls. We can better understand why income inequality has risen in cer-

5 Brandolini, A., and T.M. Smeeding, "Patterns of Economic Inequality in Western Democracies: Some Facts on Levels and Trends," *Political Science and Politics* (January 2006), pp. 21-26. According to Brandolini and Smeeding, the U.S. and the U.K. have experienced the largest and most sustained increases in income inequality, while France experienced virtually no increase. The increases in the Netherlands, Sweden, and Finland were more modest than those in the U.S. and the U.K., while the increases in Germany and Canada were even smaller. The careful reader will note that the foregoing results, as reported by Brandolini and Smeeding, don't always accord perfectly with those reported by the OECD (as presented in Figure 2).

tain countries by examining which sectors of the distribution have driven most of the change. For example, in an important set of studies, Thomas Piketty and Emmanuel Saez have shown that much of the recent change in the income distribution of English-speaking countries (the U.S., the U.K., and Canada) has occurred at the very top of the distribution, with the fraction of total income going to that top fraction rising dramatically.[6] Other countries, such as France and Japan, have experienced only minor increases in top incomes in the modern era.

We will not attempt to provide a protracted account of the political, economic, social, and cultural sources for this complex pattern of change. Although the consensus view continues to be that much of the increase in inequality stems from a rising demand for skilled labor and a corresponding increase in the payout to such labor, it's likely that other sources are also implicated, such as globalization, market liberalization, changing tax policies, financial innovation, changing social mores, deunionization, changing corporate governance, market failure, and shifting demographics. It is well beyond the scope of this book to offer new evidence on these competing accounts. Rather, we would like to present the *accounts* of rising inequality that business, political, and labor elites tend to mention.

Why are these accounts so important? The most obvious reason is that business, political, and labor elites have a special vantage point that scholars, the usual purveyors of scientific analysis, cannot readily access. If, in other words, you *really* want to know how executive compensation is generated, it's probably useful to ask those who have observed its workings intimately and on a daily basis. Likewise, if you *really* want to know how the pay of workers is set, it's probably useful to at least ask those who are intimately involved in firm governance. The observations of business, labor, and political leaders can be used in this way to produce a better and more informed understanding of how inequality evolves.

But these accounts are also of interest in their own right. Indeed, even if elites held grossly misleading views on how inequality unfolds, it is still important to understand their views precisely because they are so influen-

---

[6] Piketty, Thomas, and Emmanuel Saez, "Income Inequality in the United States, 1913–1998," *Quarterly Journal of Economics* 118 (2003), pp. 1–39. See also A.B. Atkinson and Thomas Piketty, 2010, *Top Incomes: A Global Perspective*, Oxford: Oxford University Press; A.B. Atkinson and Thomas Piketty, "The Evolution of Top Incomes: A Historical and International Perspective," *American Economic Review* 96 (2006), pp. 200–205.

tial. When regulatory, tax, and other policies are crafted, the opinions of elites tend to be especially influential and carry special weight, thus making it important to understand how elites view inequality and their recommended policies. The simple premise, then, behind this book is that we do well to understand how those who can influence inequality tend to view it. We have set out to provide just such an assessment "from the top" of why there's inequality, why it's increasing, and what, if anything, should be done about it.

In the summer of 2009, the authors conducted in-person interviews with a cross-section of top business and labor leaders in Europe and the United States, the resulting roster including some of the most influential leaders of our time. The interviewees are:

Europe

Josef Ackermann, CEO and Chairman, Deutsche Bank

Bertrand Collomb, Honorary Chairman, Lafarge

Gabriele Galateri di Genola, Chairman, Telecom Italia

Jürgen Hambrecht, Chairman, BASF

Maurice Lévy, Chairman and CEO, Publicis

John Monks, General Secretary, European Trade Union Confederation

Sir Mark Moody-Stuart, Former Chairman, Anglo American; Former Chairman, Shell

Poul Nyrup Rasmussen, President, Party of European Socialists; Former Prime Minister, Denmark

United States

Fred Smith, Chairman, President and CEO, FedEx

John Sweeney, President Emeritus, AFL-CIO

William Weld, Partner, McDermott Will & Emery LLP; Former Governor, Massachusetts

James Wolfensohn, Chairman and CEO, Wolfensohn & Co.; Former President, World Bank

Jerry Yang, Co-Founder and Chief Yahoo, Yahoo!

The centerpiece of the book is our interviews with these thirteen leaders. The transcripts, presented in unexpurgated form, provide a rare and important glimpse into how world leaders consider inequality.

In Part 3 of the book, we summarize the analyses and recommendations, as offered by our thirteen elites, and attempt to distill them into a set of principles. We then return to our central question, "What should be done?" in Part 4 of the book. We do so by contrasting the views of Roland Berger, Founder, Roland Berger Foundation, with those of David Grusky and Christopher Wimer, both U.S. academics within Stanford University's Center for the Study of Poverty and Inequality. The key question here: Will representatives of the business and academic world react similarly or differently to this unique body of evidence? We leave it to our readers to make the final judgment on this matter, but our suspicion is that some may be surprised by the amount of common ground.

Part 2: Interviews

Josef Ackermann
CEO and Chairman, Deutsche Bank

"My personal view is: To regain trust, we in the financial industry have to make sure remuneration is well-deserved and based on proven and solid lasting performance."

Since 2002, Josef Ackermann has been the CEO and Chairman of the Group Executive Committee of Deutsche Bank. Prior to joining Deutsche Bank, Ackermann worked at Schweizerische Kreditanstalt, now Credit Suisse, and in 1993 became President of the Executive Board. In 1996, Ackermann joined the Board of Managing Directors of Deutsche Bank with responsibility for the investment banking division. Under his leadership, the business unit developed into one of Deutsche Bank's principal revenue sources and entered the top tier of global investment banks. He is a member of the Supervisory Board of Siemens (Second Deputy Chairman), a non-executive member of the Board of Directors of Royal Dutch Shell, and a member of the Board of Directors of Zurich Financial Services (Vice Chairman). He also plays an active role, among various other activities, in the Initiative Finanzstandort Deutschland (member of the Initiators' Group), the Institute of International Finance (Chairman), the World Economic Forum (Co-Chairman of the Foundation Board), the St. Gallen Foundation for International Studies (Chairman), and the Metropolitan Opera New York (Advisory Director). Ackermann was recently appointed Visiting Professor in Finance at the London School of Economics, and Honorary Professor at the Johann Wolfgang Goethe University Frankfurt.

R. Berger et al., *The Inequality Puzzle: European and US Leaders Discuss Rising Income Inequality*, DOI 10.1007/978-3-642-15804-9_2, © Springer-Verlag Berlin Heidelberg 2010

Is the level of inequality in Europe and the U.S. about right, or is there too much or too little? What do you think about the current level of inequality?

In order to answer this question one must look at the prevailing socio-economic environment. Before the financial crisis, inequality was probably perceived differently from what it is today, and once we return to stronger and more sustainable growth the perception might change again. In the current socio-economic environment, there seems to be a broad consensus that the present degree of inequality is too high, less in terms of wealth than in terms of compensation. This certainly holds true for the United States, but also to a lesser degree for Europe. Even in the business community, this view is widely shared, especially regarding the financial industry. My personal view is: To regain trust, we in the financial industry have to make sure remuneration is well-deserved and based on proven and solid lasting performance.

You mentioned the financial crisis; do you think the crisis has had an impact on the level of inequality?

To a certain extent, no doubt. The concentration of wealth and income was mainly driven by the financial industry. As a consequence of the financial crisis, remuneration there as well as asset prices have come down, so the trend of increasing overall inequality should have been stopped if not reversed. However: When you are in a stagnant or recessionary environment, when people have to fear job losses or major salary reductions, inequality is perceived much more clearly. Discussions about income distribution and inequality are always more intense in such times.

If we talk about Deutsche Bank and the inequality of pay, would you say that the pay differentials between different levels of employees are just about right or are there aspects you would like to see changed?

It is essential that pay truly reflects performance and provides the right incentives. Deutsche Bank's compensation system has long been among those in the industry with a longer-term orientation. As a consequence of the financial crisis we have improved our system further by establishing a robust governance structure, introducing risk-adjusted metrics, and ensuring a significant proportion of variable compensation is deferred over three to four years and subject to stringent clawbacks. Having said this, the financial industry is very competitive and our people are our talent so we have to be cognizant of the actions of other firms in order to ensure that our pay levels and structures remain competitive.

When you read about inequality, you definitely see that there are positive and negative effects. Do you think a different level of CEO or board remuneration at Deutsche Bank would affect the profitability of the bank?

If you want to grow as a company and create profits you have to have the support of the society in which you are operating, you have to meet the requirements of your shareholders, but also of your other stakeholders. One has to take this into consideration when it comes to compensation at the board level in particular. We at Deutsche Bank are fully aware of this. However, I'm a bit concerned that the regulation of compensation systems might go too far. In the end, pay has to be based on merit, and it has to be competitive. There is a war for talent out there, and we see that some banks are losing good people to non-regulated institutions that do not have to disclose compensation packages. That is why regulation has to be industry-wide in order to avoid competitor distortions.

If you follow data like the Gini coefficient, you will find that inequality measured by this indicator has increased in many, but not in all, OECD countries over the past twenty years. What do you think are the reasons for this trend?

Let me take the financial industry. Today we are recruiting talent globally, in New York, London, Hong Kong, and many other places. This has led to higher compensation levels in many countries which were lagging behind internationally, like Germany. Secondly, public disclosures of compensation have made it possible to compare one's own pay with that of others. That again put upward pressure on compensation levels. Thirdly, for many years, our industry aligned executive pay to shareholders' interests by linking a certain portion of the remuneration package to the company's share price. Until the recent crisis, we had seen significant growth in share prices, which created unprecedented wealth for executives.

With the benefit of hindsight, perhaps there should have been more stringent limits to compensation. This is something that our industry has recognized and dealt with by better aligning compensation to sustainable value creation.

But let's not forget: We operate in a very competitive market, and this market situation as well as the compensation practices of our peer competitors also contributed to the rise in senior executive pay. We have to offer competitive packages to attract and retain the most talented people.

Besides executive and high-level compensation, we are also interested in the pay of rank-and-file employees lower in the organizational hierarchy. Is their pay about right or too low?

I think pay here is broadly appropriate and linked to the position, performance, and also seniority of these colleagues. The current discussion is mostly centered around highly paid people, but these are only a small minority. It is wrong to believe that bonuses in general created bad incentives. For many bank employees, their bonuses plus fixed salaries taken together are not more than the salaries they would receive in other industries.

Turning to wealth, which, according to the data, has also become much more concentrated among fewer people, what are the reasons for this development?

Wealth, in my opinion, has become so concentrated because financial assets have experienced this tremendous rise in prices. If you were invested in financial assets, shares, or real estate, you benefited enormously from the inflation in asset prices we had until the crisis hit. Meanwhile that has been corrected, of course.

What do you think about the future? Will this concentration leading to increasing inequality in terms of income or wealth continue, or will we see a reversing trend?

Remuneration as well as asset prices have come down, or will come down. Political and regulatory pressure will increase, and that will probably lead, on a macro level, to a different trend. But overall, as long as we are operating in a market economy, those who have a higher net worth will benefit when asset prices rise again. Therefore, I would not expect the correction we have seen over the last twelve to eighteen months to continue. On the contrary, we will see certain values recover and that will help wealthy people in creating more wealth, which is already starting to happen.

You noted that pressures to regulate remuneration will likely increase. Do you have any suggestions as to practical, effective, and appropriate regu-

lations? Do you have any cautions about types of regulation that might prove counterproductive and should be avoided?

Basically, in a market economy, companies should be allowed to set remuneration levels and structures at their own discretion, governments should infringe as little as possible on private contracts. Therefore, the regulation of remuneration should be limited to setting a framework. The proposals issued by the Committee of European Banking Supervisors (CEBS) on remuneration in the financial industry provide a good basis for this. Essentially, these proposals define the requirements for transparency, the principles for remuneration structures, as well as the minimum standards for setting up remuneration structures within firms. Establishing such a framework is, in any case, better than to trying to enshrine specific rules, such as absolute pay limits or caps on the tax deductibility of pay. Experience has shown, such mechanisms will only lead to attempts to circumvent them.

Moreover, as far as the financial industry is concerned, there is also a need to differentiate between various functions. Performance-based pay has a different impact depending on whether it is used, for instance, as an incentive to sell retail products, as an incentive in proprietary trading or risk management operations, or at the board level. The key issue here is the extent to which performance-based pay affects the risk situation of the firm.

Finally, it would also be wise to keep regulation limited to broad principles, as there is a need to differentiate between industries. Arguably, there is greater justification for setting rules on remuneration in the financial industry, where – as we have just experienced – there is a greater likelihood of the state having to step in to prevent a systemic crisis than there is in other industries, which are also less likely to receive state assistance at some stage.

Turning to recommendations, what, first of all, should the private sector do? Are there any practical actions the private sector should pursue?

Again, let me speak about my own industry: The financial industry is particularly dependent on trust. For this, transparency is key. Second, we must take a long-term perspective, remuneration must be based on real, bottom-line contributions to earnings, not on revenues, with vesting over several years. I think the more critical part is really to establish some sort of claw-back mechanism in the system such that if people make a lot of money in one year with very risky activities, they do not get the full payout if the company loses money on these activities in the following years. In that sense, compensation should be based on a longer-term analysis of your performance. We also have to avoid paying big bonuses to staff making good profits for the company in a year when shareholders suffer. But that is easier said than done when you have high-performing entities on the one hand and loss-making entities on the other. In the end, the bottom-line should restrict the bonuses you are willing to pay.

Do you also have more general advice about how to design better remuneration systems, how to better align performance and pay? Although mention was made of the excessive "short-termism" of compensation packages, are there other problems to address?

As the Chairman of the IIF, I have been advocating more sustainable remuneration practices with a longer-term orientation for quite some time now. There might be different ways to achieve these goals. For example we could use more risk-adjusted metrics and compensation plans structured accordingly. A lot of companies already have such structures in place, but they need additional fine-tuning and alignment with the risk profiles of the business they are in. More generally, I think that all aspects of a performance cycle should be covered. This means you need short-term pay for performance as well as longer-term pay structures to ensure, and compensate employees for, the company's sustainable success.

If we look at inequality in terms of poverty and limited opportunities for those at the bottom of the income scale, do you think there is anything the private sector should do?

Absolutely. I strongly believe in equality of opportunity and social mobility. If you are a child in a very poor family but very talented, you should be able to go to the best universities and maybe become CEO of Deutsche Bank one day. The feeling is growing, especially in Germany and other European countries, but probably less so in the United States, that people with a modest social background don't have the same opportunities. This is creating a tremendous amount of frustration. Deutsche Bank therefore contributes to making it possible for hundreds of talented people, children from more modest backgrounds, to obtain a university education, and that is something we will be promoting even more going forward. I believe that programs like these make an extremely important contribution to the very fabric of our society.

What can the government do to address the issue of rising inequality?

The government should invest as much as possible in education. This makes a country more competitive on a global scale, but it also gives its citizens the feeling they have opportunities in life. I think there are a lot of talented people who cannot live up to their full potential compared to other people who can, simply because they are brought up in a different environment where they get better input and are more challenged.

It is also important to invest in the very young (from the ages of one to five). And it is also very important to invest in technology – especially information technology, for example, to improve learning skills.

Aside from investing more in education, are there other recommendations for improving education in ways that would increase opportunity?

Money is not everything, you can and should, of course, invest time and talent, for example, in mentoring programs.

Should the government address the issue of inequality, or focus more on the issue of poverty?

Above all, governments should address the subject of equal opportunity. I believe this is key. To some extent, of course, this also means fighting the root causes of poverty, but it is just as important for people to have the feeling that they have the same opportunity to succeed if they are talented. If that is the case, inequality of wealth and income distribution will be much more widely accepted.

What are some practical ways the private sector and the government can work together to bring about more equal opportunities?

To give you an example, at Deutsche Bank we team up with different institutions to foster the financial education of young students to help them to effectively manage their personal finances. People from disadvantaged backgrounds quite often lack the most basic financial skills, which adds to their disadvantages.

Are there any policy recommendations, any actions of the private sector in the U.S., that could serve as a model for Europe?

With its many private foundations, in the U.S. clearly a lot is done to help the disadvantaged. We are learning from this in Europe. On the other hand, the U.S. is presently running the risk of losing some of its former advantages. For example, the country was always very open to talented people, wherever they came from. Meritocracy always played an important role, as it does at Deutsche Bank, where we look for the most talented people, whatever their background, which was very important for our success. But in the U.S., we are now seeing a trend in the opposite direction. For instance, there are restrictions on hiring highly skilled foreigners. If these were allowed to continue, the benefits of meritocracy and diversity would be lost.

Bertrand Collomb
Honorary Chairman, Lafarge

"You like to be CEO for a lot of reasons, maybe for power, maybe because you want to be useful, maybe just because you are a natural leader and you want to lead, I don't think you do it for money, in the typical company. But once you're there, then you won't accept being treated as a second-level guy, so as always, money becomes a status element."

Bertrand Collomb is Honorary Chairman of Lafarge, a worldwide leader in building materials. He has been with Lafarge since leaving the French Ministry of Industry in 1975. Collomb became Chief Executive Officer of Lafarge in 1989 and Chairman in 2003. He is also a director of Total, ATCO, and DuPont, as well as Chairman of the French Institute of International Relations and Chairman of the Institute for Studies in Science and Technology. He is a member of the Governing Body of the European Institute of Technology, the European Corporate Governance Forum, and the Institut de France (Académie des Sciences Morales et Politiques). A graduate of the Ecole Polytechnique and the Ecole des Mines in Paris, he holds a French law degree and a Ph.D. in Management (University of Texas). He also founded the Center for Management Research at the Ecole Polytechnique.

How would you describe economic inequality in North America and Europe?

When I look at the model of the globalized free market economy it has a certain number of drawbacks, or difficulties. But for most of those drawbacks or problems, I can see what the solution could be, and so I am not

R. Berger et al., *The Inequality Puzzle: European and US Leaders Discuss Rising Income Inequality*, DOI 10.1007/978-3-642-15804-9_3, © Springer-Verlag Berlin Heidelberg 2010

uncomfortable even if it's difficult. Inequality is probably one of the drawbacks of our system where I do not really see exactly how we can handle it. I see it personally as the most difficult issue for the social acceptance of our model which otherwise is extremely efficient. I mean, I won't talk here about the excesses in the financial world, because that's also relatively easy to correct if there's a will to do it. Conceptually – and I may be wrong – it's not a big issue for me. The inequality issue is more difficult.

Until four or five years ago, the perception that there was too much inequality in the system was only limited to some circles, let's say continental Europe, some emerging markets, or the anti-globalization, or alternative movement. The Americans were not feeling there was too much inequality and they've always been less sensitive to that than other people. And the British the same, even for New Labour, inequality was not too much of an issue. I would say the French probably were still more sensitive than others to this issue.

What is interesting is that two phenomena have happened. One is the U.S. has joined the fray. I was interested and surprised, with a certain amount of irony, when I heard and saw Larry Summers at the centennial celebration of Harvard Business School denouncing with almost a revolutionary tone that 1% of the richer American was getting 25% of the national income, which was about the rate in the 1920s and two-and-a-half times what it was in the seventies. So while the richest 1% was getting 10% in the seventies, it had now moved to 25%, which was about the same amount as in the twenties. The same Larry Summers, I remember clearly in discussion a few years earlier at Davos, was absolutely not uncomfortable about most aspects of our economic system. When I was trying to question some of its aspects, he was defending it. So this is a new phenomenon.

The other new thing, of course, is that this inequality debate has focused on executive compensation, which is a part of inequality which is easier to see and probably that people find easier to handle. In the past, in the thirties, for example, in France, the debate was about the "hundred families," the hundred richest families. So it was heritage money which was supposed to be the most unequal and the worst. Now in the debate on executive compensation, if you own your company, nobody is blaming you for being extremely rich. But if you just are a manager, then people are shocked by the fact that as a manager you can make so much more than they do, which is a complete reversal. There was a time, not so long ago in France, thirty years ago, inherited money was bad, money made by your work was good. Now it's reversed, which is very intriguing.

I have a friend and a classmate who is a philosopher, an engineer turned philosopher. His name is Jean-Pierre Dupuy, he is a professor both at Ecole Polytechnique in Paris and at Stanford, and he wrote a book about the importance of the sacred, what is called "le sacré" in French, I don't know how to translate it. He says there are things which are not of an economic nature, they are of a symbolic nature, not symbolic, he says "sacred." He had a chapter on inequality, and says economic inequality is not economic anymore. It's being seen as a matter of social symbol, or social rule, and people are reacting to it in a non-rational way.

My own feeling is that I've not been very comfortable with this increase of inequalities. I have the traditional European view, which is that too much inequality is not good. At the same time, I've understood why it happened, and my feeling is that it's very difficult to curb it in a way which is not economically totally inefficient. So that's maybe what the issue is.

For me, executive compensation is only a tiny piece of a larger problem, but of course is focusing a lot of attention now. The reason why there is rising inequality in our system is clear. In a free system, and a free global system, there are large differences in what you may call either "the contribution of people to value creation" if you are defending the system, or "the ability of people to capture part of value creation" if you are more critical. But anyway, this capability is much more different between individuals, or different situations or different countries, because you have the same issue between different countries.

If you are in a position to contribute a lot, or you can capture a lot, you get much more than other people. Traditionally, the Social Democrat's answer to that, or the communist, socialist answer to that was to have a state-controlled system which would reduce, suppress that. The Social Democrat route was to redistribute through tax, and what happened in Europe in the fifties, especially in the U.K., at the time of old Labour, showed the limits of redistribution through tax, because it was clearly killing economic initiative. It was indeed killing a lot of initiative when you had a marginal tax rate of 70% like in Sweden, or even more in the U.K. at the time. In the seventies, when I was a young Ph.D. student in the U.S., I remember my fellow British students were saying they didn't want to work in the U.K. at any price!

So too much redistribution through tax is killing the generation of economic value. And when people can move around, then you cannot tax them significantly more than the average worldwide tax rate, or even much more than what the acceptable tax havens would do. So that doesn't work anymore.

Do we have other means to reduce inequality? If redistribution doesn't work, can you reduce inequality at the source of revenue? Social consensus, maybe? If it's not acceptable, or if it's considered to be excessive to make too much money, will inequality be curbed? I am not sure, in a free market economy you can control the phenomenon. Take the traders, for example. I've had some discussions with my colleagues in the financial sector about the traders. I asked them why they pay the traders so much. I have a lot of very good engineers in my plants. I never had the idea that I should pay them a percentage of the profits that the plant is making. What's so different with your traders? They tell me that a good trader is really different from a not-so-good trader. And if the traders leave, they take their ability to make money with them and they will make money with a competitor. When one of my engineers leaves, if he doesn't have the plant, technical equipment, etc., if he makes more money with me than the competition, I mean, if he creates more value from me than the competition, if he leaves, it doesn't mean that going to another plant he will have the same money creation potential. So there is a rationale for paying the trader a lot. I don't know how much the answer I received is true or not. It's probably true to some extent, it's probably exaggerated to some extent.

But anybody who can be paid at a commission rate is going to make lots of money over time, and any company that has been paying its salesmen on a commission rate knows that after a while, if the business grows, then you have to reset the counter because then your sales people get over-paid. So I don't see in that context how you can have a limitation of remuneration for salary people at the source. And for financial guys, you can probably make it a little more difficult to make money by reducing leverage, or reducing opportunities to do things. If you reduce innovation, if you limit the number of financial opportunities, you will probably reduce a number of opportunities to make a lot of money. The bankers in our world have always made the most money, even in the 19th century, even in France. Look at the museums, which were formerly the private homes of bankers who were making much more money than anybody else.

Until now, my conclusion had been that – but that was before the financial crisis, so that was when there was no consensus, the Americans, the Europeans had a different approach – my conclusion was that there was no way you could limit inequality, meaning the capability of some people to make much more money than others. But what you could work at was to try to make that inequality as fluid as possible, so that it would be an inequality of the current situation, but not written in stone forever, so that people would have opportunities, or could think they have opportunities, to go up on the ladder. Historically in the U.S. the relative indifference to inequality has been due to the fact that everyone believes that they can be on the winning side, the American Dream. So I was kind of a little bit thinking that what we can focus on is to give everybody the best chance to develop his own value creation potential and accept the fact that the range of remuneration or income or wealth would be still greater than it was in the fifties.

But now this seems to have become unacceptable even in the U.S., or at least it was said to be unacceptable by the Democrats in the Obama campaign. It's not sure by any means that will lead to a significant change. Obama will probably increase taxes, not for inequality reasons, but because he will be obliged to for budget reasons. There is a little bit of a window that they can use without going too high. The marginal Federal tax rate is now at 39%, it can probably go to 42, 43, or 45. 45 plus the average state income tax would be about 50. If your marginal income tax rate doesn't go above 50% altogether, it's probably acceptable in terms of economic value creation. People will not probably leave the country because they're taxed at 50 and they could be taxed at 40 somewhere else. But if you go to 70 or 80, clearly they will leave. And if you go to 50% total, which means 45 federal, that doesn't give you a lot of potential for redistribution if the system still creates a lot of inequality at the source of income. So I don't know whether that will solve the problem.

How do you view executive compensation?

The current focus on executive compensation is not totally logical. The main reason why people focus on it is because it is known, public, and probably because they don't understand why there should be so much difference between the boss and the rest of the people in the company. On that, I agree with them. I don't understand why the boss should have a remuneration so completely out of line. Personally I believe there is probably an ethical problem when you see a CEO who's paid ten times more than the number two, and I can understand the negative reaction. In a situation where the whole scale of salaries has been extended, but in a reasonable way, which means if the CEO is within an acceptable system, like maybe twice the number two, something like that, even three times if you add long-term incentives, I would consider that as acceptable. I think that people would probably accept that better.

That's the first reason why the current situation is seen as unacceptable. It is probably also the reason why people are not so sensitive to the case of owner-managers, because then you are a different type, you cannot be compared with the managers.

Actually you have to take into account the reaction of three different categories: public opinion, shareholders, and the managers themselves. Public opinion is not aware of the real scale of inequality of income which exists and is shocked when it sees the numbers which are being publicized. We knew that in France, and that's one of the reasons we were not so keen on disclosing executive compensation ten, fifteen years ago. I remember there was a poll asking people how much their boss was making, at the time the figures were not public. Even though the compensation was not at all then at the current levels, the answers were about one-tenth of the real number. Because somebody who makes a thousand euros a month cannot imagine that anyone would make more than ten thousand. Of course they could imagine even less that an investment banker would make ten million, but they don't know it, it's not public. The only thing they know, other than executive compensation, is the compensation of the football players, sometimes the movie actors.

Some executives defend themselves by saying they are making less than a football player. But that's absolutely not acceptable because football players are considered to be extraordinary people. Even if the average football player among five hundred football players may not really be an extraordinary guy, they are considered to be people who have a special talent. Managers are not considered to have a special talent, for some reason, because they are not seen as different. If you are the number two of a big company and you become number one, so what? Especially political people do not recognize the exceptional value of the CEOs! In France it's even worse because some of the CEOs have been in civil service when they were young, so the public sees them as improved civil servants, and they don't see that they would be different. That's the perception of public opinion.

Now shareholders, at least in the old paradigm, were not so concerned about executives making too much money, as long as they were making a lot of money for the shareholders as well. In the seventies economists and financial people thought the managers were taking too much care of the company as a nice place where you can manage, live in harmony with the unions, and were not defending enough the interests of shareholders. The shareholders decided collectively, through the thinking of some economists, that the managers should be incentivized by giving them a big chunk of the value that was going to be created for shareholders. I believe it was done on purpose from the shareholders' side, and it clearly worked, for better or worse. CEOs or executives are now much more conscious of stock price and value creation for the shareholders. It worked for the best when it worked to build a good company which is creating value for shareholders over time. It worked for the worst when it came to a company clever enough to do window dressing and get the stock price to a high level so that the boss can exercise his options and bail out. But the shareholders can do the same. So, in the worst case, the CEO's interests are aligned with the interests of the short-term shareholders, and of the long-term shareholders in the best case.

The shareholders are reacting mainly against excesses where compensation is not linked to performance. Public opinion is also sensitive to those situations, but reacts also to absolute levels. At least in France, public opinion finds absolute levels too high. And even if you are very good and if your company is doing very well, they find it is too high. The shareholders understand better the situations in which companies and boards can find themselves. Institutional investors will understand, for example, that you pay something to get rid of a guy who is not good enough to keep, but not bad enough to just say: "Goodbye, fire him," and not give him anything.

I lived through an interesting case, when I was on the Board of Vivendi after Messier. He had a contract giving him ten million dollars in case of departure, which obviously had not gone through required Board approvals, so was not legally really established. There was an arbitration with American arbitrators judging according to French law. French law says if a contract is irregular, it's not void automatically, but it can be voided if it is detrimental to the interests of the company. And the arbitrators said that it was not detrimental to the interests of the company to pay ten million to get rid of Messier, because otherwise the company would have been bankrupt! So Messier was going to have his ten million, but the Vivendi Board decided not to pay anyway and the SEC forced Messier to give it up in a settlement.

Another case arises if you ask somebody to take over a company which is in extremely bad shape. To lure him out of a good job, you may have to give him the guarantee that even if he doesn't fully succeed, you will have to give him something. The shareholders can understand that, but public opinion doesn't, and call it a bonus for failure, when it's actually a bonus for not achieving as much as we would have liked.

If I look at the view of the executives, they live in an unequal world and they've seen inequality rising. They know what public opinion doesn't know, that their investment banker is making millions, that their lawyer is making millions, that the fund managers are making millions. They generally work in a world where their Brazilian partner belongs to a very wealthy Brazilian family. When they are French, they see their American colleagues making ten times what they are making, etc., etc. So they don't feel rich and they don't feel over-paid. They feel that given the amount of responsibility they have, it's not abnormal to be among the people who have a high compensation, not necessarily the highest, because a lot of people are paid more, but in that league. So I feel many mistakes made in executive compensation are rooted in the feeling that they don't feel over-paid by comparison. I believe they are sometimes over-paid if they compare themselves to the rest of the company, but very few companies have the principle of comparing the compensation of the CEO with the compensation of the rest of the company.

I know only one company, DuPont, which has a so-called "equity principle," saying that the CEO will not be paid more than x times the next level. In Lafarge that was not written in a policy, but it was clearly a principle that we had in mind. But even DuPont was obliged to increase the ratio. I think originally the ratio was twice, and after some time it was too much out of sync with the market and had to be increased to three times.

At Lafarge also the ratio changed over the years with the changes in compensation structure. Initially, when I started as a CEO, the fixed salary of my direct report would be set at 60% of mine. Then we increased the bonus rate, and the maximum bonus rate initially was the same for both levels. You'd have up to 100% of your fixed salary, so the ratio was still the same. Then under pressure from my compensation committee who said, no, no, you're not in the market, my bonus maximum increased. It went to 160% for the CEO, and only 120% at the next level. The gap increased with the stock options, where it was three times. So because the company and the market were doing well, stock options generated more than anticipated, and, clearly, the ratio increased. But in our case, we did not like it too much and were always trailing the market.

In my career, I've been chairman or member of compensation committees of several companies, and in every company I've been in, it was not the CEO who was pushing his compensation up, it was the compensation committee. Probably because I have been associated with companies which have a certain type of culture, a certain profile. Whether I was at Unilever, Total, Dupont, Lafarge, the CEO was always thinking about this balance with the rest of the company and the compensation committee was saying, look at the benchmark, look at what Towers Perrins is telling us, we have to bring you up. Their feeling – which I shared as a director – was that their responsibility to the company was to deliver enough compensation to the CEO, even though nobody was thinking that the CEO would leave the company if he wasn't paid enough. I don't know whether it was a feeling of justice, or part of the standing of the company, but if you are

CEO of this company, you should be paid normally, or else something is wrong!

What if compensation had not been transparent?

I think it was the same, in the French case, it was already the same when it was not public. Because even when it was not public, we had the benchmarks. Now the publicity initially probably made it worse, reinforced the idea that you had to keep up with the Joneses. But I'm not sure it changed a lot, because even before it was public, we had the benchmarks and the argument, taking the case of Lafarge: "You are the 27th largest company in the CAC 40, and your salary is only the fiftieth, it doesn't work."

Is the compensation committee concerned about ratio with the average worker?

No, never. It's the union people who are expressing the CEO salary in centuries of minimum wage. I found that a magnificent communication idea, the first time somebody said the CEO was paid two centuries of average worker's wages.

There is one CEO in France, Louis Gallois, who was associated with the Socialist government initially, was then the head of SNCF, the French railroad company. Because it is a state-owned company, he had fairly low-level pay. When he was appointed CEO of EADS, he refused to have a salary within the range of other CEOs and he refused to have any stock options. But of course it's much easier to do that if you come from a lower salary because you're not intoxicated. For myself, I was a little bit like the frog which is in the water when you increase the temperature slowly. The frog gets boiled because it doesn't have the idea of jumping out of the water. When you put the frog in boiling water, it jumps immediately. In my experience, I had a remuneration package rather below market; it increased considerably with the market, but I adjusted my spending to that. I'm not active CEO anymore, but if I was, and if people would tell me, you are a humanistic manager, you are a Christian, you should reduce your salary by half, my wife would tell me: but we have this house there, we are used to doing that, how are we going to do it? Of course, we are not talking about the level of U.S. financial people who have made hundreds of millions, and who can only spend a tiny part of their income. We manage to spend most of it!

Another factor which is very important for CEOs is the style of life that they are used to because of the style of people they meet. If you go to New York, you're supposed to be in the best hotels, which is not at all what, initially, I would have done as a private person. But then when you have done it for ten years, you cannot imagine doing otherwise. I'm not talking about big private planes, because that's a contentious issue and I find it really unacceptable to see people crossing the Atlantic alone on private planes costing tens of millions of dollars. Because it's not functionally really necessary. If you are in a very special period where minutes count, I can understand. But on a regular basis, it's not reasonable.

How has the financial crisis made a difference?

It has made a difference in the perception of inequality, and in the fact that for the first time in the U.S. there has been some general discussion about the issue. Also that compensation of the financial sector has been pinpointed as one of the reasons why the financial crisis happened, rightly or wrongly. I don't think it would have changed very much if the compensation system had been different, but that's another story. But it certainly increased the incentive to make a lot of money quickly and to underestimate risk. So for those two reasons I think it's more on the agenda than it was before.

And is that true for Europe?

It's true for Europe, where the perception of inequality in general is more negative. Actually, when in France we hear more about executive compensation, I am not sure if it is about the issue itself or about inequality. We also have a controversy about our tax system. In addition to a fairly high income tax, we have had a wealth tax, since Mitterrand in 1981, which was ended by Chirac in '86. Chirac lost the subsequent presidential election, and still thinks he lost because he had abolished the wealth tax. It was put back by the Socialists, and it has a significant impact, because the rate goes to 2% of the real market value of your assets – not the historical value like in Germany. Now even Sarkozy doesn't dare to get rid of it, because it is popular, even though it led lots of people to go and live abroad.

To mitigate the issue, Sarkozy has created a "bouclier fiscal" a fiscal shield, by virtue of which nobody should be paying in total taxes more than half of his total income – in a broad definition including all tax-exempt income. Even that is highly contested by the left, by the unions, and probably by a majority of public opinion. This shows how sensitive the French are about inequality of income.

What about the public's view toward CEOs who are seen largely as caretakers?

If you look at successful CEOs, those who have been over ten years in the job, there are not many who may be called caretakers, at least when I look around. Recently I was chatting with journalists and with the chairman and CEO of Eiffage, Jean-Louis Roverato. He was recalling the time when he took that company as a spin-off of a big group, and it was a pretty tiny company with very limited business. Fifteen, twenty years later, it's a completely different company. But I think in the public perception, if you are heading a big company, and if you're not an owner, if you are a manager, you're not taking any risk, you are a caretaker. It may be true sometimes, but it is not true most of the times. There is as much risk-taking and as much stress in leading a big company nowadays as in being a private entrepreneur, and maybe more!

Could you please discuss accountability when there is diffuse share ownership?

In those companies the responsibility of the CEO is enormous. When you have some identified major shareholders, you are not alone to decide what to do, you need agreement by the shareholders. When share ownership is diffuse, you have almost the same responsibility as if you owned the company, except it is not your own money. Of course you are accountable to a board, who represents the shareholders. But we all know that the board ultimately works well only if the CEO wants it to work. So, to a certain extent the CEO has to organize his own accountability.

A lot of people believe that the small entrepreneur takes much more risk than the boss of a large company, because he puts his money at risk, and he can lose everything if he makes the wrong decision. But actually the CEO of an established company has a lot at risk too: not only his financial situation, but more importantly his reputation, his feeling of achievement. By experience, I can say that it does not feel like a comfortable, assured position!

How do you see inequality trends evolving?

I believe the level of inequality that has developed over the last twenty years is probably excessive. This is true in western countries like the U.S. or Europe, but even more in emerging countries. It is also true between countries, with the poorest countries being unable – more for social reasons than economic reasons – to catch up with economic development.

At the same time we had a period where economic growth has been remarkable, and where most people, and most countries, have improved their situation somewhat. But there has been too much difference between the different groups, or the different countries.

What will happen now? There will probably be a little more redistribution through higher taxes – they will be needed anyway to deal with high budget deficits! Will there be a reduction of the amounts paid before tax? I am not really sure.

There will probably be some social consensus for reducing a little bit, and there may be some financial regulation. Because all that starts from the financial world. If the financial world was not generating extremely high compensation, the CEOs of companies which are not financial would not have the idea of such extreme levels. But I don't know exactly how much it will be moderated. Will we go back to the level of the eighties? I'm not quite sure.

What would you recommend?

If there is more financial regulation, that means that the opportunity to make extra gains by things that you can invent and do very quickly before the others is going to be smaller. I think it's necessary not for the compensation issue, not for inequality issue, it's necessary for stability issues, to get a little more stability in the system, or less instability in the system. But it will probably have at the same time some impact on reducing inequality opportunities. Then it's likely that the industry habits may evolve a little bit, even though I'm not completely sure, because we see Wall Street starting to say, well, you don't like bonuses, so I'll double the fixed salary of my people. I believe we'll probably have a vote of shareholders on compensation policy one way or the other, which will have a certain impact, not a drastic impact. But that means that before you increase, you have to discuss with shareholders, etc.

I think executive compensation is only a consequence of inequality in general. I think more discipline in the financial world is probably useful, because it is generating the highest inequalities, I would say. On tax levels, we may also go back to the higher estate taxes we had in the U.S., for example. There'll be a little bit of tax increase, clearly. It's always difficult to ask a business person to recommend a higher tax level, so I'm not sure I would recommend it, but I think it will happen and I won't fight against it in the U.S. In France, I would fight it because we are already at a level which is too high.

I guess things which are being done against tax havens are going to improve the inequality situation. Things which are being done against corruption are going to improve the inequality situation. But if we have again a growing economy, if we have a lively economy, there will be still a lot of opportunities to make a lot of money by having a good idea and developing it. I don't think we want to hinder that. So I don't believe we'll go back to the fifties, because in the fifties there were much less opportunities for people to make a difference, and that was not good. Because the systems were much more rigid, social, financial, and the technological development was not so strong.

I don't think in the fifties you could develop Google or Microsoft in ten or fifteen years like they did, because a lot of countries were socialist, because if you had a product you couldn't sell it worldwide, because communication was not developed to the point where in six months you can sell a product through the Internet all over the world. Which is why there are more opportunities for somebody who has an excellent idea to make a lot more money in the short term. But of course if we have less instability in the systems, it will also reduce a little bit the opportunity to make money on that volatility.

Speaking about innovation and entrepreneurship, I still remember how, at the time of the Internet bubble, I was shocked by my conversation, over lunch, with the head of corporate finance in a big investment bank in New York, while we were talking about start-ups. He said, oh, start-ups, the main issue is to know exactly when to bail out! Obviously that was true, but that was shocking to me, because I still had the philosophy of the entrepreneur who starts something to develop it as a successful company, not to choose the right time to bail out. And a few years later an art dealer in New York was telling me that many of his customers were precisely those whom I would describe as false entrepreneurs who started a start-up based on an idea, didn't care whether the idea was eventually going to materialize in a business or not, bailed out at the right time, sold it for very much money, and then were able to spend it at art auctions in New York.

It is true that if you have a little bit more order in the world, that will reduce the opportunities to create unequal situations. But hopefully not too much, or else the real opportunities to make legitimate money will be constrained as well. So that's why I'm not comfortable with this inequality issue, because I don't think there's a good solution.

What would you recommend for executive compensation?

I think executive compensation has to be more streamlined in terms of process, and we need some type of "say on pay" for the shareholders. What I would like is to go back to the situation where the CEO is not paid ten times, fifteen times the number two of the company. I think the range of remuneration within the company will probably remain open, because that's part of the overall inequality system, but to treat the CEO as a special case outside of a normal compensation scheme has always shocked me. But again, it will depend very much on the financial system, because if the traders continue to be paid at an extremely high level, that justifies paying the CEO at a high level too. Then if the bank CEO is paid at a very high level, why not the cement company CEO, etc. So it's interesting to watch what is going to happen in the financial industry. I have heard some financial executives very happy to have the opportunity to rein in the remuneration system of their own people, but in the next minute saying they will not be able to do it because of competition!

I don't see legislation coming, especially in the U.S. I'm not sure that there will be a complete overhaul of the system because the system makes sense. If we take the three components of compensation, fixed salary, variable compensation, and a long-term incentive they make some sense – even if we should not forget that bonuses developed because the U.S. Congress made fixed salary higher than a million dollars non-deductible! We'll probably see the performance criteria of stock options, the performance criteria of restricted stock a little bit tougher. And if the market is not as good as it was during the last twenty years, that will lead to a level of gain which will be more acceptable.

My personal thinking is that each time one of the components of remuneration becomes out of line with the others, it leads to excess. So stock options are fine, and they are good, not only for management, not only for the CEO, but for a lot of people in the company, because they lead them to share the objective of increasing the stock price. But they should be dimensioned in such a way that in case of a successful company – let's say a stock increasing 10% per year and doubling its value in seven years – the option gain should not be more than twice or three times the fixed salary level, but not one hundred times, not even twenty times. And I am not saying the Black-Sholes value of the option, which is meaningless, but the real gain on the options!

And for the bonus, I was very happy when the maximum bonus potential was 100% of the fixed, maybe 150%. But when I see people having uncapped bonuses, which can reach three, four, five times the fixed, that's too much, I think everything is a matter of measure, of balance. However, I'm not quite sure the average level will decrease dramatically. It will probably increase much less than it has in the past, even may be frozen for some time, but as soon as the good years come back, I would imagine that there will be pressure to raise the level.

Is there a level the public won't accept?

I think it will depend on the overall political, social situation. Again I don't think executive compensation is the real problem, the real problem is overall inequality. If, as I imagine, a little more organized or regulated system reduces the opportunities for too much inequality, if the tax system is catching a little more of the high-level income, there could be some limited reduction. The highest 1% was getting 25% of the global income in 2006 or 2007, versus 10% in the seventies. We may go back to 15%, 20%. But the public feelings do not always reflect the statistics. Will we still have in our countries a significant part of the population which is undereducated, underskilled, and being paid at the level influenced by the competition from the emerging markets' workforce, or are we going to get better skills in our population? I go back to my initial answer to inequality, which is social mobility. If we were able to develop social mobility, it would make inequality more acceptable.

The problem is we've had more inequality and less social mobility, at least that's the feeling people have in France. Even in the U.S., I'm not sure that the blue-collar worker feels he has the potential for social mobility. Probably less now than before, because they are disenfranchised from the rest of the country. You have pockets in the U.S. of people who are living by their own standards, the skill level of the blue-collar labor force is not very good.

At the same time, it is true that the feeling of the lack of social mobility is much stronger here in Europe than it is in the U.S. And we see that in our universities here, or our *grandes écoles*, the percentage of people originating from the lower social quartile has reduced significantly in the last twenty, thirty years. Of course one of the reasons is that the quartile in question is not made of the same people. There are more immigrants in the lower quartile, and more people who are not benefiting from the education system, because the system fails, they go to school, but they don't get really educated. So I think that, as we cannot solve completely the inequality issue, addressing social mobility and social discrimination, notably through education, is absolutely necessary.

Why were large financial incentives not needed several decades ago?

Everything is relative. At least in France, in the fifties, the big men were the civil servants and the political people who don't get paid very much. So if you were the CEO of a company, if you were paid more than the top civil servants, you considered that you were paid very much. I remember in the sixties, the people who were making money were the small business people, the great doctors, medicine professors, and the great lawyers. These were the professions where you could really make money. Not so much the bankers at the time, because the banks were nationalized.

Now things have changed, and business people – at least until recently – had a much better standing. The money has come with it, even though people are not working only for money. You could pay the CEO ten times less, he would still do his job, provided no peer was paid more. You don't do that job for money. Whether a trader does his job for money, I don't know, I've never been a trader. So I don't know if these people do to job for excitement rather than money. The excitement is so extreme, destructive sometimes, maybe the money is the true motive, I don't know.

But you like to be CEO for a lot of reasons, maybe for power, maybe because you want to be useful, maybe just because you are a natural leader and you want to lead, I don't think you do it for money, in the typical company. But once you're there, then you won't accept being treated as a second-level guy, so as always, money becomes a status element.

I remember when I was in the U.S., as CEO of our U.S. company. It was listed on the New York Stock Exchange, so my salary was public. At the time, the French salaries were not public. We were among the Fortune 500, so my salary was listed in *Business Week*. There was my picture and my salary was not very high because, within Lafarge, I was paid as an executive, number four or five of the group. And in addition, I had only been there for nine months, so the number was even lower. When my daughter was shown *Business Week* by one of her school friends she asked me: "Dad, why are you paid at such a miserably low level?" So you understand how it works! And we always had a problem that the CEO of the U.S. subsidiary wanted to be paid more than the CEO of the Group!

That being said, I'm surprised to see how American compensation committees are so protective of the system and always fear they are not going to have the best people if they don't pay them at the best level, etc. The belief is strong that there is a market and good people need to be paid, and if we are not paying well, we won't get good people. What I'm telling you, not very many CEOs at that level are working for money. But I could never say that at an American Board!

I remember, almost ten years ago I was asked to write a foreword for the French translation of a book on human resources by Harvard Business School professors. I was slightly worried, so I asked to see the book before accepting to write the foreword. I was very surprised. We were in the middle of the excitement about shareholder value, financial motivations, etc., and they were writing things like that people were working not for money only, that things were not as simple, that people are not unidimensional. All the good old things that we've known for a long time, but that were getting forgotten. So I was happy to write the foreword to that book. There was such a discrepancy between what they were saying about the way a company works, and the image of a company devoted purely to building shareholder value, and making sure everybody was in line through appropriate monetary, financial incentives. It was striking.

But to answer your question more appropriately, some theoretical economists were not happy about that complexity of management motives. They wanted management to be concerned only about shareholder value, and they advocated the systems of financial incentives, which developed so well that they created the current situation.

Gabriele Galateri di Genola
Chairman, Telecom Italia

"The world has survived ages of tragedies and disasters and of confidence and development, because every action produces a reaction that tends to stabilize or recreate equilibrium. So even in this field I think that what has happened will create a better equilibrium in terms of speculation and remunerations, and more generally in terms of diminishing inequalities."

Since December 2007, Gabriele Galateri di Genola has been Chairman of Telecom Italia, Italy's largest telecommunications company whose operations span Europe, Brazil and several other South American countries. Galateri received his MBA from Columbia University and joined the Banco di Roma initially as Head of the Financial Analysis Office. Over the course of the next thirty years, Galateri helmed major divisions of prominent companies across Europe such as the Saint Gobain Group, FIAT and IFI. Appointed CEO of Fiat in 2002, he became Chairman of Mediobanca in 2003. He serves as non-executive board member at several financial and holding companies, as well as the Accademia Nazionale di Santa Cecilia – Foundation, European Institute of Oncology, and Accor. He is member of the General Council and of the executive board of both Confindustria and Assolombarda.

How would you characterize the amount of inequality in the U.S. or Europe?

It is difficult not to sense that inequality in recent years has increased, rather than decreased. When I was younger, I thought that the world was

R. Berger et al., *The Inequality Puzzle: European and US Leaders Discuss Rising Income Inequality*, DOI 10.1007/978-3-642-15804-9_4, © Springer-Verlag Berlin Heidelberg 2010

actually moving, on average, toward an objective of reduced inequality and improved equality, in general terms. This probably happened in the western world after World War II. But certainly the last few years have highlighted in many areas, typically finance, that this was not completely the case. This is particularly true for the United States and Britain, where in the last two to three decades the disparity of income has increased. The present economic crisis has created further evidence of inequalities around the world.

I would like to preliminarily make two fundamental statements to illustrate my opinion on this subject: the first is that inequality has arisen not only from the lack of rules, as many people suggest, but also and mostly by a reduction of what is called, unfortunately in too generic terms, a sense of ethics. Undoubtedly further regulation in certain areas would have helped and will help. But I don't think that the basic situation can be changed unless we restore an ethical sense, a commitment of the human being toward a correct behavior that otherwise would be very difficult to promote strictly by regulation.

We wouldn't reduce the number of people stealing by adding rules that say you must not steal, and if you steal you go to prison. You have to start much earlier by teaching young people that stealing in itself is a wrong act. This prescription has been with us since the Decalogue, without any parliament, police authority, or juridical process to enforce its validity. This reduction of pressure, or constraints on individual actions through diminished respect for what was called natural law, has had important consequences. For example, the fact that guys forty, forty-five years old, who were earning as much as twenty or thirty million euro in one year, went completely unnoticed and did not give rise to perplexity in anyone. It could be a touch of luck. If you play the lottery it can be understood. If you work in a normal company then it doesn't make any sense. But there has been a sort of addiction that made us accept this as a fact of life, instead of saying that there was something wrong going on.

I think it reflects a much wider problem than corporate governance. There was an overall worldwide cultural movement that has slowly taken over and reduced the importance of many rules, legal or natural, that kept people on track. Why do morals matter, if growth, profits, and jobs are assured? It was all fine, having the "huge air of the world" rush through without real limitations, except of course the legal order, it was a fantastic period of anyone's life, but I don't think it really was the right way.

And this brings me to the second basic statement that I would like to make, which pertains to education. An ethical life starts very early in the education of people. The values, the examples absorbed day by day within the family: the first and the most efficient antibodies are developed there. And then comes school. When I was young we had tough teachers, highly respected by scholars and families. Their role was much more than teaching subjects: they taught responsibility for life, and they were acknowledged and appreciated as an important social resource. Moreover, we had a school subject, one hour of Educazione Civica or civics, which really taught certain basic things about living together, rules that had not the force of law, but were recognized by everyone as the rules that let us live peacefully, constructively, and positively with the rest of the society. Nowadays, many people have lost the understanding that society is built over time. It is not created out of the blue by law, decree, or whoever. Restoring a different attitude cannot be done in six months, one year, or two years. The task requires almost a generation, starting with young children in elementary school, continuing through junior high school, high school, and on to the university. So, ethics and education are two areas where we should pay much more attention, starting from rebuilding the parents' sense of responsibility along all the course of life of their children from childhood to adulthood, and restoring the key social role of teachers.

I would like to make another point. All indicators tell us that income inequalities have risen not only in the United States but – with the exception of continental Europe – all over the world. They have risen in Brazil as well as in China, in Argentina as well as in South Africa. But I think that this growing gap in income – which represents a serious political issue to be addressed – is somewhat less important than the human development index trend that shows an improvement for all these countries. In my opinion this is due to globalization: the more a country is integrated in the global economy, the more are the growth dividends for its citizens. If I look, for example, at Brazil, I am impressed by the greater number of people who have gone to the market, who are now participating actively into the marketplace. I went to China fifteen years ago: I remember that masses of people were living in the fields, in the farms with a bowl of rice. I saw them. Now they tell me that you go to the huge cities and you find millions of people. If you look at the entire world, not at each country individually, and you consider how many people have improved in terms of participating in global wealth compared to twenty-five years ago, the quality of life is not really worse than before.

The ongoing debate about inequality has recently focused on issues of executive compensation. If executive compensation at companies was re-

duced slightly or substantially, would that likely affect executive performance and ultimately corporate profitability?

Executive compensation is the red flag that shows this inequality. We heard incredible things recently that cannot allow anyone to say that there is not inequality. Once we were shocked by the news about U.S. executives' compensation. I never understood whether they were real or not. For at least ten, fifteen, twenty years, from time to time, you could read that Mr. So and So, chairman, made 200/300 million dollars in one year, without knowing if it was salary, stocks, bonds, or whatever. But, because of what I said before with regard to international differences, while it was shocking, it was almost a vagary of the world without specific impact in terms of actual inequality.

Over the last ten years, in Europe we started having those kind of situations that were really impressive. I was in charge of companies and remuneration committees. I participated to support programs of stock options and so on, that in my opinion were, in themselves, reasonable instruments to promote incentives for management to create value for the shareholders. Over time, however, they proved to be short-sighted because they were built in a way that was not correct. No problem if and when the company was indeed developed and creating value in a solid and sustainable way, but in a few cases those plans brought to the recipients an enormous amount of wealth just because of short-term stock evolution.

Another problem was to discover that the stock option could have had a sort of boomerang effect. The moment you produce that amount of wealth, you give an incentive for people to leave the company instead of staying. When one has made such amounts of money, what is the reason for that person to remain with the company? This was the first consideration that left me really puzzled, and that is why the Italian government introduced later certain changes.

There was a time in Italy, when stock options enjoyed a very positive fiscal treatment, so you would pay, if I remember correctly, 12.5% tax instead of paying the usual 43% of tax on the capital gain. There was an opinion in the country that this had to change. So the Minister of Finance proposed a rule that passed a few years ago, that said there had to be a vesting period of three years which was not mandatory before. In addition, a particular rule was that the capital gain that you would have made after the vesting period, in order to receive the fiscal advantage, had to remain invested in the stock of the same company for another five years. So at least, maybe it's still wrong to give the stock options, but you would have an eight-year period of loyalty guaranteed by this, because you had an inducement to remain in the company to maintain the performance over the five years subsequent to the vesting period. It was not particularly appreciated by managers, but I thought that it was the minimum modification to help control this sense of inequality, in terms of fairness with the rest of the company and the market.

Executive compensation is a very big issue. I think that meritocracy should be reflected in remuneration, and this is an instrument of capitalism which I fully support. You cannot pay everyone the same amount because you would never have the right incentives. I'm not shocked by the fact that there is a strong level of remuneration for some executives, as long as this is clearly tied to medium and long-term results and makes a minimum of sense. I don't know if the top manager remuneration has to be a maximum of 20, 50, 100 times the lowest level of remuneration, but there has to be some logic in the level of compensation.

Do you think companies offer about the right amount of inequality of compensation across many categories of workers? Or would you favor making changes in compensation practices? If so, what types of changes?

In many companies crazy things have been done in the past at the top level. But, I would like to share with you how we, at Telecom Italia, have moved toward bringing back the group's compensation policy to a more credible and transparent level.

Over the last year Telecom Italia has striven to substantially reduce executive compensation, moving from third quartile to approximate median market positioning. Furthermore, Telecom Italia has been more selective in executive variable pay, awarding bonuses which better reflect company performance.

In 2008 Telecom Italia non-management remuneration level grew at a faster rate than management remuneration level. In addition, the disparity in rates of salary increase between Telecom Italia non-management employees and management was greater than in the general market. Therefore, in our company the equality has increased.

In order to reduce inequality to sustainable and appropriate levels, we are promoting remuneration policies which are closely linked to company profitability and effective individual high-performance/potential. We cannot change things from one year to the other. But the clear policy of the company is to create a rank of executive and non-executive remuneration that responds to performance and has a certain logic in terms of relations between management and non-management compensation.

I have to say that our remuneration committee, and in general the board and the governance of Telecom Italia, are among the best I've had to run. And I've been on the boards of U.K., French, Italian companies. I don't know whether it is just the evolution of the system or this particular case, but Telecom Italia remuneration committee really functions so that each director is independent from other directors, and they are independent from their original association in terms of shareholder structure: so everyone works with the sense of being fully responsible for his own decisions. In the committee as well as in the board, dialogue is extremely open.

How might changes in executive compensation affect company performance?

I think that money is not the only way to motivate performance, which depends very much on your culture, your past, your future, your age, your experience, and so on. Of course, remuneration levels certainly affect the company performance in the sense that in a competitive market the inducement of making money is certainly a strong motivation for executives. If you pay them too low, they will move to another company.

I have to say that for me, for example, the economic motivation was a strong push when I joined the job market more than thirty years ago. I remember when I went from the business school at Columbia University to work in a bank in Rome: I was quite happy. I was bringing the new theories learned in the business school to this bank, and I was considered like a messenger of God because I was introducing concepts like ratios – the ROE, the ROI, and so on – that were totally unheard of in Italy. But after I was at the bank two or three years, a former colleague of mine from New York City proposed that I move to Milan to become the finance manager of an industrial company. I have to admit that the key motivation for me to accept his offer was probably the fact that I was doubling my salary after three years' work. It was not the only reason, but it was certainly a very important reason.

Today, I don't think that I would move from my position to another company just for the sake of making twice the salary. I consider that the possibility of strengthening one of the leading companies in Italy in a technological field like telecommunications, participating in a game with huge potential in terms of innovation and contribution to the solution of the economic crisis, is, I'm not saying as important, but certainly very important in terms of my global satisfaction. If I could retire from this company in the future by leaving it stronger, successful, and well-positioned in the market, that would give me an enormous satisfaction, compared to the fact of making even bigger my salary.

Will inequality continue to increase into the near future? Or will the trend soon stabilize or even reverse itself?

I would expect certainly not an increase in inequality, because I think that what has happened has opened the eyes of a lot of people. At least in our world, inequality will stabilize or decrease. The main cause of all the turmoil we lived in the past two years and a half – financial speculation – is well in the foresight of governments, central bankers and public opinion. And I don't think that we will see the excesses we have seen in terms of compensation and speculation. I've seen this already happening in some of the companies in which I am involved. People are much more attentive, much more respectful of the rules of the game in terms of remuneration connected with performance and with overall equilibrium. Basically I'm optimistic because I see this improvement linked to a sort of natural reaction that probably regulators, parliaments, could never have orchestrated by themselves.

The economic crisis has produced an enormous disruption that forces people to act. Therefore I think, at least I hope, that there is an in-built mechanism which corrects imbalances. The world has survived ages of tragedies and disasters and of confidence and development, because every action produces a reaction that tends to stabilize or recreate equilibrium. So even in this field I think that what has happened will create a better equilibrium in terms of speculation and remunerations, and more generally in terms of diminishing inequalities.

In addition to ethics and education, certainly there will be some new regulation. While I said before that regulations alone will not solve the problem, I didn't say that they are useless. For example, if only top management remuneration will have to pass through the shareholders' meeting and be approved by the shareholders, not just by the remuneration committee, this simple act might improve the situation.

Globalization is another trend that will help restore equilibrium, if governments will resist the mermaids of protectionism. I think that in a globalized world, putting all these markets in contact with each other, in principle, should advance greater transparency, and therefore greater competitiveness, and greater action of market forces.

A few years ago, the widespread conviction among economists, entrepreneurs, and politicians was that the basic economic trend in the developed world was oriented toward more services and higher value-added productions, leaving industry to the developing countries. What has happened recently is not exactly in that direction. We have become dominated too much by services, particularly by financial services, and we have forgotten too quickly the real economy. I think that bringing back a different concept of the real economy and financial services is advisable. I'm not suggesting we should continue producing our own iron ore or steel, but it will be more difficult to imagine that countries can live only by financial services or pure services, forgetting the other economy. There will be a better equilibrium in terms of subdivision of labor among countries.

Another example of the need for a better balance is that too many people in services have never known really the industrial arena. This introduces a related issue with regard to compensation. When I was working at FIAT, I recall the effort, the complexity, and the risks of creating and running a factory in Brazil when the company started its presence in Betim, near Belo Horizonte. I remember the face and the effort of the man who was building this factory, and I remember, more or less, what he was paid. I compare his situation with people in the financial services business who at noon or one o'clock, instead of going under a tree to eat some roasted chicken, go to a nice place in London and Milan to take a sandwich while earning maybe a hundred times what he was making. This has always been questionable to me, and given a sense that something was not right.

What practical actions, if any, should the private sector undertake to address rising inequality?

I believe flexibility, mobility of management, is certainly a way through which the private sector – on top of paying attention to the education area as I said initially – can address and partially improve things. Together, as I said before, with more ethics and more globalization – and sometimes also more courage. With regard to more courage, I speak in terms of becoming more independent upon these clubs of top people that have formed in the different countries and that are very much interlocked.

We should have more flexibility and more interconnection between the sectors of activity. In the United States you have much more dynamism than you have in Europe. People spend some years in the government, some years in the financial industry, and maybe some years in industry. This creates a knowledge of the economy, and a sense of where the problems and the solutions are, much more real and credible than what you can imagine by always operating in the financial services, always in the industrial sector, or always in the governmental sector.

What practical actions, if any, should the government undertake to address rising inequality?

Governments should try to reduce poverty, the reasons for poverty, with sound politics that foster growth and the distribution of growth dividends. Easy to say, much harder to put in place. In general terms, I think that a well-balanced welfare with an effective social protection, and more education and more social mobility should be three key political goals. We must create a system of equal opportunities. I don't see any injustice in offering everyone the same opportunity and accepting the fact that some will take it, some will not. If they don't, if there is a choice, there is nothing wrong with that. I mean, some people might prefer to sit on top of a mountain and pray, rather than work in Wall Street to make money, and this is acceptable and correct. I don't see any problem with that, as long as it's offered in a context where you're not leaving aside the weak. Of course there are people who are less fortunate and society will have to take care of them, but this is a different case, it is not what we are talking about.

Jürgen Hambrecht
Chairman, BASF

"In the current crisis, it's true to say that the poor are being hit disproportionately hard worldwide. Aside from the current downturn though, we should not forget our societies are becoming increasingly prosperous, and we need to ensure that as many people as possible participate in this prosperity so that they can benefit socially and economically. Government intervention should, in my opinion, be kept to a minimum, but it's also important for businesses to live up fully to their social responsibility."

Since earning his doctorate in chemistry in 1975, Jürgen Hambrecht has spent over thirty years at BASF, the world's largest chemical company. BASF has nearly 100,000 employees at approximately 385 production sites across the globe, posting annual sales of more than 50 billion euros. Hambrecht now serves as the Chairman of BASF, a position he has held since 2003. He also serves as a member of the supervisory boards of Daimler and Lufthansa, as well as Vice President of the German Chemical Industry Association, and Chairman of the Asia Pacific Committee of German Business.

There are long-standing debates about how much inequality is the right amount of inequality. How would you characterize the amount of inequality in Europe? Is there too much, too little, or about the right amount?

The fact that the global financial and economic crisis has not resulted in serious upheavals in Germany is, I believe, due in large part to the success of our social market economy: Thanks to its social systems and flexible work practices, we have so far managed to avoid the mass unemployment

R. Berger et al., *The Inequality Puzzle: European and US Leaders Discuss Rising Income Inequality*, DOI 10.1007/978-3-642-15804-9_5, © Springer-Verlag Berlin Heidelberg 2010

and poverty seen in the thirties. Nevertheless, the social market economy is a system in which inequality is inherent.

The strength and dynamism of a successful social market economy are based on competition, in other words the constant search for better processes, better products, and higher productivity. And competition is natural in a free society – it's human nature. Competition promotes diversity and creativity, and the results of such competition are unequal per se. Inequality is thus part and parcel of any democratic society. A look at the history books will quickly show that all utopian attempts to abolish inequality have failed in the long term: a performance-based approach has prevailed over efforts to achieve equitable distribution. And we see the same in nature, where qualities such as strength, beauty, or intelligence are not equally distributed.

Although some inequality is of course needed to increase incentives, effort, and output, too much may generate resentment, disengagement, and even unrest. What are your thoughts on this?

As you say, a certain amount of inequality is necessary as an incentive to perform. I therefore believe it would be wrong to reduce such incentives. We should do our best to reduce inequality, but we should do so by working to ensure that opportunities are fairly distributed, and we should avoid extremes of inequality. In Europe, there is a tendency to use the word equality in the sense of equitable distribution of wealth instead of equitable distribution of opportunities. We would do better to focus on the latter, since this is a prerequisite for social mobility.

I also feel that there is a tendency to think somewhat one-dimensionally and to view this issue only in terms of economic inequality. I think that this is why the term inequality has a very negative connotation for many people. I prefer to extend the idea of inequality to include dissimilarities in the sense of diversity. What is important here is inclusion: Enabling people to display and develop their various talents and abilities in the interest of both societies and businesses. This has long been something we have focused on at BASF. We have successfully intensified communication to a wider audience through a special Diversity & Inclusion project and are now beginning to harvest the fruits.

The ongoing debate about inequality has recently focused on issues of executive compensation. If executive compensation at BASF were reduced slightly or substantially, would that likely affect executive performance and ultimately the profitability of BASF?

Times of economic crisis require special efforts from BASF's management to guide the company successfully through turbulent waters. There was a reduction in executive compensation at BASF as a result of the downturn in 2009, since total compensation contains a significant performance-related component that is linked to our return on assets. Moreover, we elected to freeze salaries for senior executives worldwide.

Financial incentives are important, but money is not the prime motivator. The motivation it provides fades fastest. In my experience, the most important source of motivation comes from within – our "inner spark," so to speak. In the crisis especially, we need to work harder than ever to ensure the best-in-class performance of our company and the well-being of our employees and their families. If we succeed, we will be rewarded for our success. If not, then the rewards will be fewer.

I am opposed to the idea of limiting executive compensation. Legally imposed limits for compensation are diametrically opposed to the principles of a free-market economy. We need courageous individuals who are willing to take the risks needed to develop new business opportunities and markets in the face of increasingly tough global competition. In a social market economy, free and responsible entrepreneurship plays an essential part in ensuring and promoting the growth and prosperity of our society. The existing Corporate Government Codex we have in Germany is widely accepted and a new law on Management Board Remuneration (Gesetz zur Angemessenheit der Vorstandsvergütung) came into effect in August 2009. It ensures that executive compensation contains long-term incentives and that it is tied to the success – or lack of success – of the company.

The media is much enamored these days with issues of executive compensation, yet one should also consider the entire spectrum of compensation at all levels within a firm. Do you think BASF has about the right amount of inequality of compensation across its many categories of workers?

You're right: We shouldn't just be looking at executives. At BASF, compensation is based on a combination of market rates, the respective function, as well as individual and company performance. At our companies in Germany, for example, we have an integral system made up of fixed and variable, performance-related components at all levels – from non-exempt employees right up to the top tier of management. The proportion of variable compensation increases, the higher employees are in the company hierarchy and the greater the responsibility they bear. This provides employees at all levels with an incentive to perform and show what they can do. We also have a very transparent system, since the performance-related component for everyone is tied to BASF's return on assets.

Why has economic inequality increased substantially in North America and many European countries over the past two decades? What role has globalization and other forces played?

Globalization has created a huge amount of wealth that is, of course, not equally distributed. The primary effect of globalization, however, has been to provide millions of people throughout the world with better living standards and better access to basic needs, especially in emerging markets. This has helped to lift many people out of poverty.

People in developed economies are also quick to forget how they benefit from globalization. For example, hardly anyone considers that products from China have helped to keep inflation down in Europe and the U.S. Instead, many people now want to start building fences. But that can't be in anyone's interest, and we can't ask for easy access to other people's markets and then start building fences around our own.

We need more globalization, not less: real political solutions for more free trade, more climate protection and more sustainability globally. As the world's leading exporter, Germany benefits especially from globalization. Globalization generates new markets. Ultimately, the opening up of these markets results in prosperity and helps to secure jobs in Germany.

Will inequality continue to increase into the near future? Or will the trend soon stabilize or even reverse itself? If you do expect stabilization or reversal, will this occur because of changes in the business cycle, because of direct political intervention, or through some other means?

Inequality is something that will always be with us and will fluctuate somewhat over time with economic cycles. And as I said before, nature provides all of us with different gifts and talents. Where influence is possible, I think it is important that we work to avoid extremes of inequality that undermine social cohesion and harm society and the economy.

In the current crisis, it's true to say that the poor are being hit disproportionately hard worldwide. Aside from the current downturn though, we should not forget our societies are becoming increasingly prosperous, and we need to ensure that as many people as possible participate in this prosperity so that they can benefit socially and economically. Government intervention should, in my opinion, be kept to a minimum, but it's also important for businesses to live up fully to their social responsibility.

Has inequality increased to a point at which the public might start to react against it?

I think that the negative effect of inequality on social trust is due more to a sense of unfairness than to a sense of inequality in itself. This brings us back to the importance of ensuring the fair distribution of opportunities that I mentioned earlier.

What role might the media play in either supporting inequality or fanning discontent?

I don't think that the media really have a position on this issue, even though they are fascinated by it. The borders between admiration and contempt are blurred, and there's a general lack of critical analysis and serious discussion. The mass media demonstrate an unhealthy interest in people at both extremes of the economic spectrum. They show us either celebrities who receive vast amounts of money for doing apparently very little or people who slog their guts out and earn next to nothing. We rarely see the vast majority who fall somewhere in between – for example, hard-working individuals and families who invest in the education of their children. I think this skewed depiction in the media does more harm to society than the social differences themselves.

What I also find disturbing is that we only ever seem to get snapshots – there's hardly ever any background. We see the high-earning manager, but not the years of study and hard work that put this person where they are today. And the same applies at the other extreme.

Why do you think this is so critical?

I believe that people are more willing to tolerate differences in wealth if they can see a correlation between what a person earns and what they contribute to society. The mass media, however, show us a world in which there is no longer a link between performance and status, prestige and income.

I distinguish between two types of envy: productive and unproductive. Productive envy is a form of competition: We emulate our role models and are determined to achieve our own success. Unproductive envy, on the other hand, does not spur us into action. It makes us resentful and bitter. Today's media create unproductive envy, since they suggest that we can all become something without ever having to work hard; they offer us role models who are rich and famous for doing nothing. This does not sit at all well with ideas of fairness and social mobility.

What practical actions, if any, should the private sector undertake to address rising inequality?

A business cannot be successful in the long term if it does not act responsibly toward the environment and society. That is why sustainability is an integral part of BASF's strategy. We have initiated a number of projects in the area of corporate social responsibility that could be broadly construed as efforts to improve access to education, health, and business opportunities.

One example is a social business joint venture that we have established in Bangladesh with the Grameen Healthcare Trust together with Nobel Laureate Muhammad Yunus. The aim is to offer affordable solutions to meet the basic needs of the poor in Bangladesh. These solutions – sachets of vitamins and micronutrients, and impregnated mosquito nets – tie in with BASF's product portfolio.

Through this joint venture, we want to enable poor people to participate in business life, while providing them with better nutrition and protection against insect-borne disease. The joint venture is intended to cover its own costs and recoup the partners' initial investment. Any additional profits will be ploughed back into the business. But we are not a charity: We also benefit from healthier and better-educated employees and customers. And it allows BASF to explore new markets and customer groups.

What sort of educational initiatives is BASF involved in and what is their impact on inequality?

Initiatives related to education have long been part of BASF's social responsibility efforts and go back far longer than the term social responsibility! Education is also an area that is very close to my heart. I think it is very important for young people to acquire the skills they need to succeed and thrive in today's highly competitive society. In 2005, BASF was one of the founding members of an initiative in Germany known as the Knowledge Factory that now has seventy member companies. It involves a number of educational projects at the preschool, kindergarten, and elementary levels. The projects aim to encourage an interest in science and nature and promote language and arithmetic skills; in addition, we want to teach economic fundamentals. All of these things are crucial to success at school and beyond. To implement these projects, the member companies have established more than 1,000 partnerships with daycare centers, kindergartens, and schools to date. We also aim to promote entrepreneurship through a mentoring program in which employees of the member companies provide professional support and advice to young entrepreneurs.

Projects like these play an important role in ensuring that opportunities are more equally distributed, especially for children and young people with a migration background. But here again, we are not acting out of sheer altruism. A German study has clearly shown that investments in early education offer the highest returns. I believe these are real win-win-win projects that benefit the participants, society and, ultimately, companies in the private sector. After all, companies like BASF will hopefully profit from a larger pool of scientists and engineers.

What practical actions, if any, should the government undertake to address rising inequality?

In my view, the role of government should be to promote opportunities for social mobility and provide incentives to perform at all levels in society. I would therefore like to see much, much more spending on education. Intelligence and talent are characteristics that are not equally distributed. Education has and continues to play an important role in the social mobility of individuals from communities lacking in economic resources and social connections. Neither should we forget that there is a linear correlation between education and reasoning power.

A good education is only one side of the coin, however. The other side is discipline and hard work, unpleasant as those terms might sound. And that is why I wish governments would place more emphasis on the importance of a positive work ethic. Our welfare state in Germany is something that we are rightly proud of, but I think something has gone wrong when some people seem to consider doing nothing to be a career option.

What practical actions, if any, should regional decision-making bodies (e.g., the EU) undertake to address rising inequality?

In Europe, I would like to see the EU working harder to implement its Lisbon Strategy. I wholeheartedly support these efforts to promote innovation and a learning economy. What needs to be done has long been clear, but action is still lacking. Innovation is all about our future.

Should the private sector and government focus on reducing poverty rather than inequality? Should they focus on equalizing opportunities to succeed rather than equalizing outcomes themselves?

I don't think that reducing poverty is a means in itself, and the results tend to be very variable. As I said before, I am convinced that efforts to ensure the fair distribution of opportunities are more beneficial to society in the long run. Charity can demean and stigmatize the poor. Social businesses, like our joint venture with Grameen, and similar microcredit schemes on the other hand empower people and allow them to play an active role in business life. We want to shift the emphasis from institutional help to self-help. Governments are trusted when people perceive them to be working to establish a better life for all their citizens. Equalizing opportunities play an important role here, but populist wealth distribution schemes are another matter completely!

What types of policies and programs are or would be most effective in reducing inequality to desirable levels? What types are the least effective?

At whatever level – government or corporate – the best schemes in my opinion are those that leverage the opportunities offered by human diversity in all its forms. Such schemes encourage healthy ambition and help people to make the most of their innate skills. The least-effective schemes in my view are those that promote egalitarianism and simply end up giving everyone a small but equal share. We need to focus on making the cake bigger rather than distributing it equally.

Our last question is rather personal: We know that you have four children. How have you responded to their different talents and abilities?

It's a great joy as a parent to watch one's children develop, and with four children you get a real sense of their individual differences. I have tried to give each of them room to find out where their talents lie and have encouraged them to develop their individual potential and ability. They're all young adults now, and each of them is finding his or her own way in life.

I'm sure that they will be successful, whatever career they choose to follow.

Maurice Lévy
Chairman and CEO, Publicis

"You have people who are ambitious, and those who are not; people who are hard workers, and people who are not; people who are entrepreneurs, and people who are philosophers. People who are very happy looking at the horizon, the sunset, the sea, eating just one fish a day that they have caught themselves, and people who are fighting hard, who are wasting or spending their lives building something because it's their nature. So we cannot say that what has been generated by one should necessarily go to somebody else. ... What I do know is that inequality is good when earned, when it is the result of exceptional talent."

Maurice Lévy is the Chairman and CEO of Publicis Groupe, the French advertising and communications company. He has been at Publicis since 1971, acting as Chairman and CEO since 1987. The company is now the world's fourth largest advertising and media firm, advising clients through offices in almost 200 cities across more than 100 countries. Lévy helped turn Publicis into a global powerhouse through a series of important mergers and acquisitions, notably the 2000 acquisition of the British superstar advertising firm Saatchi & Saatchi, the 2007 acquisition of Digitas, and the 2009 purchase of Microsoft's Razorfish. The Anti-Defamation League recently recognized Lévy for his commitment to promote diversity and tolerance in the workplace. He is a member of the International Advisory Board of the Council on Foreign Relations, the World Economic Forum Foundation Board, and (since June 2006) the Supervisory Board of Deutsche Bank. In 2010, he was elected President of the French association AFEP (French Association of Private Companies) that represents top French listed companies. He has also served on the Advisory Committee of the Banque de France and the French Government's Commission to

R. Berger et al., *The Inequality Puzzle: European and US Leaders Discuss Rising Income Inequality*, DOI 10.1007/978-3-642-15804-9_6, © Springer-Verlag Berlin Heidelberg 2010

Combat Drug Addiction. In 2005, he co-founded the Institute for Brain and Spinal Cord Disorders.

How would you evaluate income inequality changes over the past two decades?

Honestly I don't know if inequality per se has increased. I know that there have been a very small number of people who are making a huge amount of money, giving the idea that inequality has increased. But if we look at it from a global standpoint, in fact we can say that there has been, at best, an improvement in inequality. At best, because there are hundreds of millions of people who have been able to attain a much better situation, much better revenues, and much better life than they had prior to globalization.

If you look at France, where President Sarkozy has asked for a report on how added value is shared, what this report – produced by independent economists – has demonstrated is that things have remained relatively stable during the last twenty years, with very small differences. Obviously inequalities in salaries remain. Where a huge difference is evident concerns in fact a very small number of people, 1%, maybe less, mostly CEOs. I believe this small number of people with huge revenue packages, particularly at a time when the economic situation has worsened, have fueled the feeling of inequality, and more importantly, of injustice. It is both a real problem and one of perception; people felt that there was unfairness in the way wealth is distributed.

If we look at things statistically, as we should when we are doing a survey on macroeconomics – obviously I can speak only for France – there is certainly a relatively stable situation and in some areas a small improvement. But we cannot ignore that despite what statistics tell us the feeling of injustice and inequality has increased. Clearly there are some elements that have given the idea of a worse situation.

What are some of these other elements that have changed society and perceptions of inequality?

If you look at the way people were spending money in the seventies – taking the example of France – you had roughly between 25 and 30% for housing, approximately the same amount for food, and then you had all the other aspects, and maybe less than 10% devoted to culture, leisure, etc.

Today, things have changed dramatically: there are communication costs which have risen enormously (pay TV, mobile phones, Internet, etc.). And thanks to the progress in electronic and banking systems, people do not measure how much they spend. At least in France, suppliers can take the payment directly from your bank account. Add to that what one can buy through credit cards and now Internet and you get the picture. To summarize, inequality is very difficult to assess and understand. The first aspect is real: lots of people are having a tough time and live with revenues which are insufficient. This is a reality and is exacerbated by the fact that they don't see how their life can improve with the current state of the economy. It can only get worse. It is also exacerbated when they see in the press the millions that executives are making, including when they fail. And it is normal that they have this feeling of "injustice" and get angry. What is left in their pocket is much less and they have the feeling that in reality the purchasing power is reduced and they blame governments, companies, and employers. ... TV was free, now it is quite common that everyone has to pay something. Phone communication was either through a fixed amount, or a relatively low figure, it was fixed-line communication. Now with mobile phone companies people are talking non-stop, and sending SMS and data. You can go on the street and see everyone chatting away on their mobiles, and obviously they are going way beyond the minutes of their subscription. So they are paying extra costs, and this reduces their revenues. There are many examples of kids using their mother's or father's credit cards and buying stuff on the Internet. Individually each of these items is not very costly, but when you add it all up, it is biting a hefty amount of money out of their paycheck.

There is also something much more important, which is that we have entered what we call in France the "leisure civilization." People are living much better, are going much more often to concerts, sports, and public events, on weekends, vacations (even if they are short vacations), and this is taking a share of their revenues which is much bigger than that in the seventies or eighties. So what's left in terms of real purchasing power is much less or feels much less. They have a terrible feeling that they have less money. This is why it is an issue of both perception and reality.

I mention these other aspects of inequality, purchasing power, etc., because all these are notions which are mixed, it's not something which is that simple. You cannot just look at the numbers from a macro-economic point of view without going into some level of detail. For example the new phenomenon that value or price have absolutely not the same meaning as before. Because of a yo-yo game coming from rebates, promotions, etc., people no longer know the real value of the goods they buy. In the good ol' times, they had a few products for which they knew the price by heart. When they went to the supermarket, if they saw the cost of a bottle of oil had increased, they knew prices had increased. So they had a few references – coffee, oil, bread, etc.

Today the variety and number of products, the range, are such that they simply don't know. The only thing they know is that they were filling their trolley for a certain amount of money, and now when they fill their trolley it costs more, a lot more. What happened two years ago when the oil price climbed to 160 dollars has led to the use of green oil, agro oil. Prices of corn, wheat, milk went through the roof. We saw riots in many countries. Now that the oil price is back to a more reasonable level, people do not understand why the price for the consumer is still so high while the price for the producer is way down. Another aspect that generates a bitter feeling of inequality is the fact that a lot of people do not care about cost due to their favorable financial situation. They are filling their trolley without watching the price, while others are struggling. You should observe people in a supermarket. You learn a lot about human beings, jealousy, envy, and bitterness.

How will levels of inequality evolve?

Inequality is here forever. Again, if we look at how the value-added generated by production is distributed, I believe that things will remain stable. If we look now at the high-end, I think that there is a – in French we would say a *prise de conscience* – of the boards and the CEOs that there is bit of an exaggeration here. Recently in France we witnessed a lot of CEOs abandoning their bonuses, their stock options, even if they were entitled to receive them due to their company's performance. They said, "We understand the situation, it is too difficult for so many people and we need to contribute." I think we will see in the future an approach to CEO compensation which will be more measured. Do not expect to see an alignment or a very serious decrease but you can be assured that people will be more reasonable.

What is the right level of inequality?

From an ideological point of view, there should be no inequality. Particularly if you are born French, you have been raised with the idea that everyone is equal, *liberté, égalité, fraternité*. The key question is what equal means, what is equal? Honestly, I don't know. What is fair? Today we are in a situation where all this is decided by what we call *les forces du marché*, the market conditions. So I'm not sure that someone can say from any standpoint – could be a philosopher, a sociologist, a politician, or a man in the street – what is equal, what is not? Why the wealth which is generated when I am the owner of a company is something well-accepted and the wealth one can make by generating growth, developing a company is less well accepted? So we understand that if you own a company, are an entrepreneur, and you take risks, you can make a lot of money. If you do exactly the same running a company as a CEO, the money you are making is less accepted by the public opinion.

I think that there is no clear answer. Anyway, I consider that I'm not in a position to say what is the right level of inequality. Ideologically, I would say as we are born equal, we should live equal. This has a name, as a political system – communism – and this political system has collapsed and proven to be a total failure. Would that political system have worked if people had not been deprived of their freedoms? I don't know. In fact, what was at the origin of the collapse of socialism? Is it because the system was not right, or is it because it was a dictatorship? It is difficult to know if the experience would have worked with freedom.

We see this new kind of communism in China, where it is difficult to say that there is total freedom. The Chinese system is interesting: free entrepreneurship with a few key things which are under the control of the state, including information. The system has generated a lot of wealth, a lot of rich people, a formidable new middle class, and incredible inequality (maybe more than capitalism). We see that communism is not always the enemy of wealth generation and generates inequality. I think that if there is a country that has generated more inequality than any other country in a very short period of time, it is clearly China. But it is also a country which has taken hundreds of millions of people out of poverty. As you can see, things are not simple.

Is there an ideal political/economic system we should strive to create?

I'm not sure that there is one single political system which is so great that we can say, "Yes, that is the solution." I think the world will never be equal. It's not something that I say either with pleasure or cynically. The world will never be equal, simply because men are different, one man or woman is different from another, has different dreams, different approaches to life, different conditions, etc.

You have people who are ambitious, and those who are not; people who are hard workers, and people who are not; people who are entrepreneurs, and people who are philosophers. People who are very happy looking at the horizon, the sunset, the sea, eating just one fish a day that they have caught themselves, etc., and people who are fighting hard, who are wasting or spending their lives building something because it's their nature. So we cannot say that what has been generated by one should necessarily go to somebody else, who, by the way, doesn't care. That is the reason why there are social systems that create some "amortization" of the differences through redistribution of wealth. But imagining that the world should be the same level for everyone, I believe is a utopia and probably wrong. When you look at some of the history of very ancient times, you have men who have fought to eat, to create fire, to hunt, and you have people who have not. That's the nature of mankind, and you can't say what is the right level of inequality. What I do know is that inequality is good when earned, when it is the result of exceptional talent, work, idea, inequality is good but to a certain extent.

How does this affect executive compensation?

It's interesting to first have a look at what happened and why we have seen a huge rise in the way executives are compensated. At the beginning things started in the U.S. There are huge corporations out there and their boards considered that to build these corporations, to grow them and to grow the economy, they had to incentivize people. Incentivization is something which has been not only accepted, but praised. The fact that people were making a lot of money was celebrated, and was part of the American dream.

Beyond incentives, which had led to "cash" bonuses, they created stock option plans and thanks to performance of corporations and the stock market the gain became real big. The big packages became generalized outside the U.S., including in France (albeit to a lesser level) and a lot of executives made a lot of money. Then two things happened. One was what we can call the Wall Street era, which started in the eighties, and we saw very bright people going to Wall Street. The best young people, the top quartile from Harvard, Yale, etc., were going to Wall Street instead of going to marketing, or to production. And these bright, young people were making a lot, a lot of money, just gambling with stocks and shares, and you'll remember the formidable Olivier Stone movie with Michael Douglas epitomizing this period.

After this phase came another with Silicon Valley, the dot-com era. You could make a large amount of money, not by salary, but by joining a company with a name ending in dot-com. The stock market was enamored with these dot-coms. Suffice to have a dot-com behind your name and you had a multiple which was infinite compared to the real production or the real value created by the company. This has generated the idea that people can get rich easily. Obviously corporate boards wanted to keep their good people, so they had to raise the compensation of these people, give them more stock options, etc., and by raising the compensation of these people, they had to raise that of the whole hierarchy, including the CEO. We have seen in these two decades a huge inflation of packages under the influence of these two elements.

In Europe, and particularly in France, we have been faced with the consequences of transparency. What happened was that salaries or compensation were benchmarked and adjusted to the highest-paid person. New experts appeared whose analysis was that if you wanted to keep your people, you had to be in top quartile, etc. ... The transparency which was meant to moderate has in fact created a serious inflation. Not to mention that transparency has helped headhunters to hunt the best talent with perfect knowledge of their compensation. It's easy then to make an attractive offer.

On top of this with globalization, jobs became more global and people were receiving job offers from any given place. So instead of comparing on a country-by-country basis as we did in the old days, we are comparing with the American executives, the German, the British, etc. This has been another factor of inflation.

And last, but not least, in 2009 we saw several initiatives going in different directions, which are creating big trouble for the general public: on the one hand, we saw, particularly in the banking industry, big bonuses coming back, as if the economic crisis never happened! On the other hand, some companies and CEOs publicly said that they will reduce (or manage differently) bonuses and incentives. This has created confusion and put compensation on the front pages of newspapers.

How have cross-country comparisons affected compensation at Publicis Groupe?

Our own people are making the comparison. Why the guy who is doing the same job in the U.S. is paid more than me. Globalization has provoked inflation of salaries, even though people were not traveling (I mean moving from one place to another). Headhunters are coming to poach our people irrespective of the place they work. We have to deal with that issue which has an inflationary effect.

This phenomenon is not limited to us, it is shared across many companies. In the past, it was very, very rare to see a Frenchman playing a major role in an international company. Today you see many French people hired to have an executive role outside of France. How many French engineers do we have in Silicon Valley? Even if relatively limited to some jobs or qualifications, there is a global market which has an inflationary consequence on compensation.

In our industry there are some jobs for which knowledge of cultures, languages are less indispensable: for example, art directors, digital experts. You need to keep the cohesiveness of the workforce and as soon as there are global jobs, it has consequences on the whole organization.

Have you seen other changes in how your employees approach compensation?

I remember when I was recruiting in the seventies. I was always putting the following questions to candidates: "You say you want to come work with us, you say you love the agency, so what are you willing to sacrifice to join us?" Often people were sincere and really wanted to join and accepted a pay cut to show how sincere they were. Sometimes it was just speech and I had to make a judgment, do I hire a mercenary or a foundation for the future? Obviously today the world has changed and often candidates are "marketing" their talents.

How have globalization and the financial crisis influenced public views of inequality?

Globalization has brought some great things, among which hundreds of millions of Chinese and Indians and several million Brazilians and Russians have greatly improved their lives. That's great, fantastic. Growth has been remarkable, fueled by low wages in developing countries. In developed markets there has been some backlash with the destruction of jobs in favor of outsourcing to low-cost countries. This situation has generated angst, bitterness as people did not understand why they had to pay the price.

Now, we are in an economic and social crisis which originated in the finance industry. A lot of CEOs of banks have been fired, and some went away with a fat package. The person in the street has lost his house, his job, sometimes he's literally in the street, homeless, and he sees that these people couldn't care less. If you want to talk about inequality, you have here a good example. Suffice to see this discrepancy and you understand the anger, the "no, this is not fair."

We are certainly at a sort of tipping point; we need to rethink our society model which for centuries has been based on More and More. We know that it will not work that way in the future because it's not sustainable. We need to reinvent the economic and social model of our society. We need to keep in mind how the world is changing very fast. And which kind of answers and solutions will fit with this new paradox? In our developed countries, the life-style standard is high and people have legitimate expectations; but we also see a sort of new poverty emerging in our countries. Today, the new trend is to ask everyone to move to a more sustainable way of life (with individual and collective efforts). But, in all emerging countries (BRIC but not only), the new citizen-consumers who get more money have the same expectations that we had several years ago. They want to enjoy their new way of life with mass consumption and luxury goods and if this exacerbates inequality or consumes more energy or destroys the environment, so be it. They do not understand why they should not enjoy this new life.

What can business or governments do?

Inequality is not an easy issue and regulation is almost impossible, or at best very difficult. I think also that we should be very cautious because we should not point fingers at people making money thanks to their hard work. In our societies they are the growth drivers, and we should be cautious and not destroy our growth capabilities.

I think that governments have already done something very important. Sarkozy, Obama, Merkel, have said loud and clear what their feelings are about compensation when governments are helping, rescuing companies. Some banks are in a hurry to get out of the TARP (Troubled Assets Relief Program) just to resume their old habits, or be able to compete for talents.

In the nineties and in the last decade compensation went too high and sometimes out of proportion to the value created. I'm in favor of very good compensation but clearly linked to measured performance.

For my own compensation there was a question put to the board two years ago at the AGM. The head of the Compensation Committee explained the structure of my compensation and the stockholders applauded. And at the last AGM we were the only public company in France where no questions, not one question was put on the compensation of the executives or the CEO.

I think that it is very important to act reasonably, *avec mesure* as we say in France. It is clear that we have seen an escalation and it would be a good thing to bring compensation to more moderate levels, to have a bonus system based on performance, part paid in cash, part paid in shares, and part deferred.

I am of the opinion that the years to come will see the return of great values like ethics and the fading away of cynicism. I believe that this would help change behaviors particularly if appropriate didactic communication is applied. The effect on moderation of compensation would be much more important than any regulation.

How does Publicis Groupe design its incentive plans?

Our long-term incentive plan (LTIP) is based on three-year performance, and it is earned after three years, not year-by-year. So we tell people at the beginning of the plan, we are granting you X stock options or free shares. You will get them based on two criteria: organic growth and profitability. In both cases, compared to the top tier in our business. After three years we measure the criteria, the numbers are audited and the Compensation Committee reviews the results, and the final numbers are decided purely on metrics. As we had a not-so-good 2007, in our view (though a lot of people would consider it was a very good 2007), people lost close to 40% of the grant because we reward only super-performance, and not performance per se.

In 2008, due to the crisis, we decided that we would not award any stock options. We distributed no stock options, despite the fact that we delivered the best growth and the highest margin of our peer group. We considered that we are facing one of the world's toughest crises and we might well have to take some decisions to adjust, so we could not distribute stock options at a time when we had to adjust our workforce and let go some people. By the way, in 2009 all the members of the Directoire (Management Board) decided to forego their bonuses.

To conclude, what is making us a little different is that we originate from a family business. Marcel Bleustein-Blanchet, our founder, ran the company as if it were a family business. And things have continued that way right up to the present day. I run the company as if it were my own business, caring about clients above all, but also about the shareholders' money, about the wellbeing of the employees, and trying to find the right balance between all the stakeholders. We – the board, the managers – still have that spirit, one of the things of which we are very proud.

John Monks
General Secretary, European Trade Union Confederation

"The person who comes along and invents an engine that's readily available, quite cheap, and very green and clean, is going to make an absolute fortune, and deserves to, I don't care about that. So never mind the undeserving poor. I can acknowledge a deserving rich, and I'd like to find some way to separate them from the undeserving rich, many of whom are fairly ordinary people who happen to be working in certain areas and do what everybody else does, and make a fortune."

John Monks is the General Secretary of the European Trade Union Confederation (ETUC), an organization established in 1973 to represent trade unions across Europe. Monks has held this position since 2003, prior to which he served as the General Secretary of the Trades Union Congress, a similarly purposed United Kingdom organization. With the rise of the European Union, Monks has helped make the ETUC the primary organization working for collective bargaining, good working conditions, business-labor dialogue, and worker consultation on business topics. The ETUC works with all EU governing bodies to address these issues. He is a Visiting Professor, Manchester Business School, a member of the Councils of the European Policy Centre, Brussels, and the Centre for European Studies, London, and a Fellow of the City and Guilds of London Institute.

R. Berger et al., *The Inequality Puzzle: European and US Leaders Discuss Rising Income Inequality*, DOI 10.1007/978-3-642-15804-9_7, © Springer-Verlag Berlin Heidelberg 2010

How would you judge the amount of inequality today?

Far too much. Since financial market deregulation in the mid-1980s, the gaps between rich and poor have widened dramatically. I believe too that the concern the people at the top have for the wider society has also become correspondingly less. They're in a bubble. We've just seen now that the system has had a heart attack – the financial markets have collapsed. But the minute there's any talk of any regulation, they're all talking about emigrating to somewhere or other. Switzerland is a favorite, West Indies is a favorite, and I just find it repulsive. The levels of inequality, the ratio of the upper quartile to the lower quartile, are back to where they were in the late 19th century, and that was before the invention of the welfare state.

I think we know that pay levels are not just about how much you get, but about how much you get relative to what other people get. The level of dissatisfaction is relative. Seeing people in financial services, and seeing people at the top of other organizations who want the same as the people at the top in financial services, people in the public sector want the same as people at the top in the private sector, who want the same as the top in the banks, has led to this widening of the gap. I think it's very divisive.

It is not the politics of envy. The rich, super-rich, not all of them, but too many of them, have completely forgotten those responsibilities and obligations. Mention the word tax and see what their reaction is. Charity is different, but with a few honorable exceptions, like Bill Gates, charity payments are a lot less than the tax payments would be. So I'm very hostile. I think the trend has been a disaster. Reagan, Thatcher kicked it off; it spread to other countries to varying extents. Inequality in Europe is not as pronounced as it is in the United States, though Britain is getting pretty pronounced, and I think France is about the same. In the Second World War, and the period after the last great economic crisis, we did develop a sense of greater mutual obligation. I wouldn't say it was a golden period, it wasn't, Roosevelt, the New Deal and all that. But it was a kind of system which kept a check on the rich and powerful, and I think those checks have largely disappeared.

Has globalization also played a role?

I think being able to whiz your money about has played a part. If you are a Richard Branson, all your tax arrangements are somewhere in the West Indies, company and personal. Funnily enough, I don't think it's got much to do with China, I don't think it's got much to do with trade. I'm much more relaxed about that, and unlike some of my American colleagues, I'm rather a free trader. But the free movement of capital has been exploited ruthlessly to the detriment of the tax base in a lot of countries, and this has helped create a significant number of people in the super-rich category.

Once there were a few, a tiny percent, less than 1% – but now, there are a lot of millionaires and billionaires around. They have a major effect on inflation, on the macroeconomic picture. Their pay has been way beyond any measure of performance that could be objectively established. It's been scratching my back, scratching your back, setting easy, ludicrous targets, and paying each other a fortune. And it affects even little things, like how much time a Board of Directors spend talking about their own remuneration arrangements, a huge part of the time.

I don't mind people getting rich, I don't mind real entrepreneurs being well paid. It's not class envy. But these guys did what they did in the banks to such disastrous effect, convincing themselves that they eliminated risk, which just shows how stupid they were. They've wrecked their banks and they've done a considerable amount of damage to the Western economies. It came from them and it has rippled out into the other areas, right down to what a chief executive in a local authority might pay himself, with ludicrously easy targets to achieve. I'm extremely angry about that, passionately scathing about the people, and very concerned that governments have been so tolerant of it and scared in front of it. If they want to pack off to Switzerland, let 'em go, is my general philosophy.

Do you think the current crisis will change anything?

That is extremely interesting, because if we go back to the G20 meeting in early April in London, everybody was going to regulate the new financial economy. As far as I can see, the British Government, apart from hoping to develop transparency and to increase taxation, is going to do little on the financial sector. They're protecting hedge funds and private equity against European regulation. They're not going to do Glass-Steagall, they're not going to restrict the banks. They're thinking about capital ratios, what banks might keep, but they're looking very much at what the United States does on that. They might try to keep London less regulated than New York, despite the fact that the AIG operation was London-based, the bit that collapsed, and the Lehman Brothers bit that was particularly culpable was in London. So this is not a sub-prime, just made in America crisis. London had a significant contributing role to play and the British government have a commensurate responsibility too.

I've just read a book by Gillian Tett of the *Financial Times* who spotted much of this going wrong about 2004 and nobody paid any attention. I was the General Secretary to the British TUC, all of three miles from the City, and while I followed macroeconomics intently, I chucked the markets bit of the *Financial Times* in the bin, what's happening to some company or other, funds and so on. It wasn't until my daughter's then boyfriend got a job with a hedge fund and I asked him what it was that I really got interested. Because after he told me, I said, "Is any of that legal?" As far as I could see, it was gambling with other people's money. I gave the Aneurin Bevan lecture in 2006 that was mainly on hedge funds and private equity, and what they were up too, loading huge amounts of debt onto companies, with Goldman Sachs and others making a fortune out of the fees.

It's been particularly bitter for me that the Glazers in Orlando, Florida bought Manchester United, and landed it with 700 million pounds debt, an annual interest rate charge of 67 million. We won the European Cup in 2008, finalists last year, the English league last year, and we are still in debt. Before we weren't in debt at all, but we were one of these quaint companies who owned its own property, had a small mortgage on its latest new stand, and was ripe for being asset stripped, which was done by these Glazer brothers. And again, Goldman Sachs, the Royal Bank of Scotland, they made a fortune. God knows what happens to Manchester United if they don't win, there's no margin for any error.

I think the excesses of capitalism are the biggest threat to capitalism. Cheap money did it, to some extent. But the greed of the people is what comes out in this Gillian Tett book. JP Morgan seems particularly an exception, they invented credit derivative swaps, but they were much more cautious and were aware of the downside risks. Merrill Lynch, Bear Stearns, and just about everybody else, just piled in. The book reads like a thriller, it will hold your attention.

Will inequality increase?

What checked the rise of inequality? One was politics and the rise of the organized working class demanding a bigger share, demanding political change, and welfare states before the First World War. Secondly was prolonged recession where there was simply not enough profits to generate high pay in the late twenties and thirties. And thirdly, the post-war period, huge taxation rises on the rich, 98p in the pound in the U.K. – not too many people paid that – but that was the top rate. But after a flatter rate of tax was introduced and capital markets liberalized, then there's been no limit to rising inequality.

It should be checked by this recession temporarily, but people don't just want business as usual, they want bonuses as usual. I don't detect any sense that many in the financial services world even now understand. Gordon Brown commissioned Sir Win Bischoff, former chairman of Citigroup, a British guy who's working in Wall Street, to discover what went wrong with the banking system. And he totally unsurprisingly and predictably reported back, "We made some mistakes, we have some lessons to learn, but we don't want any more regulation, thank you very much." Of course that's what he would say. There's a huge, huge lobbying effort launched against the American government, against Europe, in favor of trying to restore business as usual, with the message leave us alone. However, the fact is that the taxpayers are into this to 2030, minimum. We've lost three trillion dollars. But bank profits are not looking too bad, they want to pay the governments off, then tell the governments to keep their hands off. Of course, there is the Sarkozy-Merkel criticism of the Anglo-Saxon model which I generally support. But that's portrayed, certainly in London, as the French want to move our City to Paris. But I think that misses the point that this crisis will be the cost of a major war, and it's due to the behavior of the financial services sector.

Is there a right level of inequality?

There is no rigid formula. We used to talk in the 1970s, when a Swedish economist proposed that chief executives should get no more than five times what the lowest paid employee in his company should get. Well, multiply that now by hundreds. But let me make clear – I'm not trying to remake East Germany, I'm not trying to restore the Soviet economy.

What could be done with regard to executive compensation?

"It is difficult" is the answer to that. But I do think that executive compensation is at the heart of the poor levels of performance that have taken place, that people take so much time maximizing their own take, under the mantra of shareholder value, they actually screw the shareholders. Ironically, shareholders didn't care much about what they were doing because I don't think shareholders are long-termist. How do you get people to think more long-term, about the growth of the business over a period? I posed these questions at a seminar in the City of London and some bright spark put his hand up and said, "I've got some long-term investments, Mr. Monks. They're short-term investments I can't get rid of," he said with a smirk on his face. "As soon as I can sell 'em, I will." That's the traders;

they have taken over from the organic growth. They've made generally far more money with far less risk than the people who are really building businesses.

Nonetheless, I do think the answer will be found in a combination of some pretty well-enforced taxation and some linking of executive pay to longer-term growth. Rather than short-term shareholder maximization, linking pay to growing market share and activities that encourage organic growth, rather than selling off your buildings just before your annual report has to be written, not satisfying your short-term targets by creating long-term weakness in the company, which is what many have been doing.

In that respect, I think the United States has done better than Europe. The States has an ability to generate new businesses in new areas to a much greater degree than the European Union – IT in particular has been spectacular. Private equity is venture capital, and not just related to mergers and acquisitions as it's tended to be in Europe. For example, venture capital was 10% of private equity in the U.K., but this is a small business compared to mergers and acquisition, asset stripping, stuffing results in the short-term to make returns look attractive. I'm not a Soviet communist, but I do think the behavior of these bosses has resembled the Bourbons in their last years. If they carry on like this again, and especially if there's any repeat of what we've just had, I'm not sure how many Western economies could pay for that or people would stand for it. I'm still not sure that all countries can pay for what we're going through.

There will be a reaction, I don't know what it will be or exactly what form it will take. The U.K. is interesting because the bankers were really in trouble, and then the *Daily Telegraph* managed to find all this stuff on MPs' expenses that lasted for about three or four weeks and everybody forgot the bankers. If you were a PR guy for the banks, that was the finest diversion operation that's ever been done. I could be paranoid on it, but I wouldn't be a bit surprised to find that the timing of that exposure was down to some City PR company that thought, right, give it to the *Telegraph*, providing they stretch it out and then nobody could remember who Fred Goodwin (the discredited ex-boss of the Royal Bank of Scotland) was anymore.

What about setting a limit on executive pay?

It's hard, isn't it, I don't know how you do that. If you were in the Gates position and you had a fantastic product that the whole world wanted and was virtually unchallenged, and you make an absolute fortune, what can you do about that? I don't think you can do anything about that. But in a way, this is a weakness of our position, we try to divide the ones who've done something from the ones who've done nothing, apart from improve the returns for their bank or whatever, often by rearranging their tax affairs. The person who comes along and invents an engine that's readily available, quite cheap, and very green and clean, is going to make an absolute fortune, and deserves to, I don't care about that. So never mind the undeserving poor. I can acknowledge a deserving rich, and I like to find some way to separate them from the undeserving rich, many of whom are fairly ordinary people who happen to be working in certain areas and do what everybody else does, and make a fortune.

Have we seen any popular reactions?

I don't think in a period when living standards were generally going up, people noticed. In Europe, minimum wages, with the exception of Germany, have been going up. The United States, for the average and below, they have probably been going down, which is a big difference. The fact that top pay was going up, I'm not sure that people really noticed or cared. I think they're noticing now what has happened to top wages when the economy's gone right down and who are the people responsible for the collapse? The money was made in the heart of institutions where people put their life savings and their mortgage, and so on, and it was being traded like a badly run casino. Meanwhile, for whose benefit was that being done? Certainly hasn't been the shareholders, it hasn't been the workers, it hasn't been the customers, it has been the executives. Outside people have been noticing, and if I can do anything to help them notice more, I shall certainly do so.

What should the private sector and government do to address rising inequality?

I think much of this lies in corporate governance. It's very difficult for one company to take action in isolation from the others, which is where I think the state, and perhaps beyond the state, Europe and North America, have to do something concerted. But I do think it helps having shareholder organizations demanding that pay is more long-term related. There are different elements to consider. It has long been the case in Germany that you didn't just get your bonuses linked to shareholder value, you get it from market share, which was something real and could be measured – the social market concept that you have to show organic growth, not just financial chicanery. I wouldn't say that Germany is a model of corporate governance, it isn't, but I do think that is the direction I would like to see people going, trying to structure business rewards so they are not just linked to short-term shareholder value, mergers and acquisition deals, many of which go wrong. The majority of which go wrong and you have no shareholder value at all. I think that's probably where the heart of it is, but I wouldn't say we're totally confident we would stop it by those things. We're not.

The other area would be tax, a stronger progressive tax agenda with a major effort in relation to making them pay their tax, which most of them don't do fully at the moment. If you've got a multinational company the chances to shift your money to avoid tax are considerable, as you probably know. Corporate governance and taxation are the two most important areas.

What can labor unions do to address inequality?

One is be strong. There is a correlation between strong unions and employers behaving themselves. Strong unions keep employers more honest. That's one of the reasons why there is so much anti-union sentiment in boardrooms around the world. They don't want strong unions. They don't want strong unions because they may interfere with managerial prerogatives. They don't want the scrutiny and the independent challenge they get when the unions are strong and tough. So be strong and be interested is the first thing. How many employers get away with saying we want to be one team, we want to be the best team, but the rewards structure is being elongated? That's not fair, that's not right.

Is there anything you can do to put that on the public agenda?

We try. I think, at the moment, this is the biggest opportunity labor unions have had for a long time, because our opponents have had a heart attack and are on life support courtesy of the taxpayer. Workers are paying with their taxes, with their pay cuts everywhere, and in some cases jobs. I think we should have a heavier degree of public support. When things were going very well, I can remember talking to Tony Blair, about the City. He said, look, you're the Prime Minister, you've got everything going wrong, foreign policy, someone breaks out of jail, health service does the wrong thing somewhere. When something's going well, you're rather relieved, you don't go looking for issues because they come along and clout you around the face. I understand that, but it now has come along and clouted them all around the face. Because of the degree of the problem, the banks are virtually under national protection, the taxpayer is the banker of last resort. That's happening in the United States, Britain, and some other countries.

Is there a best measure for addressing inequality?

The evidence of previous attempts shows that taxation does have an effect, that it is a signal of public policy about inequality to have high levels of personal taxation for higher incomes. Of course, you get, "Our incentives are being reduced, so we're probably going somewhere else to do it," and all the rest of it, and that is a risk, that is a risk I would take. You probably lose some of the talented and keep the mass bulk of them who are dross. So there is a cost to it, but I think that would be the route I would prefer.

Have you seen signs of resentment in the labor movement?

The place where it should have started the most was in the States. The AFL-CIO has got some very good guys, very good people in the States, but they're more relaxed with inequality than in Europe. Whether it's the relative absence of a class structure, whether it's the American love of success, the American Dream, "we're all immigrants, we'll all make it," "we're not jealous of people who make it, we'd like to be like them." Whereas with the greater cohesion of European societies, the traditions, their conservatism, their welfare states are strong.

Perhaps I haven't said enough about the different European countries. Watch France, particularly as it is the most socially minded country in Europe, probably in the world. Belgium, by the way, is somewhere not far behind. Watch France, Sarkozy is talking about the failings of capitalism on a daily basis at the moment, threatening the Anglo-American style of capitalism. He's just cancelled some bonuses.

If I had a forecast to make, I'd say, we're in a Keynesian counter-cyclical era where governments are spending hugely to keep up demand in the economy without any particular regard for the deficits, apart from the Germans who are not fully in the recession yet but already clearly concerned about the deficits. When we come out of the recession – and by the way, all this talk about green shoots, share prices up, banks getting back to normal, is a massive public relations exercise to show they don't need regulation. When the economy recovers, the governments will turn and look at each other and say we've got to pay back all this money.

France has just gone to 80% debt of GDP. Euro rules say it shouldn't exceed forty. At that point, the public sector will get hit hard.

There will be huge cuts in public spending, there will be probably rises in taxation, probably on the middle earners because they're the ones who tend to pay it. There will be a period of considerable misery as we try to get public expenditure back under control. That's the most dangerous phase. It is extremely hard to judge when to do that. Today, apart from these people losing their jobs, it's relatively painless. Prices are low, there is a bit of deflation, governments are not doing what they did in the thirties, they're not cutting benefits. There are some wage cuts, but they're not cutting benefits. But give it a year's time, say, pessimistically maybe two years, they're going to have to cut back very hard. I see the figure this morning from the Chartered Institute of Personnel and Development in the U.K. was that 350,000 public sector jobs to go in the next five years, starting next year. Real tough battles will take place with the labor movement on that. I don't think we're there yet, but there is a gathering storm sense about some of this. If at the same time the bankers are back to normal and whacking in their claims to their big bonuses when all this is going on, which they're perfectly capable of, they don't learn anything, then I think this will be a much bigger issue than it has been until now.

Sir Mark Moody-Stuart
Former Chairman, Anglo American; Former Chairman, Shell

"Outrage and media coverage only has an impact on the most visible and also on the more responsible or on those sensitive to public opinion. It has no effect on the invisible or indeed on the completely brazen."

Sir Mark Moody-Stuart was Chairman of Anglo American, a global mining and natural resources company, from 2002 to 2009. He is currently a Director of HSBC, Accenture, Saudi Aramco, and the International Institute for Sustainable Development. From 1998 to 2001, he was Chairman of the Royal Dutch Shell Group of companies. Moody-Stuart is a member of the United Nations Global Compact Board and was Chairman of the Global Compact Foundation in 2006. He is also Co-Chairman of The Global Business Coalition on HIV/AIDS, Tuberculosis, and Malaria, and Chairman of the Innovative Vector Control Consortium. He holds a doctorate in geology and originally joined Shell as an exploration geologist.

How do you view income inequality today?

You have to begin by defining how the inequality arises, because that makes a big difference. Basically you have three forms of inequality arising from well above average wealth – leaving on one side for the moment the low-pay end of the range. The first is caused by old wealth, inherited wealth, which has been with us always and always will be, and generally keeps its head down and is not particularly visible. The second kind of inequality is generated by entrepreneurs, owner-operators such as

R. Berger et al., *The Inequality Puzzle: European and US Leaders Discuss Rising Income Inequality*, DOI 10.1007/978-3-642-15804-9_8, © Springer-Verlag Berlin Heidelberg 2010

Bill Gates or the founders of Google. I think that this form of wealth differential, in general, doesn't cause issues. Most people consider that these are people who invested their own money, took risks, retained a share, and maybe got people co-investing. Their wealth fundamentally comes from a significant shareholding in something they created, which will eventually elide into old wealth as it did with Rockefeller or Carnegie.

I think nobody begrudges the wealth of people who are owner-operators, who created something. Of course, what they then do with it does make a difference as to how they are perceived and also to some extent how they made it, whether in a reputable or disreputable way. But if you assume that somebody made money by creating something useful which society wanted, innovating or inventing, I don't think people are concerned that someone like that is a multi-billionaire while other people are working for normal wages in the organization, provided they have good working conditions and so on. The differential is not seen as relevant because the difference is between an owner, a capitalist as it were, an entrepreneur, and the workforce.

Where the issue of inequality comes to the fore is with regard to a third group of people who are essentially managing public companies. Historically they've been people who ran and administered companies owned by other investors. Such people may also be very creative – they may grow the company, they may do all sorts of things – but essentially, they're doing it with other people's capital. The current issue has arisen because in the last ten or fifteen years there has been a growth in the differential between these people at the top of major public companies and those within the company or in society at large. I think that is where the strains begin to grow. If on top of that there are issues resulting from failures of these major organizations, in other words, fundamentally a failure to steward the investment, the problem is exacerbated. Everyone in the Western world has a stake in such companies, in the form of investments through pensions, through employment directly, or in suppliers and so on, so society's feeling of betrayal in the case of failure is then greater. But the problem existed before the current downturn, it's not just something which has come to light because there have been major failures. It was quite clearly growing over the last decade or more and not just in banks.

I think in the last ten or fifteen years there has been a tendency for the base salaries at the top of major organizations to rise. In this country, for example, senior executive salaries have tended to grow in the 5 to 10% range, not above 10%, but in that range. Wages in the organization as a whole have tended to grow more in line with inflation or inflation plus a little bit, so say 4%. If you do that for ten years, it exaggerates the difference and is manifestly unsustainable. You can't go on doing that forever. This differential was further exacerbated by increased amounts of performance-related pay, bonuses and long-term incentives at the top. People designed remuneration structures which reflected short-term and long-term performance. I sit on several remuneration committees, and in my experience the incentive schemes are very often quite well designed and do reflect performance. They work in the sense they deliver what they're supposed to do. I'm not saying they work in all cases, but the idea, which is common, that these systems are all just a bunch of flannel and that they have no real meaning and performance targets are not tough, is not generally true. While it is clearly true in some cases, in the companies I've been involved with, the schemes don't pay out when performance is poor, so people don't get anything. In that way, within their framework, they're perfectly fair.

Is the level of inequality unacceptable?

It's just in that third category that it has become unacceptable. Inherited wealth is not a problem – I think the vast bulk of the population who save and try to pass something on to their children or give their children a better life don't get too excited about it. And since most of the people with seriously inherited wealth sensibly tend to keep their heads down, with some notable exceptions such as Paris Hilton, I think it's not been a big issue. The entrepreneurial class is also not, I think, a big issue. So if you ask me whether the levels of inequalities in those two areas are too high, I would say no.

It's this third area of employees that the strains develop. In my Shell career, I referred to us all as the employees, because even when I was Chairman or a Chief executive I was an employee. One tried to encourage this feeling that we were all employees of Shell; we were all paid to work on behalf of shareholders, but to produce something useful to society. I think that the divergence of remuneration between the top and bottom of an organization is now causing strain in society.

What are the reasons for the rise in senior executive compensation? Was it due to globalization?

Only partly, although due to globalization there has been a certain amount of increased mobility. In the financial industry, for example, remuneration in the United States was generally higher and that flowed across the Atlantic to Europe. That is a consequence of mobility and the market. In a strange way this was exacerbated by the greater transparency on pay in company annual reports, certainly in this country. So now everybody knows what their peers are paid, and that has probably led to an upward competitive movement. It is an entirely unintended and unexpected consequence of giving shareholders what you think would be beneficial, a right to comment on pay, as they have in this country. And of course in order to comment, to vote on it, they need to see the figures and the systems. I think that this public reporting has been a small contributor, but I'm not in any way against transparency because I think transparency coupled with a shareholder vote on pay is a good thing.

The correction, in the end, lies in that transparency. There are only two ways of correcting excesses of pay. One is by legislation, which I do not support because I think it would result in an enormous amount of effort being put into devising ways to get around the legislation. When we had so-called pay restraint in the seventies in the U.K., it resulted in very complex pay packages, benefits-in-kind and all sorts of stuff which took years to remove. The other way to control remuneration is self-regulation under the pressure of a) shareholders and b) public opinion.

What shareholder pressure has clearly done is to help ensure that the variable elements are reasonable and generally have sensible performance conditions. There is no doubt that this could be made more active and effective, but it has had an effect.

Public opinion can also have an effect on the level of remuneration, but probably only when it reaches the level of outrage. Public outrage is not a very pleasant sight and has unintended consequences because it operates in a capricious way and often hits people and organizations who are not the most guilty of the egregious offences, but who are merely most visible. There is no doubt that public outrage and media attention has had an impact – many organizations and individuals waived bonuses in the last year, but not everywhere. Outrage and media coverage only has an impact on the most visible and also on the more responsible or on those sensitive to public opinion. It has no effect on the invisible or indeed on the completely brazen.

If people at the top of banks, or at Anglo American, were paid less, would it make any difference to the amount that they worked?

The answer depends on whether they were the only ones or not. If they felt that their peers, people in other companies or similar situations, were being paid more, then it would make a difference. Because as we all know, whatever level you're at in a company, remuneration is only a factor when you think that you are being taken advantage of – being screwed relative to the competition. If there is a genuine reduction across all similar companies, it wouldn't make any difference at all, because the size of remuneration at the top of major corporations is such that you could live a perfectly happy, comfortable, affluent life on significantly less. So the root of it has been this competitive relative growth. That's very difficult to deal with.

Why did the inflationary pay spiral start?

Probably for two reasons. First, based on easy credit, we have been through a period of remarkable growth of global GDP. So there was a lot of profitability around for a long boom period. The second reason was the increased mobility of people, so the market became freer. Mobility between companies increased, which in a sense is positive. But of course, if you sit on a remuneration committee, you then have to be concerned that your best people might go and work for someone else. While mobility is in principle a good thing, in many corporations I think there has also been a decrease on both sides in long-term commitment and loyalty. Companies became more focused on financial returns and forgot about all the other issues. I think that was another aspect influencing changing attitudes toward pay.

In discussions with shareholders – and as chairman of the remuneration committee of a bank I have a lot of these discussions – I often explain to our shareholders that on the high remuneration end of a bank, as a remuneration committee we did a number of things to ensure that our remuneration was effective and competitive. There are quite simple measures such as tracking what proportion of offers to experienced hires are accepted – if everyone accepts your offer you are just leading the market. Or, for example, ensuring that the bonus of the person you're hiring in comes out of the existing bonus pool, so that the hiring group has to believe that the new hire will really contribute to the overall business. Then one needs to look at the return on the additional investment you are making through hiring people over time, because these are significant sums. So I would explain with some pride to our shareholders that we put into place a number of measures that made sure that we were not spending excessively on recruiting experienced talent and that we were deriving benefit from it. But then I would also point out that the real problem with all of these measures is that you can start to look at them as if they are the controlling mechanism, and that the whole thing is driven by remuneration. Because when you start to treat people like a financial investment – if you just add some more money here, the following happens – that's exactly what you don't want. The more you devise these crafty mechanisms, the more you forget that pay is only a little piece of the whole motivation of people. The really important bit is how you build the spirit and the ethos of the company. And it's as companies began to lose that spirit and ethos that the unwelcome bits of mobility, the weakening of loyalty, increased.

Mobility is a good thing. The days when major companies regarded somebody who left to do another job as worthy of being cast into outer darkness and felt that there must have been something the matter with him (in those days normally him and not her) compare unfavorably to the present. Today, when somebody goes, and has found a good opportunity, you say, "fine, you've done a great job here, when you want to come back, you're welcome." But what you really want is to have your people, the people in your organization, being the people everybody wants to hire. The competition will make them tempting offers, but your people will say, "No, thank you, I'm very happy here. This is such an exciting job, I know you'll pay me one and a half, twice what I'm earning, thanks very much, but I'm happy." That's where you want to be. But that, of course, is also a dream. We can achieve it in places. I know many individuals who have been offered multiples of their salary and they come and say I received such and such an offer. Then what do you do? They know you're not going to say, "OK, we'll double your salary," but you probably do give them an extra big rise or something, although they're not actually asking for that.

So this question of remuneration becomes in part a reflection of how your contribution to the team is perceived, a kind of gesture. At Shell, I think the first bonus I was paid was sometime in the nineties. I remember thinking, oh, this is really a very nice thing. They didn't have to give me the money, but they did; it wasn't a huge amount, but I thought, that's really very nice. Gradually, of course, that wears off and people get grumpy if they don't get a bonus. Then you get the spiral.

What can be done to correct this trend?

It is clearly unsustainable that the differential should keep on growing as it has done for ten years or more. Certainly the growth in disparity between top and bottom has to stop, but reversing or switching back will be very difficult. So we have to make sure that remuneration moves toward more investment in their company's shares by the most highly paid people. The majority of their performance pay should be in equity, in shares in the company. I think this is a positive trend which begins in a way to move the people from the third category into the second category. Of course, in a major corporation no employee will ever be a significant shareholder, but at least you can make sure that a significant amount of their wealth is tied up in the fortunes of the company. I think that would be the key and that's the principle I have always worked on, that as an executive one's variable remuneration becomes an investment in the company.

If I was a controlling shareholder of a major company, I would pay people a pretty generous basic salary. I would then give significant bonuses, varying with their performance and the performance of the company or their part of the company in the last year. I would say to them, you get a bonus but three-quarters of it goes into shares of the company. You've got to hold those shares for a very long time. You'd have to make sure they built up a very substantial pot in the company, so that they really are linked to the company.

Would those shares remain if they left the company?

I think they should lose some of them, but not all of them, because if someone works for twenty years and then decides to work somewhere else, it would be quite unreasonable not to allow them to take basically their savings. If they're being hired by someone else, of course, the guy hiring them has to pay them. They go and say, look, I had all these shares which only vest if I stay, I'm losing them, what are you going to do about it? The answer will be, OK, then we'll give you shares in our company instead. You can't tie people by money, but I do think you can align them.

What other aspects affect attitudes toward appropriate compensation?

I come from a slightly previous generation. My executive service stopped in 2001 and it was only about five years before that when things began to take off in remuneration terms. You have, of course, to look at the other side of the coin. If you go back in time, although I was never remunerated at the sort of levels that senior executives are now, I had a very generous final salary pension scheme and those have gone now. Nowadays most highly paid executives don't get final salary pension schemes, they have to look after their own retirement funding.

That gets us into the philosophy of final salary pension schemes. The changes in pension schemes started in this country when the then Chancellor changed the taxation of pension funds, which took several billion pounds a year out of the pension industry. That caused trouble, reducing reserves. This was a bad move, because it actually damaged something useful. I think those pension schemes were a valuable benefit for a very large part of the population. Quite plainly, because of changes in life expectancy and so on, one needs some modifications. But I think a move which basically says to the vast mass of the population, here's your money, you're on your own as far as pension goes, is a bad thing. A certain amount of enforced saving is very good. For highly paid executives to have a large proportion of their savings tied up in shares of their own company is a good thing, but for much of the rest of the organization a secure pension is an important element of remuneration.

Since we got ourselves into this crisis, people tend to blame the banks. This is unfair as Western society as a whole is guilty of an orgy of credit-based expenditure. Everyone who topped up their mortgage and had a big credit card debt is just as guilty of mucking up the system as are the banks. The people who are really guilty are the financial regulators who allowed it to happen, because that's what regulators are there for.

Does the financial crisis have an impact on the third category of people and the other two groups?

Yes, it plainly had an impact on inherited wealth, but that will come back, it's a dip. In the great scheme of things, some of them will be wiped out if they had all of their funds invested foolishly, but those with good, solid advisors would have seen a reduction, but it will come back. Those in the second group have obviously also seen their wealth damaged by share prices, particularly if their fortune was largely tied up in a single corporation. Market declines have impacted many foundations. Every non-profit that I have any involvement with has had to scale back. So it certainly has an impact on the not-for-profit sector. Those in the third group, the senior executives of corporations, have also felt the pain. They have received less variable pay, their shares in their own company are also worth less, and in some cases they have lost their jobs. The crisis has affected everyone.

Does charity affect how people view inequality?

Yes, something we haven't talked about is what people actually do with their money. The United States for many years had a very high level of personal philanthropy so people always saw this need to donate, whether it was related to their alma mater or other causes. They donated sometimes in a rather visible way, which is to some extent part of the process, but very much expected in the United States. That has come more slowly in this country, but it is coming now. It has lagged behind the increase of corporate remuneration. Although I know it sounds judgmental, but I know from approaching people for funds that in some cases it lagged quite seriously. A colleague of mine said once, "you can tell how much it lags because if you give a thousand pounds to one of the big mass charities, such as Oxfam, you go on their major donors list." That may be an exaggeration, but it's not far from the truth. That doesn't mean, of course, that people are not donating in other areas. People who are trying to give their money away intelligently don't necessarily give it to mass charities that have a capacity to raise funds from a much wider base. They probably – and that's personally always been my approach – try to find things which are really worth doing but are not able to get money from anywhere else, or organizations which are in a crisis and really need untied help. I think people are much more tolerant of high remuneration if they feel the person earning it actually does something with it other than just spending it. Behavior, of course, makes a difference. It is always interesting to look at sponsorships of charitable marathons and cycle rides in companies. You would expect higher level folk to do higher levels of sponsorship. Not to give ten pounds, but two hundred or more, because that's at least the ratio in pay from bottom to top. I don't think the ratio in generosity generally matches that in the U.K.

How can we change that ratio?

I think it's coming, actually. It's coming slowly as people begin to realize the satisfaction that it can give; when they can see something worthwhile and exciting that some organization is doing and in which they can become involved. Of course, we've been talking very much about people at the top of organizations. Some of the highest paid people are not at the top, they're within the organization. Certainly in the banking industry, you get young people who are paid very substantial amounts of money in performance bonuses. I think that they're beginning to realize that pleasure is not just a Ferrari or expensive wines, which is the kind of conspicuous consumption which upsets people. Many of those people are realizing there's more to life than this, and that personal satisfaction or fulfillment is more important.

Will the values change come naturally?

In part, but I think it can be encouraged by tax incentives. I was asked to take part in an interesting survey the other day commissioned by the U.K. Treasury on the taxation of charitable donations. I confess I was deeply suspicious. I get asked to participate in a lot of surveys, but I did this one quite carefully because they were basically asking what my response in giving would be if the government reduced the tax efficiency. Under the U.K. system, if you're a higher-rate payer and you make a donation, the charity gets back the tax paid at the standard rate and all the higher-rate tax comes back to the donor. The questions in the survey were testing what would happen if the government played around with this. They asked, for example, what would happen if we didn't give the higher-rate taxation back? Would you reduce your contribution? Or if, for example, we gave all the tax to the charity, would you reduce your giving? I was carefully looking at my answers to indicate that provided the tax went to the charity it would not matter whether any tax came back to me or not. You want the charity to get a certain amount of money, and whether you get some back or not, is neither here nor there. What's important is what goes to the charity. If I thought the government was simply pocketing something they had previously let go, then I would be upset.

In general, the fiscal arrangements here in the U.K. are as generous as in the United States. The only difference is that in the United States I believe that you can give the money away in the future and get a credit for it now. That you can't do here, you only get the tax credit when you actually give the money away, which seems quite fair to me.

How do you see the level of inequality evolving?

I would hope that inequality in general would not further increase, partly as a result of more restraint at the top. But we have not mentioned the other end of the scale which involves raising people out of poverty. It depends how you measure inequality. If you take the physical gap in dollars, plainly if everyone increases by x%, the numerical gap increases, that's mathematics, so that gap will probably increase. But I would hope in percentage terms, in multiple terms, the gap would not increase. In part developments will depend not just on developments at the upper end of the pay scale, but on the lower end and on how good countries are at encouraging enterprise and employment. There are also social issues. In this country there is a significant element of people who are poor, disadvantaged, deprived, and entirely dependent on state aid. I'm not saying it's their fault, but they're stuck in it, they're in a trap, an aspiration trap, or an example trap, or the trap of a lousy education system. I mean an education system which has been manifestly failing them, an education system which actually has failed partly through the search for equality.

As an example, some time ago every few years the *Economist* would look at the top jobs in Britain, although as the publication has become more international they probably stopped doing this. They defined the top jobs as the Prime Minister, Cabinet Ministers, senior civil servants, various professions, and the chief executives of some major companies (the comparison is now more difficult because some companies have disappeared). They took two hundred benchmark positions, influential people in the country, and looked at their educational background. If you go back to the fifties or sixties, when I was in school and at university, the key positions were all held by people who had been educated at private schools, attended a significant institution. So Hugh Gaitskell, leader of the Labour party, was educated at Winchester. Whether you looked at a Labour party cabinet or a Conservative cabinet, most were educated at private institutions.

This then progressively changed, and you could see that increasingly these positions were held by people who were educated in the state sector, not in the private sector. They were educated at grammar schools which were selective and somewhat elitist, the great grammar schools such as Manchester grammar school and other well-known, really good state-supported schools. But then with the creation of the comprehensive school system there was a movement against academic selection and selective grammar schools – we should have no selective education. And basically, whether because of the principle or because of the implementation – I do not know which – there was severe damage to the education system. The peak of state educated people in the *Economist* benchmark was about in the nineties, and then it turned round and started to go the other way. I would guess that it's seriously going the other way now. Entrants from private sector education are dominant in the major universities, however hard the major universities try to adjust the ratio. So here was an effort at increasing equality, which has actually in my opinion damaged social mobility, which is a huge tragedy.

I don't necessarily blame it on the concept of comprehensive education. But manifestly in this country it was a product of what we did, which has not worked. It may be how we did it rather than the fact that we did it. Unfortunately round the world we see that when you do something and damage the education system, you can damage it extremely quickly and it takes decades to recover. We are now in a situation where our examination system is seriously flawed, such that the major universities are now saying they have to invent their own exam to get differentiation because the major exams in science and technology are now such that, properly taught, anyone should be able to get straight As. There's no differentiation. How do universities see whether one person's straight As are better than another person's straight As? As there is no significant differentiation in public exams, universities have to develop their own methods of differentiation.

If we want to have less inequality in the future, what do you recommend?

For the long term, you have to start doing something about the education system, you need to make sure the education system gets everyone properly educated, but paradoxically also allows for differentiation, because people are not all the same. We need a system which allows people to develop their talents. Because what's extremely disruptive in inequality is not just inequality itself, it's when individuals feel that they are trapped in the unequal half of the equation. If they feel they have an opportunity to achieve, then I think it causes less stress.

So a feeling that there is fairness in the system is important. I am not a sporting person, but I suppose that is why in sports salaries, the large difference between top and bottom causes less stress and outrage. If you look in football, soccer, tennis, golf, the top are extremely well remunerated and there is a long tail of people who struggle to make a living from their sport. I suppose that society finds that acceptable to some extent because people feel if they're really good, they will get to the top and they have the dream that they can actually access the top. Then, at a certain point, they think, well dammit, I am plainly just not good enough. They come to terms with the fact that they're not a great footballer while so and so is, and good luck to him. I think this feeling that you have the opportunity and that there is mobility is very important.

The education system is very important, but systems within companies are also enormously important. Within companies we need to work carefully on diversity, making sure that there are no hidden barriers, that there are not people with advantages because of who they are or where they came from. That's hugely important in a corporation. In a well-run corporation, you have a very strong feeling of corporate unity and common purpose. There is complete acceptance that people at all levels contribute. If there are people who others in the organization feel are not contributing, that's extremely disruptive. Almost every company has somewhere in its values the concept of respect for people. If you have people who are contributing financially, whose business performance is very good, but who are doing so in a way which is out of line with the company's professed values, that is damaging. For example if you have such people who manifestly do not have respect for people and you don't kick them out or make them change their behavior, then I think you get a very damaging erosion of the company's professed values.

People within the company want their team at the top to be well paid, but they probably don't want them at the very top of the salary leagues and being attacked for being fat cats. But they don't want to be at the bottom of the pay league either. They want the feeling that they're somewhere in the right place. It's going to take a while to change, but equity is the key.

So internally, I would work very hard to make sure that compensation is seen as equitable and that the variable pay systems are seen as equitable. There are group systems which bind people together and yet still acknowledge differentiation and the need for team leaders and specialists who should earn more. So it's the style of leadership that I think will make a difference. Furthermore, for people who earn a lot, what they do with the money is important. It's an entirely private matter, but I think it's nonetheless socially important.

Are there issues of inequality you feel that Anglo American should address in less-advantaged parts of the world?

This is something we tried to address in my Shell days, but I've also thought about here. In Shell when I was there, we used to publish in our Shell sustainability report the youngest person who was working for the company and the person who earned the least. Interestingly, after a while we stopped doing it because it got so difficult in terms of understanding. I remember at one point the person who earned the least was something like a security guard somewhere in the Horn of Africa. I don't think in cash terms he earned a great deal more than two dollars a day. But if you looked at it in societal terms, the guy was probably a well-respected member of the community and the society, he had a job. I would guess he had a uniform and he probably got lunch, quite likely he might get educational support. In the end just looking at a salary in isolation is meaningless; you have to look at the context.

We considered, briefly, whether we should commit to a global minimum wage. We dropped the idea because it would just lead to economic disruption in some of the countries where we worked. You can't say that you shouldn't have anyone who earns less than, say, ten thousand dollars a year. In some countries you would grossly distort income patterns in the economy. If you started doing that, you would end up with inequality and envy which is already an issue in international companies operating around the world.

This is caused by what have often been called islands of affluence. If you run an operation in a poor country and you want to run a world-class operation, you need world-class standards. You need education, you need food, you need housing, you need training, etc. That immediately puts someone with a job in this organization, if they're lucky enough to get a job, as working at a kind of Goldman Sachs of Africa, as it were. If you're not careful, if you provide facilities where your operations are, you'll end up with a migration gradient as people swarm into the area.

I remember going to a mine in a remote location in Namibia. It had been there for quite a while and as I always try to do, I looked at the schooling and housing, because if you want people to work in a remote area, you've got to fix all that. There was a beautiful, well laid-out township. Neat streets, trees, houses, a bank, supermarket, clinic, a school with strong corporate support, and a community supported by the government. But then if you went a little bit further, just behind the next hill, there was basically a shanty town. I asked, what's that? Ah, well, I was told, because of this island of affluence, there was a certain amount of work available and services also. So people came and they didn't have anywhere to live, so they knocked up a few walls. You look at this and say, this is really bad news, and then you think, why did it grow? The answer is that although you may think this place is unattractive, people walked and migrated to that place because it was better than wherever they were, and probably very much better than in a major urban area. Then you say, OK, now what have we got to do? Can we in some way begin to formalize this, because if, of course, you built another township, there'd be another shanty town next door to that township to serve this second township. Somehow you have to address these things in a wider context and in conjunction with the government concerned. Certainly companies in the extractive industries have begun to think much more holistically about this, as we have done, and we've learned a lot in the last forty years.

One of the things you learn is the importance of the role of government. I was just this morning at a breakfast about British investment in Africa. People were saying if you have income from oil and so on, it helps, and the economy booms. Yes, it does help, but actually what really helps more is sound government and sound governance. In the absence of these, a sudden flow of income into a country, whether from resource revenue or aid, leads to misuse of funds, corruption, and indeed increased inequality.

Poul Nyrup Rasmussen
President, Party of European Socialists; Former Prime Minister, Denmark

"Not only cleaners, taxi drivers, and unskilled workers have rights and duties; this also applies to CEOs, the bankers, and hedge fund managers. We should introduce new ethics based on rights and duties. ... When a plumber is underperforming he's either dismissed the next day, or the employer says, 'You can't have the same salary as you had yesterday.' In the financial sector you do not have similar consequences for those who are in positions of responsibility."

Poul Nyrup Rasmussen was the Prime Minister of Denmark from 1993 to 2001. He became a member of the European Parliament in 2004, where he sat on the Economic and Monetary Affairs Committee and the Foreign Affairs Committee (until June 2009). Since 2004 he has been President of the Party of European Socialists (PES). He is also Co-Chair of the Global Progressive Forum. In December 2008, he oversaw the unanimous ratification of the PES European election manifesto, People First: A New Direction for Europe. Rasmussen has been active in calling for better regulation and supervision of financial markets, and in 2009 he placed fifth on *Financial News*'s annual list of the 100 most influential people in European capital markets.

R. Berger et al., *The Inequality Puzzle: European and US Leaders Discuss Rising Income Inequality*, DOI 10.1007/978-3-642-15804-9_9, © Springer-Verlag Berlin Heidelberg 2010

How would you characterize the level of inequality in Europe and America?

With regard to the United States, I have several observations. One is that the living standards of the average American have been unchanged in the last eight, nine, ten years until the crisis. They're only now beginning a tentative recovery after the deep fall of the crisis. If you take real wages and income, you see that the number of poor people in the United States has increased dramatically, and you see that in the top 5%, 10% of the American income pyramid, they have had extreme gains in income during the last years. For example, if you take *Fortune* magazine's yearly statistics, you will see that the five richest people in the U.S., within the financial industry, have a yearly income corresponding to 22,000 times an American industrial worker's yearly income. This is real inequality, which means American society is divided, with a corresponding threat to social cohesion.

In terms of inequality within European member states, we have during the past five to fifteen years seen accelerating inequality between different socio-economic groups. Income tax – which has been a classical welfare state instrument from a social democratic point of view to ensure a certain contra-inequality policy – has increasingly failed to play its redistributive role, which has led to rising inequalities. The deterioration of the quality of work, precarious working conditions and low wage increases in many member states have served to further widen the social divide. Furthermore, the top 25% of earners have gained disproportionately. And the upper tenth has moved even faster. This is happening to an even greater extent in the United States.

Therefore, you could say that on all the major parameters on how to measure inequality, the arrow is pointing in the same direction, which means increasing inequality. Now, if we take inequality between countries, I would say in Europe there has been an even more complex picture. During the crisis here during the last two years, there has been increasing inequality with respect to the average economic performance and actual economic living conditions among people. The demarcation line between the new Central and Eastern European Member States and the others is especially marked. This crisis has showed us how vulnerable the newer member countries are in Europe.

There are widening inequalities between countries in the European Union as a result of the crisis. This is despite the EU being one of the more economically robust parts of the world. Normally, one would expect the well-developed public sectors to act as a stabilizer during a downturn in the business cycle. In 2009, there was a contrast of a 5% drop in economic growth in Germany compared to 18% in Latvia.

On a global level the crisis has increased inequality between Europe and developing countries, particularly the poorest countries in Africa. However, some of the emerging countries, especially the BRIC countries, have moved faster than the rest of the world has done, so you have a mixed picture. People in developing countries that lack strong democratic governance and established welfare systems have been extremely hurt by this crisis.

Coming back to Europe, the number of poor people has increased, but let me clarify what I mean by poverty. In Europe we define poverty in relation to the average income in society. We consider individuals living in households with an income of less than 60% of the average income to live at risk of poverty. Now it's about 85 million people out of 500 million inhabitants. We have no figures on how the number of people living at risk of poverty increased as a result of the crisis yet, but it is likely that it has been considerable, not only caused by rising unemployment but also by increased pressure on public households due to cuts to welfare systems. A recent Eurobarometer study also shows that 75% of EU citizens believe that poverty has increased in their home country in the last year.

Another aspect of inequality is what I would call those who are excluded from society, not least those who are excluded from the labor market. Increasing numbers of the young generation have found it extremely difficult to enter the job market, resulting in them being marginalized, dropping out of their educational system, and not managing to reintegrate. The barriers preventing young people from getting this crucial first foothold are significant.

If we take minority groups, unemployment is alarmingly high. Some countries are doing better, for example Sweden, Denmark, and partly Finland, but in other countries such as in regions of Germany or France, the numbers are much lower. In Spain, they did try, with some success, to integrate minority groups, and to eliminate social exclusion, but this crisis has had a very negative impact on these policies.

Rising mass unemployment will have a huge impact on inequality in the U.S. and in Europe. Already by the end of this year we will have reached a new peak of 24 million unemployed in Europe, a figure which could go up to more than 28 million in the next five years, if the cuts and "austerity only" approach advocated by the European Commission and Conservative governments is implemented.

Unemployment figures in the U.S., according to two American professors, Nobel Prize winners both, are even more concerning than official reports indicate. They told me: "Poul, it's not around 13%; it's 20%, if you add to the official figure all the illegal immigrants and the informal sector." If you ask who's become unemployed due to the crisis, the answer is certainly that only a very small part of it is coming from Wall Street, and they will survive, one way or another.

The economic recession here has shown us the underlying fragility of our advanced service-based economies and societies. As we have seen earlier in our history, when you have recessions and business downturns of this kind, those who are hit first – poor people, vulnerable people, minorities, immigrants, those with the lowest incomes, those without any education – have a weak attachment to the labor market.

What can be done to lessen inequalities?

Unfortunately, there is no one-size-fits-all answer. There are some common answers, and then there are some specific answers depending upon which part of Europe we're talking about. Europe is more diverse today than it was before our last enlargement. Ten new member states coming from Central and Eastern Europe has altered the dynamics. We need what you could call a pro-convergence strategy which makes the economic demarcation line going through Europe less pronounced.

What can be done? Unemployment and precarious working conditions are key reasons for the existence of inequality and poverty. Especially in times of crisis, stronger efforts need to be made to provide people with decent jobs. Measures to support job creation and to introduce higher standards for the quality of work must become a priority. Especially in future sectors, such as renewable energy, nano-technology, and IT, creating new jobs will have positive effects on social cohesion and economic competitiveness alike.

A number of additional measures could be implemented with respect to the EU budget. The funds available need to better utilized. Improving the mobility in education systems must be a priority. The Erasmus project could be expanded to cover all young people, by giving them an opportunity to live for half a year outside their own country as a part of their general education, and not only for university students but also for those doing vocational education. This would give them valuable transferable skills, such as language skills.

The second point is to reform the European Social Fund, the Cohesion Fund and the Globalization Fund. The social fund should be restructured to focus on three points. The first is funding education and training projects, in a broader context than the Erasmus project. The second is to use the social fund as an instrument to help those excluded from the labor market back into it. The third element in the social fund context is to help our member countries finance projects to integrate vulnerable groups into society – immigrants and minorities for instance, and the long-term unemployed.

The Globalization Fund needs to be expanded in scope and become a permanent financing instrument to aid workers hit by restructuring and to facilitate structural change due to globalization, technological change, and the current crisis.

Additionally, European legislation could be strengthened, for example to make the free movement of labor become genuinely free. It's not free today. For the major part, those who move are forced to move for economic reasons. When the Polish worker goes to Britain, it's not because he loves to go to Britain, it's because he needs to go there for higher earnings, to go back home to buy his house, help his wife, his kids. I'm not saying it's wrong, I'm only saying how do we do it in a better way to ensure we achieve equal pay for equal work and full respect for collective bargaining agreements.

What we need in legislation is the so-called equal pay principle, that no matter where you are, you receive adequate wages, have access to social insurance, pensions, and can benefit from high workers' protection standards. So when Polish workers go to Germany, they are treated according to the German rules and when German workers go to Denmark, they enjoy Danish standards. If you take the northern German slaughterhouses, each Monday morning there's a bus, or two, or ten, coming with Ukraine workers. They come into the slaughterhouses and work from six o'clock in the morning to late at night, and they work for less than half the wages of German slaughterhouse workers. Then they go into the local park and sleep in containers there. They work until Friday, and Friday night they go back to the Ukraine. This is not my concept of what Europe should be.

The so-called posted workers EU directive is another point of debate. It is a controversial one, particularly in Scandinavia. It has to be revised and we need to close the loopholes. We have to avoid the kind of situation whereby an employer sends his own team of employees to another member country, to do a job for a certain period of time, but only pays the minimum salary of the country these workers come from and therefore undermines the right of equal pay for equal work. Such behavior not only exploits these posted workers, it also puts pressure on salaries and working conditions in the countries the employees are sent to. The posted workers directive has been interpreted by the European Court of Justice to allow such abuse and therefore it needs to be revised.

Finally, even though I know this is difficult, we should define a common standard for minimum wages across the European Union. Of course we cannot determine that from Romania to Luxembourg the minimum salary must be €8.50. But an agreement should be found that in each member state an adequate minimum wage should be introduced, either by law or by collective agreement. This way we can begin to define a distribution policy in the future. Minimum income initiatives are essential if the poverty reduction targets of the Europe 2020 Strategy are to be met. We must understand that you can't develop economically and sustainably in the future without dealing with inequality. Having adopted a European standard for a minimum wage, you can then begin to combine this policy with the European Social Fund to tackle inequalities more comprehensively.

As a second general principle, also at the European level, we need to develop the concept called Social Europe. What is our social model? What can be done? Flexicurity has been part of that debate, but the Danish model cannot just be transposed across Europe. Some people would say they would like to do what I did when I was Prime Minister from January 1993 to November 2001. I brought unemployment down from 13% to 3.9% and I reformed the whole labor market in Denmark. I introduced the flexicurity concept, which means that we have today the highest mobility in any labor market anywhere in the world, and at the same time we have the highest social protection in any part of the world. You see that the combination with the right kind of social policy based on rights and duties is, in effect, saying, "I'll give you an offer you can't refuse."

To integrate, step-by-step, this concept at European level, the following measures are needed: It's not about ensuring that a person will have the same job for the rest of their lives. Today's generations will have to change their jobs ten times as much as my father and mother, or even I did. No, it is the transition from the old job to the new job, which is our focus. Making this period as short as possible, as enjoyable as possible, as intensive as possible and as demanding as possible, is the challenge. This means, changing from one job to the other should be based on a relatively high unemployment benefit. We don't want you to be squeezed, so that when you lose your job you don't have anything.

We want to protect your income. In my country, unemployment benefit for the lowest income workers corresponds on average to 78% of their income. For the average workers, it's 69%. So that's number one, unemployment benefit, because if you're not secure, you don't dare to take the leap. Especially during the crisis we have to be careful that the opposite doesn't happen, that unemployment benefits aren't reduced.

You only dare to take a leap to try something new if you don't have anything to lose. This is not only a theory, in Denmark it actually works. I'm not saying that all of Europe should exactly copy Denmark, but examine the philosophy and the direction of the policy. I'm saying, "OK, employees, when you go from this job to that one, you will have unemployment benefits, but, be careful. This is based on rights and duties. You're not having your unemployment benefits if you're not doing something yourself. What do we want you to do? We want you to educate yourself, to gain new qualifications. You don't have to do that alone, you do that together with society. We're giving you an offer you cannot refuse."

"We're making a contract with you, we're making an interview with you, we're spotting what you're good at, what is your qualification in the broadest sense, and then we want you to be better at the thing you're good at. If you're a plumber, we want you to be a better plumber. You can begin to use computer techniques to find the best way to solve this or that problem, you will be better at taking on new projects. I'm not suggesting plumbers become nurses. I'm asking at each level for a general effort to raise standards and bring new technologies on board. This is tough. If you say, no, I don't want to do it, then you lose your unemployment benefits. If you can't do it, let's say you're not prepared to go into training and education, then we identify an alternative. We take you on board into a labor activity, into an activist scheme where you learn to start in the morning, you learn to go to work, and you learn to do something, and you're self-confident again. And then you move to the next level." This is good, this is my experience, and it works.

Because my philosophy of life has been that a job, employment, doing something, is the core of self-confidence, of initiative, of everything. Neither society nor the individual can afford to be on the outside, to be excluded. To have a high employment level is the secret. The Scandinavian model has the advantage of a very big public sector. Yes, we pay a lot taxes. But on the other hand, you cannot have close to full employment in a society without having a very strong public sector, and you can't have a very strong public sector without having full employment. So full employment and the welfare state go hand-in-hand.

What are your views about CEO compensation?

Not only cleaners, taxi drivers, and unskilled workers have rights and duties; this also applies to CEOs, the bankers, and hedge fund managers. We should introduce new ethics based on rights and duties, which leads me to financial regulation, and remuneration and bonuses systems.

The U.S. is probably the part of the world where the anger is not only most visible, but also most widespread among the population. Ordinary American working families, the mainstream, feel that Wall Street has simply been too greedy. You cannot expect these workers to go to work and forget all about it – that will not happen. We need to change behavior in business, within the financial sector, and we need those actors to be a bit more humble.

It's unacceptable that a CEO is receiving his bonus even when we are going through a downturn of historical proportions. Sometimes bonuses are paid to the CEO, even when you have a foreclosure of a company, or a bankruptcy. This is unacceptable. When a plumber is underperforming he's either dismissed the next day, or the employer says, "You can't have the same salary as you had yesterday." In the financial sector you do not have similar consequences for those who are in positions of responsibility. Their salaries and bonuses hardly depend on their performance at all. The financial sector is becoming more and more a little box inside society, free from responsibility. We need to change this.

For CEO bonuses and salaries, level and methods, I would say that the number one aim is transparency. It should not be a little board that deals with the CEOs and decides on their remuneration and relocation. This has to be done in the general assembly among the shareholders. Secondly, the CEO's remuneration should decrease if the company's performance decreases. We need a symmetric remuneration equating to your performance in the company and to your company's performance.

The pay and bonus level has to be negotiated on some ethical level. Having finance executives earning 22,000 times the average wage of a hard-working American industrial worker is obviously disproportionate. The European Commission is working on proposed guidelines for bonuses and remuneration. We need to find solutions, and we need to be relatively tough. I would not want to be part of, you could say, a guerrilla-like attack on all business CEOs, but we do need to solve this one.

We need to solve the tax haven problem and the general taxation problem, too. We need to ensure that capital income is treated in principle the same way as labor income. I admit that this means an increase in taxation. Why should the CEO be taxed less than the hard-working industrial worker? I don't understand that. There was an article I saw, on the front page of the *Financial Times*, where a private equity manager said, "I pay less in tax than my cleaning lady." I hope that it wasn't one of his spin doctors who told him to say that. For us, of course, it was an enormous provocation.

Coming to the regulation of the financial markets, which is a hugely important area, I made many concrete proposals during my time in the European Parliament and hopefully I continue to add substance to the debate. I was the main driver of the principal report on hedge funds and private equity. This was the basis for what is now on the table from the European Commission for private capital pools to be regulated within the European Union. It's a big story, but the short answer is, yes, we must have good regulation now, not to kill the industry, but to learn the lessons so that this crisis cannot be repeated in the future. We must do that coherently, which means that we will cover all financial actors on the market. We must do it symmetrically, which means that the classical demands to the different actors are the same kind, of course tailored to different actors, but the same kind.

Are you optimistic or pessimistic about the future, if we sit here in ten years, how will inequality develop?

There will be less inequality.

Why?

Because I and many other people want to change the way things develop. Among citizens, there is a growing willingness to profoundly change the status quo that led to this crisis. This recession has opened the door for new thinking in governments, in universities, and among the general public. There is potential for reforming our economies. But also, anger is very high, and it will not go away. I know it's going to be extremely difficult. Each day the *Financial Times* is filled with well-formulated articles from conservative lobbyists, the private equity and banking industries, and they try repeatedly to resist regulation. They have enormous resources. What do we have? We have motivated people who can organize and be organized. At the end of the day that is stronger. I cannot, of course, predict that when we meet in ten years' time I will give you a bottle of champagne and say, what did I tell you? But I can tell you that in my long life, I have to go back many, many years to see a similar readiness for change and engagement. And I see my job with my colleagues, here and in the U.S., to try to guide it, to try to be a constructive force for change.

Fred Smith
Chairman, President and CEO, FedEx

"I have asked the question, 'Do you believe if corporate tax rates were reduced from 38% to say 25%, and capital equipment and software could be expensed, do you think that the relative attractiveness of the industrial sector would rise relative to the financial services sector?' The answer to that is 100% yes. I've never had anyone disagree with that – not one."

Fred Smith is the Chairman, President, and CEO of FedEx, a 33 billion-dollar global transportation, business services, and logistics company, and the largest overnight express delivery company in the United States. FedEx was the first service enterprise to win the Malcolm Baldrige National Quality Award in 1990, and FedEx has consistently ranked on *Fortune's* industry lists, including World's Most Admired Companies, 100 Best Companies to Work For, and Blue Ribbon Companies List. Smith founded FedEx in 1971, and has since been an active proponent of promoting regulatory reform, free trade, and "open skies agreements" for aviation across the world. He has received numerous leadership and management awards, served as chairman of numerous business councils, and has served on the boards of several large public companies, as well as the St. Jude Children's Research Hospital and Mayo Foundation Boards. In addition, *Barron's* has named him among the world's best CEOs and *Chief Executive* magazine elected him 2004 CEO of the Year.

R. Berger et al., *The Inequality Puzzle: European and US Leaders Discuss Rising Income Inequality*, DOI 10.1007/978-3-642-15804-9_10, © Springer-Verlag Berlin Heidelberg 2010

How would you characterize the amount of inequality today?

I think inequality is significant, but I'm not sure that it's significantly greater than it's been many times in the past. I think there are a number of issues that make it seem to be greater today than it has been in the past. On the one hand, you have a significant increase over the past couple of decades in income in the form of benefits that don't appear in the wage statement, but that definitely improve the individual's relative income for the goods and services that they're being provided. Of course, that's the centerpiece, when you really get down to it, of the entire health care debate. The escalation of health care costs, and the fact that they are deductible at the corporate level in the United States and provided as non-income benefits, is a very big part of the story that gets left out, a very big part of the story.

Secondly, I think you have a situation today where there is a highly visible class of high-income earners who tend to be the focus of the media and their proportion of all earners is not as great as the media would lead you to believe. I think those high earners are highly focused in particular areas, the most important of which is finance. I think if you take the median distribution of wages, I think it would not be as significant as a lot of the rhetoric makes it out to be. It's a wonderful set of stories, but it's quite concentrated, really.

Does the current crisis affect inequality?

It's probably bringing inequality down because all of those huge paydays a lot of people had that brought up the top have taken a hit, although the other day as I'm sure you saw, right on point with this subject, there were five thousand recipients of million dollar compensation packages in the financial institutions that were receiving TARP money. I know of no other industry even close where there are thousands of million dollar earners in a particular segment.

I think that has created a political and perception problem that is enormously important, and it is made possible because of the government's tax policies which favor the financial sector, much to the detriment of the industrial sector. It is the industrial sector that provides the high-paying blue-collar jobs that everybody nostalgically pines for. I think that is at the root of the problem. Too much of the economy is in the financial sector and the tax code continues to encourage that. That is the source of an awful lot of the inequality that we have in the country.

How will inequality evolve over ten, fifteen years?

If the tax code doesn't change and certain educational policies don't change, then I think we'll be having the same conversation. It will be very difficult to significantly improve the compensation levels of the less-educated, blue-collar workforce.

Are you in general optimistic or pessimistic?

I am pessimistic so long as the government is so focused on the financial sector to the detriment of the industrial sector. Eisenhower used to talk about a military-industrial complex. We have a Washington-Wall Street complex, and it is at the heart of a lot of the problems.

What are the causes of inequality?

I think that you have a tax code where interest is deductible and you have the pooling of the world's savings into a single market, and that means that relatively small amounts of capital can be leveraged up incredibly to engage in financial services and speculation. Very small slivers of the revenues going through these financial institutions provide huge compensation opportunities for the people involved in those industries. As long as interest is deductible and the tax rates that the United States has on industry in general, and the punishing tax on capital investment, and the diminishing return of government investment in infrastructure – bear in mind it's gone down significantly in the last ten or fifteen years – the blue-collar sector that depends on that industrial investment or government investment is the one that takes it on the chin.

It's very difficult to produce high-paying blue-collar workforces without capital investment. The fundamental difference between our highly compensated pilots or pick-up and delivery people, than somebody in Africa or Asia or Latin America carrying a load of sticks on their back, is the investment in infrastructure, the investment in training, and the investment in capital equipment. Obviously you have to have the market demand, but that's what makes blue-collar people able to sustain a reasonable standard of living, the investment in the industrial sector, and that is treated poorly by our tax code and our government policy.

What should be done?

The two things that we've advocated very publicly, including an op-ed I wrote for the *Financial Times*, is number one, bring the rate of taxation at the corporate level down. Perhaps even more importantly, allow the expensing of capital and software when it is put into service. I'm not talking about buildings which can appreciate, but a piece of equipment which is wearing out the moment you put it in service. The physical plant of the United States, bridges, ports, airports, our airlines, our railroads, whatever the case may be, is very tough to modernize and re-invest with the level of taxation and the slow return on capital that you get due to the depreciation schedules in our tax code. If you did those two things, it makes the tax shield of interest deductibility less valuable relative to the industrial sector. The only thing that happens if you allow the expensing of capital is, at worst, the government loses the time value of money, and that assumes the investment would have been made to begin with. But in bad times, the reality is most of those investments aren't made, because every board of directors when business is getting bad has the same refrain, "push off the capital, " "make do with what you have, " "don't spend," "cash is king." When many of the projects – particularly today because of technology – have a positive ROI even in down economic times, they're not funded because it takes you a number of years because of the depreciation schedule on that investment to get your money back.

So if we buy a wide-body airplane, we're out, say, 150 million dollars day one, and we can get back, I think, forty-some odd million dollars the first year in depreciation, and then we can write it off for tax purposes over a seven-year period. If we were able to expense that the day we put it into service, then it's completely irrelevant as to what the market is. You are able to make the decision on the basis of what the piece of equipment will earn over a period of time. In the second year, the government is a full and equal partner in that investment at whatever level of taxation applies. So both of those things tend to make the financial sector a much more attractive area to put capital into because you can leverage it up, and the interest allows you now, in this worldwide market, to do all kinds of things. That's really the short form of what happened to us in the recent meltdown. The speculation and over-leveraging because of that tax code created the meltdown.

What are your views about CEO compensation?

I think CEO compensation has two or three things to pay attention to. Again, going back to the comments I just made, if you list the top one hundred or five hundred CEOs' compensation in the last five to ten years, I would be very surprised if a disproportionate number of the ones who have received the eye popping packages are not in the financial sector. Second, the Black-Scholes model for the value of stock options makes compensation reports often misleading. For the first time since double-entry bookkeeping, you have an expense that is dragged through the profit-and-loss statement, and if the value of the options goes south, you never reverse the entry. That's never been done. The thing that bothers me about it is that the man who came up with this formula is one of the architects of Long-Term Capital Management, so I'm not sure I really have a lot of confidence in this valuation formula. I think the reporting of these huge option values – which are going to be taxed at whatever the top marginal tax rate is so you take that off the top, then you have the purchase of the option – vastly overstates the compensation, and there's no canceling out on the other side if the option is "under water" and never exercised.

A good case in point here is an article in the *New York Times* recently. You know, the *Times* has probably more than any other institution waved the banner on CEO compensation. It was a study by two academics, one of whom was European and one was in the United States. It said, it wasn't excessive executive compensation that was at the root of the financial problem. These people thought they were actually doing the right thing by the shareholders, and many of them rode the Titanic right to the end; I think the CEO of Lehman Brothers being the best example. He got all that "compensation" in the immediate years before the crash, but at the end the options were worthless. He had made hundreds of millions of dollars for which he was excoriated by Congress, but when you settle all the books, he had kept those options and they were worth nothing. So while there is a great amount of inequality and CEO compensation packages undoubtedly did get too high relative to societal norms, the reality is quite a bit different than the popular press would make it out to be.

Do you think the government should regulate compensation?

I don't think the government should regulate compensation packages. If you calculate what one of these enormously capable baseball players gets, I don't know, 50,000 dollars a strike out, or a basketball player, 10,000 dollars a basket, they're just mind-boggling. My guess is the relative compensation of Kobe Bryant of the Lakers to the lowest-paid person in the Lakers organization, makes any kind of such disparity in CEO compensation in the industrial sector pale in comparison. So if you're going to start regulating that, what's the government going to do? Should then a basket be regulated to be worth only three thousand dollars, or five thousand, taken to its ultimate conclusion? My belief is that if the government wants to get in that business, what the Congress needs to do is increase the marginal personal tax rate as you go up the income scale. That's a better solution than trying to regulate something the government could never effectively regulate.

What should be done with regard to education?

In my view the government should phase out federal loans and support of higher education, except in the scientific disciplines where it can be justified on the basis of national security and economic wealth generation. All of the wealth and improvement in human well-being has come from the scientists, the inventors, the entrepreneurs, the engineers, the people who have created all of the conveniences, the fundamental science that has built the products and infrastructure that we enjoy today. Eisenhower began this process by saying, we will help you get a degree in engineering, a degree in science, whatever the case may be. On the basis of our egalitarian impulses, we now allow the government to provide funding for anthropologists, theater majors, and liberal arts majors. As the father of a large group of kids, I don't think any of them would qualify for the educational benefits that I just described. But I'm not sure from society's standpoint that would have been a bad thing. One of my sons is a lawyer.

I'm not sure the government's interests are served by saying that it's a universally good thing that everyone goes to college and gets a degree in something. I think the government should instead put a lot of emphasis on community colleges where you take youngsters out of high school and teach them skills that are useful in industries where they are likely to be able to compete for jobs. A person that has an airframe and power plant license to work on these marvelous Boeing and Airbus airplanes that we have, has an extremely well-paying job, great benefits, great income, and these types of industrial jobs often go begging. There are approximately three and a half million unfilled jobs right now. If you look at the nature of those jobs, they're generally in some sort of blue-collar production, machine tool repair, maintenance, or things of that nature. I think our society has become so enamored of getting that degree from a prestigious institution, regardless of what type of degree, we have a complete mismatch between what the educational structure is producing relative to what society needs and will compensate. Building new sources of wealth in the future will be basically focused on scientific, engineering and managerial disciplines. A change in the corporate tax rate, and in the treatment of capital equipment investment would be the third thing I would recommend. Again, we need much greater focus on scientific education and support of community colleges, rather than higher education in general.

Do you have other observations about inequality?

I think if we did this, that inequality would begin to take care of itself in a lot of ways. That may include increasing the marginal tax rate as personal earnings go into the stratosphere. But you've got to get economic activity back into those sectors which longer term provide a high standard of living for the whole society and in those sectors that provide well-paying, blue-collar jobs. The tax code and the whole emphasis of this country is very much built around that Wall Street-Washington axis. It's not built around, "Let's talk about how we can boost our manufacturing sector, or how can we re-equip our industrial companies faster and allow them to reinvest in the next generation of machine tools, or fabrication equipment."

Why did this shift happen?

I think if you look at the history of the power structure in Washington, it's based mainly on the northeastern educational system and that's very much focused on the financial services industry and the government. When you talk to most political people about these subjects, you're talking to people that don't have the same frame of reference. When I started making these points about corporate tax rates and expensing, I went out of my way to talk to people on the center-left side of the spectrum. I talked to Paul Krugman, I talked to Robert Reich, I talked to Alan Blinder, I talked to Larry Summers. It's very interesting. I've never had one of them dispute what I said. But I've never heard one of them say, "You're exactly right." It's just not of great interest to them. I talked to another famous economist and described what happens in a downturn at the board level – I've been on five New York Stock Exchange boards. The problem is that you need boards of directors to accelerate business investment when economic times are bad, not have it go down by 40%. You're not going to have that unless you change the risk profile of capital investment. His response was, "You just have to try harder at the board level to get those investments approved!" He completely misunderstands what goes on in the corporation and the requirements for a board to be prudent, to exercise some level of discipline and restraint. Unless you change those fundamental dynamics, you're going to put more business activity into the speculative area which produces most of these income extremes and which, in turn, creates most of the invidious reaction against rising inequality. It's a vicious circle.

In 1983, the United States corporate share of profits represented by the financial sector was a little over 15%. By 2007, the last year before the meltdown, it had grown to approximately 35%. Now you tell me in those twenty-five years where the added value in the financial sector came from that represented more than a doubling of profitability as a share of national income. Take a hundred dollars worth of mortgages, and slice them and dice them, put some sort of an insurance component on top of them, and diversify the risk around the world and so forth. They're now worth a hundred and three. Some smart group of folks up in Wall Street, the mortgage originators and others, take a little slice of that and the total dollars are so enormous, you get this situation where five thousand people are making a million dollars a year. At the end of the day, were these securities really worth a hundred and three after they did all those things, rather than a hundred, probably really worth eighty-five, because an awful lot of the people weren't credit-worthy who were purchasing mortgages in the first place?

There is a complete mismatch between the needs of the blue-collar sector for the kinds of government policies that create investment and skill sets to increase their earning power relative to government policies that prejudice the system toward government and the financial sector. I believe anybody in the industrial sector will concur with what I just said. I have probably asked two hundred Fortune 500 CEOs in the industrial sector if they agree with these points. I've never had one disagree, never.

Do you have any figures you would like to see changed?

The corporate tax rate today is 38%, and we pay the corporate tax rate. I think on a globally competitive basis it should probably be around 25%, and my guess is that receipts from corporate taxation would actually go up. I think that capital equipment and software should be expensed on day one, again not buildings because building can appreciate in value, but equipment that is wearing out from the minute you put it into service. If you want to deal with the issue of very high incomes, then just graduate the income tax rate up. I think what you would find is that people will have much more propensity to invest. By the way, I think that capital gains is a big part of this. You can't go back on capital gains. If people aren't going to take their income in these huge compensation packages, you've got to give them some incentive to put their capital to work. I believe on capital gains the best way to do that is to have the capital gains tax fall as a function of how long you hold the asset. If the capital gains rate is 15 or 20%, I would zero it out after five years. So if you churn it, you pay. If you want to keep that capital employed to produce those blue-collar jobs, there's an incentive to do so. I think that's at the heart of income inequality, our inability to improve the earnings of the bottom half of the income distribution curve.

I personally think it doesn't make any difference what they do in terms of trying to limit compensation at the top, because the key is how to you increase compensation at the bottom. Nobody's talking about that. Now the government has tried to do it through the tax code, through earned income tax credits and so forth, so that today you have a very high percentage of the population in the United States who don't pay income tax. They're actually net recipients. They pay FICA, but that's the worst kind of tax, because that's a tax on employment, which you want more of.

Do you think the current crisis will have an impact on Ivy League education, change priorities?

No, as long as the tax codes are the way they are, people will go where they can get those million dollar pay checks. The way they get those million dollar pay checks is in financial services, which are highly lucrative because of the tax code. You can take a relatively small amount of equity and leverage it up so the potential earnings at the individual level dwarf almost any other thing that I can think of. If you're a physician, at the end of the day, you're limited by the number of consultations or operations, but there's a finite limit there. You might be a very well-compensated physician, but there's a limit. There certainly is a limit in the industrial world to compensation just because of sociological reasons, if for nothing else. But in the financial sector, there are no such limitations. That's why in 2007 before this crisis happened, the pay of the financial services folk just took your breath away. There were at least three 50 million dollar cash paydays for the CEOs of financial services companies. I don't know of anything like that in the industrial sector, other than somebody founding a company and the stock goes up. Or taking a company, like Michael Eisner did, that was moribund, and getting a lot of stock options in the early days, and then have the market cap run up as earning improved. I know of no other legitimate fields other than the financial sector – with the exceptions of a few big earners in sports, entertainment, or the law – that has equivalent cash compensation levels at the top.

What are the sociological restraints?

I think there is a clear understanding that if you run a company that has lots of blue-collar folks, there is a limit to the disparity between the lowest income and the highest income. Now it may not fit what the *New York Times* wants exactly, but it is definitely a consideration. In this company, for instance, when we went into this huge meltdown, our management took pay cuts. We took the most from the top to the bottom. That's a sociological constraint, or whatever you want to call it. If your people are seeing their hours get cut, and at the top you don't have disproportionate pain, you will have a morale problem. That's not true in the financial services sector, mainly because the financial services sector is not like an industrial company which is more hierarchical. You've got top management, you have to have middle management because of geographical or product requirements, and then you have lots of people actually doing the work. In the financial sector, it's like a dumbbell, you've got a fair number of people at the top figuring out what trades to make, hardly anybody in middle management, and then a lot of administrative support folks. There's not that same sociological pressure on the financial services or entertainment or sports world that there is in industry.

How do your fellow executives view financial services executives?

I've never asked them that question, but I have asked the question, "Do you believe if corporate tax rates were reduced from 38% to say 25%, and capital equipment and software could be expensed, do you think that the relative attractiveness of the industrial sector would rise relative to the financial services sector?" The answer to that is 100% yes. I've never had anyone disagree with that – not one.

There are only three fundamental questions in life, as best I can tell at age sixty-five. Number one, what does one person owe to another? The whole issue of envy and equity has been a driving force since the time people first put pen to papyrus, or whatever. The second, is there a God and what does God want? People have been fighting over that since the beginning of time. And the third, how are we as a society going to organize to deal with the first two questions? Everything goes back to those three points. So anybody who says that inequality isn't a big issue for the effective functioning of a society, is simply ignorant of the record of humanity. It's a huge issue. The problem is that the prescriptions for dealing with it often exacerbate the problem, in my opinion, and that's where we are in this country.

If I sat here and had this conversation with Mr. Sweeney, the former president of the AFL-CIO – he's a very nice man, I met him one night over dinner in Washington – I'm not sure where he would come out. I hope he would come to the same conclusion, because I'm on his side. It's blue-collar worker incomes that need to be increased, and the only way to do that is through better training and giving them better equipment and infrastructure investment to make them more productive. It's impossible otherwise.

A lot of people want to disregard the elasticity of demand and hope we can have 50,000 a year janitors. That's not going to happen, because once a janitor costs 50,000 a year, people are going to shrink the size of their offices, or work at home, or whatever the case may be. Society cannot afford to pay low-value-added jobs higher than some acceptable price to society, so most of the left-right discussions always leave out elasticities and customer service. That's a short-form description of what happened to the U.S. automotive companies. People within the industry came to believe that it didn't make any difference what the car cost, or how good it is, there is only a discussion between labor and management about how we divide the pie. But, people came into the market that did understand those two things. Companies like Toyota, Nissan, and Honda started building cars for the U.S., and now they have a huge part of the market because they clearly understood customer satisfaction and the effect of price on competition.

The way to make that janitor more money is to have buildings with high-speed vacuuming ports that can clean twice as fast, to have new products in the carpeting that don't take stains and so forth. It's the age-old thing. Investment and invention allow people to be more productive and make more money, and nothing other than investment and invention will allow you to do so over time.

Are there any models in Europe that could be useful for the United States?

I think Europe is, in the main, a wonderful society, but the reality is that many of the things Europe has been able to do were possible, in part, because the United States economy was different. The United States has spent an enormous amount of money, for better or worse, being the world's policeman. Those budgets don't hit anybody in Europe, they're borne by the American taxpayer. What goes into our military budget, goes into social services in Europe. I think Europe and Asia have been made wealthy over the past fifty years largely as a result of the United States opening up our markets, getting industries in Europe and Asia up to a certain point that then becomes self-reinforcing as their internal markets become robust on their own.

I gave an interview also in the *Financial Times* about a year before the meltdown took place about the theory, at the time, of "decoupling." Some people felt it didn't make any difference what happened to the United States, that the economies in Europe and Asia were so strong now that the United States was no longer the locomotive. I felt this was incorrect. No company is more in the middle of the world economy than FedEx, and so I said that's not true. It's still the American consumer, and the innovation and invention that's centered, in the main, in the United States that are the drivers of the world economy in terms of increasing wealth. If either of those stop, you're going to have a problem. Over time the same thing took place in Europe beginning with the Marshall Plan and all of the GATT openings. Europe with the EU has created a major internal market. But it will be a long time before the China internal market can produce the kind of income for the Chinese population that export markets to the U.S., and to a lesser degree to Europe, have done.

Did I give you a different point of view than some of the other folks?

Yes.

Good, the worst thing in the world is to be simply another "me too." I told you why I agreed to do this interview. I saw the subject and I have such strong feelings about it, and I'm very concerned that the current prescriptions will exacerbate the problem. The whole issue of health care is a separate issue, but it is a subset of this, because it has profound implications in terms of income and income inequality.

What would you recommend for health care reform?

I served for many years on the board of the Mayo Clinic, and we spend billions of dollars on health care [at FedEx]. Almost all of our folks get health care, even our part-timers. Based on these experiences, I think there are basically three things that must be done. Number one, you have to recognize that health care is an ethical and actuarial problem. Society can no more provide everyone unlimited "free" health care, in whatever way you want it, than we can provide everybody free food – filet mignon for breakfast! It just cannot be done. I think having a mandate is very important, like we have for automobile insurance, but that mandate should be for catastrophic events only. So everyone would be required to have major medical. In fact, when I was growing up, that was the only health insurance you could buy – major medical. Below that mandated coverage, the tax code treatment of individual health costs, however you get it, should be equalized. Also, the purchase of health care across state lines should be permitted. If these changes were made, things would happen that would rectify the problem over time. You might have seen a great article recently about Safeway where they've got different deductibles for various lifestyle choices or outcomes like smoking or obesity. That's what's happening. Everybody understands what is creating the huge run-up of health care costs. It is the obesity epidemic, the lack of focus on preventive care, and the costs of dealing with the elderly. But we can afford a lot of care for the elderly if routine medical expenses were actually subject to market forces much more than they are today and if catastrophic illness and accidents were insured across the entire population.

John Sweeney
President Emeritus, AFL-CIO

"We are living in a new gilded age, in which the wealthy few live extravagantly, while the vast majority can barely afford the basic necessities – even as they are more productive than ever and work longer hours than in the past. We have been heavily focused on executive compensation in recent years. Excessive and poorly structured executive compensation distorts incentives for executives toward short-term risk-taking and exacerbates trends toward inequality."

From 1995 to 2009, John Sweeney was the President of the AFL-CIO, the largest federation of unions in the United States, representing over 11.5 million members in 57 federated unions. Beginning in 1980, he served as President of the Service Employees International Union, where he helped expand membership from 625,000 to approximately 1.1 million during his fifteen-year presidency. In 2000, Sweeney was elected President of the Trade Union Advisory Committee (TUAC), an international organization with consultative status at the Organization for Economic Cooperation and Development (OECD). TUAC's affiliates represent some 70 million workers and encompass more than fifty-five national trade union centers in the twenty-nine OECD countries. Sweeney's initial job in the labor movement was at the International Ladies' Garment Workers, which later merged with the Clothing and Textile Workers Union, and he joined a New York City SEIU Local in 1961 as a union representative. Sweeney holds honorary degrees from Georgetown University, Oberlin College, the University of Massachusetts at Amherst, the University of Baltimore, Catholic University Law School, and the University of Toledo's College of Law.

R. Berger et al., *The Inequality Puzzle: European and US Leaders Discuss Rising Income Inequality*, DOI 10.1007/978-3-642-15804-9_11, © Springer-Verlag Berlin Heidelberg 2010

How would you assess the level of inequality in the United States?

Even before the onset of the economic crisis, working people in the United States have been left behind by an economy that is fundamentally unbalanced. Income inequality in the United States has grown to levels that we have not seen since before the Depression. The 1% of households received 21.8% of all pre-tax income in 2005, more than double what that figure was in the 1970s. This is the greatest concentration of income since before the Depression. In 1928, 23.9% of income went to the richest 1%. According to the *Wall Street Journal*, employees received nearly 2.1 trillion dollars of the 6.4 trillion dollars in total U.S. pay in 2007. This doesn't include stock options and other benefits. In the five years ending in 2007, earnings for American workers only rose 24%, half the 48% for the top earners.

We should also talk about how this is going to affect the future of social security. More and more of our nation's total pay is above the limit subject to payroll taxes. Compensation not subject to payroll tax now represents revenue of 115 billion dollars a year. This is a serious concern, since social security benefits are funded through these payroll taxes.

We are living in a new gilded age, in which the wealthy few live extravagantly, while the vast majority can barely afford the basic necessities – even as they are more productive than ever and work longer hours than in the past. We have been heavily focused on executive compensation in recent years. Excessive and poorly structured executive compensation distorts incentives for executives toward short-term risk-taking and exacerbates trends toward inequality.

Why has inequality increased over the past twenty years?

Workers have not been receiving their fair share of the wealth they create, and the gap has gotten wider and wider with the greed of the highest paid. The numbers speak for themselves in terms of what's happened here, and workers have just been left behind in this process. It took the economic crisis to put the focus on it. A lot of what's going on now in terms of trying to rebuild the middle class, and to place caps and limits on executive compensation, are steps in the right direction. But it's going to take a lot to have a fairer system as far as workers are concerned.

There are lots of reasons for what happened. The bottom line is how do you correct it, how do you straighten it out? What we've seen with the changes that have taken place in the auto industry as an example, those were all good middle class jobs, good wages, good benefits. Those jobs are gone. How do we restore a middle class in our country? How do we eliminate the greed at the highest levels? The economic crisis has dramatically exacerbated the inequality.

What do you think will be the developments in the years to come?

I hope that is going to change. I think the President has taken initiatives to move us in that direction, it's going to take a lot of doing and depends upon the political will in the Congress to provide the legislation that will be required.

Should executive compensation be regulated?

That remains to be seen what we can do about it, and whether we have the will to be aggressive enough. It's not just what can be done legislatively, but what are the shareholders going to do, how are the stockholders of these companies going to hold their CEOs accountable and restrict CEO compensation, how are they going to relate these salaries to the performance of the CEO, and the performance of the company.

How does the union movement regard inequality and executive compensation?

I think it is a serious concern and it relates to our organizing workers, doing what we can to improve the standard of living of those workers and to negotiate contracts with good wages. It's an issue we have been concerned about and raised for a long time. In individual negotiations, negotiators would be relating to whatever information they had on the latest CEO compensation or middle management salary increases and how it relates to the production line worker wages. That's been a part of negotiating strategy for many, many years.

What if unions acted in concert about executive pay?

I think that it is getting a lot of that kind of activity. In the Obama campaign, CEO pay and the inequality of wages was a big issue. The President's response in terms of the decline of the middle class and how we have to rebuild the middle class was all a part of that discussion. It's been an issue for a long time, it certainly was during the Bush years. We also work globally. John Monks is a classic example, and they haven't seen the inequality issue as bad as it is in the United States. They haven't seen the CEO compensation as bad as it is here.

Have you noticed any changes about a belief in the American Dream?

I don't think that attitude is as prevalent as it was years ago. People today are not confident that their son or daughter will automatically experience the American Dream. Based upon the experiences that workers are going through, or have gone through, they're fearful that their children are not going to enjoy life as well as they were enjoying it for a while. But there is a complete frustration with what has happened and there is a sense of bitterness over what the extreme has gone to in terms of the haves and have nots.

Why has this happened?

Greed.

How will the situation evolve over the next ten, fifteen years?

I hope it's going to be better. The election of a new Democratic President was a big step toward giving us hope. National health care reform will be a major step, and will have a strong impact on improving the economy as well as health care coverage. Alongside of health care, the most important legislation for us is the Employee Free Choice Act. The President is committed to supporting that as soon as he gets health care. It was his decision to do health care first. I don't think he thought it was going to be as tough getting health care as it is turning out to be, but the developments of the past twenty-four hours have been a little bit better.

The Employee Free Choice act is going to provide workers with an opportunity to organize and all of our polls and surveys show that the majority of workers want to be organized. They don't want to have to fear losing their jobs if they join a union, or being harassed or intimidated. There will be a renaissance for workers. You'll see massive organizing campaigns in every single industry. That's going to have a strong impact on improving workers' wages and certainly going to build a stronger labor movement, which will also give us more political power than we've had in the past.

Do you see signs in the corporate world that there need to be changes in executive compensation?

We see some signs of it. Again, with health care, businesses are facing up to the health crisis in a more positive way than when the Clintons were trying to reform health care. On the one hand you have the organizations, like the Business Roundtable and the Chamber of Commerce, putting millions of dollars into trying to kill health care reform. But individual businesses both large and small are far more interested in health care reform today, and they're feeling the pain and the cost. Employers who provide health care are also indirectly paying for the uncompensated care for the uninsured, and that affects their ability to compete in the global market. More and more they are acknowledging that and they do want to see some form of national health care reform. They also want to see some cost-effectiveness in the legislation. It's going to be a challenge to come up with a bill that really provides all of these provisions, but I think that's the direction it's going. And I think there are businesses who are questioning more and more why should they fight unions, or try to beat down the attempts of people who want to join a union, or at least want to have the chance to vote on whether they join a union or not.

Global companies accept the role of the union in every industrialized country around the world except ours. Why shouldn't workers in the United States have similar democratic processes to form unions as workers have in every other industrialized country in the world, including the north of us?

What are your views about how education might support equality of education?

We're big supporters of education at every level, including public education for every single person in our country. As the expression goes, leave no child behind. We're especially focused on worker education, including the apprenticeship and training programs that individual unions have. We have our own National Labor College, which is certified to award bachelor degrees, and which gives credit to workers who are in a certified skill training program to get college credit. We provide the additional courses that they need to get a degree in the sciences, arts, and so on. But we're also very innovative with our educational programs. Presently there is a lot of work going on training workers for green jobs. We see that as a tremendous opportunity for growth and for the improvement of the standard of living for workers in some of the industries that have suffered as a result of trade policy and the economic crisis. The labor movement in the United States has been very supportive of education at every level, encouraging our government to be focused on educational programs. The President's educational policies and some of the moves that he has been taking, and some of the stimulus money has been going into education programs as well.

The two major teachers' unions in the United States are the American Federation of Teachers, which is an affiliate of the AFL-CIO, and the National Education Association, which is an independent union. Both of them are very progressive, both of them, as you would expect, represent their members and their professions and their jobs. They are very much involved in the development of national education policy, and I don't think that they are a stumbling block to improving education in any way.

Are there ways the U.S. and European labor movements can learn from each other?

We have for years learned so much from each other. I certainly, personally, have had great dialogue with my peers, and see them regularly throughout the year. I head up the trade union advisory committee to the OECD, and so each of my peers in the major European countries, as well as the other G-8 countries, and the G-20 as well, we come together frequently enough to have these kind of discussions. Worker education, we have learned a lot over the years through the European models that we have seen. With the development of our National Labor College, we had consulted with some of the European unions in terms of their educational programs and some of them have had their own problems with funding and the expansion of the programs. We dialogue all the major issues. They come to our conferences, conventions, and we go to theirs. There are these opportunities where we can learn a lot, and now there's even more back-and-forth with members of our staff in different countries. Our political director, Karen Ackerman, recently went to Australia at the invitation of the labor movement there. They wanted to hear what we did during the Obama campaign, and were impressed with the win, what we did to mobilize at the grassroots levels, our political education. I just use that as an example. Our organizing people have been to the TUC to talk to their executive board on our organizing programs. We've learned from them as well, where we've had success, where we haven't. People are very interested in our campaign for the Employee Free Choice Act. They can't believe what we're going through, because most of them have what we're looking for. It's an eye-opener for them. But with some of the changes in

European governments with some of the conservative moves, they are also fearful there are going to be changes in some of their own laws. Going back to Australia, the Australians went through hell, not with the present administration, but the prior administration, and the changes that were made in the labor laws there. The new administration is restoring some of what they had changed. I'm citing that because we watch each other, the changes that take place, learn from each other, there's very open dialogue, exchange.

William Weld
Partner, McDermott Will & Emery LLP; Former Governor, Massachusetts

"The reason you want prosperity to penetrate is not so that everybody will have more expensive sneakers, it's so that people can participate as productive working members of society."

William Weld is the former Republican Governor of Massachusetts, a position he held from 1990 to 1997, where he pursued an agenda of tax reductions and business deregulation. While in office he also served as national co-chair of the Privatization Council. Weld initially worked in Washington as a staff member for both the U.S. House of Representatives and the U.S. Senate. Prior to his election, Weld first served as Asst. U.S. Attorney General in charge of the Criminal Division of the U.S. Department of Justice where he prosecuted white-collar crime, and then as the U.S. Attorney for Massachusetts during the Reagan administration. After leaving the Governorship, he joined the international law firm of McDermott Will & Emery, focusing on government strategies, corporate investigations, compliance, and general business advice, especially with regard to finance. He is a member of the Council on Foreign Relations and serves by appointment of the President as a member of the U.S. Holocaust Memorial Council.

How would you characterize the amount of inequality in the United States today?

It's excessive. These issues are nothing new. I majored in classics at college and the rallying cry in Greece back in the fifth, sixth, seventh, eighth

R. Berger et al., *The Inequality Puzzle: European and US Leaders Discuss Rising Income Inequality*, DOI 10.1007/978-3-642-15804-9_12, © Springer-Verlag Berlin Heidelberg 2010

century BC was *gehs anadismos*, redistribution of land. In many societies, land was the coinage that people wanted redistributed. It seems to me that the pendulum has now swung too far in the direction of inequality in this country. This becomes particularly clear because of the fantastical concentrations of wealth and remuneration at the top. Candidly, I don't see how someone can spend responsibly more than 5 million dollars a year, but at least until quite recently, on Wall Street that amount was considered an odd lot. That sort of brings the issue home.

I have somewhat conflicting impulses here because I'm also a supply-sider in economics. I've always been violently opposed to tax increases. That was my signature issue in office, refusal to raise taxes, which I never did, and we cut them twenty-one times. The result was an absolutely straight increase in prosperity and decline in unemployment in the tiny area of the world that I had, Massachusetts, 6 million people, and nothing like the poverty that exists in some other states.

Still, even then, I remember making common cause with a fellow named Jim Braude, who was a pro-tax activist. He ordinarily would be opposed to absolutely everything I was doing. But there was one issue, the Earned Income Tax Credit, where if you're really at the bottom levels, you make out very well. I think it's similar to George McGovern's proposal of a negative income tax, which people thought was too radical. I always liked the EITC, however, because it was aimed directly at people who were working at the lowest rungs of the ladder.

At the same time I'm a supply-sider, I've always considered myself a disciple of both Mill and Bentham, and Bentham is "the greatest good for the greatest number." The greatest good for the greatest number is not really consistent with supply-side economics, at least in the short run, yet I subscribe to both of them. Scott Fitzgerald said the test of a reasonable intellect is the ability to embrace contradictory propositions simultaneously, so I've always pleaded guilty to that.

I don't analyze this issue from the point of view of a Simone Weil, "I must give all my goods to the poor." I think of it from a prudential point of view: if you don't have some spreading out, some flattening of these curves, you're going to have a revolution, or you're going to have sufficient disquiet so that sand will be thrown in the gears of commerce.

Are we close to this?

Outside the United States, look at the desperate poverty in India, parts of Latin America, Africa. You can't look at something like that and think we should just sit here in New York. Yet I'm of the school that thinks foreign aid to governments is not the way out for Africa, it's got to be building economic institutions and employment.

A book recently published by an African woman, *Dead Aid*, argues that foreign aid has been a disaster in Africa; you need investment, you need a Grameen Bank approach to wealth creation. I remember when Yeltsin first came to prominence in Russia, even before he took power when he was just standing on the tank, he said, "Do not send any more aid to the government of Russia, do not send it, it will never reach the people."

In the nineties, Bill Clinton nominated me to be ambassador to Mexico. He had offered me Court of St. James, New Delhi, or Mexico City. I took Mexico because I was sick of the U.S. Congress beating up on Mexico, and it was pretty clear to me what needed to be done, which was to build big roads down into the middle and southern part of the country so that the entire country could benefit economically from the North American Free Trade Agreement (NAFTA), which I had worked on with President Clinton. The maquiladoras near the border were doing great as a result of NAFTA, but that prosperity was not penetrating. The major reason it was not penetrating was transportation. What you needed to do was build superhighways to Oaxaca and Guerrero where people were very poorly off. Those were the people I was worried about. If I had been confirmed as ambassador, which I was not because of my great and good friend Jesse Helms, I was going to go down there and make some noise. Because even from afar I had a sense this was not right.

The question is how to enable prosperity to penetrate. People often talk about it in terms of creating equality of opportunity. I'm not sure that's concrete enough. I like the example of a category of infrastructure which if constructed could have a real economic impact. Those roads and that economic development would benefit not merely Mexico, but also of course the United States, because real prosperity in Mexico is the deadly enemy of illegal immigration and narcotics trafficking.

What are the reasons behind the increase in inequality over the past twenty years in the United States?

The rich got too much richer. They got fat, dumb, and happy. Part of it was the movement of the capital markets toward increasingly convoluted and abstruse mechanisms that created vast pools of wealth and people then tithed them at bonus time, at the end of the year. It bore absolutely no relation to any real economic value. That's bad for business, because people look at that and they get sore and justifiably so. I'm a Republican, I come from the financial world. But when I see bankers with thirty-to-one leverage ratios, complaining about anybody even looking over their shoulder, I have to take a time out. I do think the leverage ratios were unsustainable, and they should have known it.

Has globalization also played a role?

Globalization is not a villain. It's an aerating device; I myself don't think it's contributed to greater inequality. Indeed, the countries of Africa, the Caribbean, what they want more than anything in the world is for markets to open up so they can sell their produce. It's one of the reasons President Reagan was so popular in the Caribbean: one of the first things he did was the Caribbean Basin Initiative, which opened up the U.S. market for Caribbean fruits and vegetables. Edward Seaga of Jamaica was the first foreign head of state to visit Reagan in the White House.

People see globalization happening, and they see bad things happening at the same time, and so they connect them. Some people in the U.S. labor movement blame globalization for a host of economic ills, but I don't believe globalization is the cause. It would be short-sighted to take a protectionist turn.

Does the current crisis have an effect on inequality?

It has one salutary effect. The amount of attention being paid to executive compensation, the excesses of the "Masters of the Universe," is becoming a lever that may get some things done.

People say, what should the private sector do, what should the public sector do? I think this is not going to be solved by charity, it will be solved through the public sector. So what the private sector should do is support some of the things that Barack Obama is trying to do. I had not endorsed a Democrat for President before, but I had the feeling in 2008, hey, us supply-siders have gotten everything we wanted for the last eight years, and look where we are, we're in the cheap seats. So it's time for a change. What the public sector should do is help people, particularly those at the most desperate economic levels, with goods and services that are relevant to survival and ability to function, notably food, health care, and keeping families together.

The reason you want prosperity to penetrate is not so that everybody will have more expensive sneakers, it's so that people can participate as productive working members of society. I do not think that government should be spending a lot of money on what used to be called welfare, which was payments to people in order not to work. I was always staggered about the rules of the welfare system, Aid to Families with Dependent Children. If a female was eighteen years of age, unmarried, and got pregnant, the government would pay for housing and food for her and her child, but only on two conditions. Number one, she had to move out of her parents' or grandparents' house, into a separate apartment. So you had to separate the child from any caregiver. Number two, once she moved out of the house and had her own place and the taxpayer was paying for it, she could shack up with anybody she wanted, she could have anybody live with her and we weren't going to question her social habits, except there was one person who was not allowed to move in to that house or apartment, and that was the father of that child. Because if he moved in, the law would assume everything was hunky-dory and all payments would be cut off. Talk about rules destructive of family cohesiveness! So I would not put the old welfare laws in the category of what we should be doing to reduce inequality.

Do you think something should be done about high levels of CEO compensation?

As I said, I think it should be impossible to spend more than 5 million dollars a year. What was troubling was that some people were making many, many millions of dollars a year without creating value, as a result of obscure flows of capital. I don't think we have to have a national solution about how do you organize compensation within a corporation. I have some views: I've never liked lock-step compensation in a law firm, I've always sought out firms that rewarded entrepreneurial approaches, and not everybody gets paid the same. But should people be making a 100 million dollars a year in salary? I don't think so. That wealth would belong to the corporation if it didn't go to the CEO. Does that have to be legislated? I would hope not.

Where will the pressure come from?

Maybe in part from public opinion, aka "the market." People may decide that they don't want to buy the stock of a company that consistently overpays its executives. That will get the attention of the board of directors, if nothing else does!

How will the world look in ten years, will we have more or less inequality?

We're not going to have more inequality than today. We've got an inequality hangover from a multi-decade booze party. I think people are getting a bit more serious. I also hope we're going to get the kinks out of globalization and immigration, and permit smoother flows across markets. The victimization of the immigrant pool is an issue I find galling. When dozens of people looking for a better life suffocate to death in the back of a truck coming across the border, I am reminded of Hitler's Germany, of Jews hiding in terror in attics and crawl spaces.

Like a lot of people, I took heart from the election of Obama. I gave a presentation at a meeting of former world leaders in Saudi Arabia in April, 2009, and every single one of them expressed great, great hope. Khatami, the former president of Iran, gave a marvelous speech and the word Obama was in it about twenty times. The President's nickname in the campaign was "no drama Obama": he would never give people sneering sound bites, or mere palaver. I was amazed, but delighted, that he was elected.

Why was he elected?

I think people appreciated that he didn't seem to be pandering. Mrs. Clinton was more than a worthy adversary in the primaries. I was a bit surprised he got past her. I know two people whose names are Clinton who were also surprised.

Are there useful foreign models for improving inequality?

One is the Grameen Bank model, programs that put a little bit of money into the hands of people who've shown they're interested in being economic operatives. If that showing has been made, then you can do it with straight cash, because you don't have the risk you have with foreign aid, that it's all going to disappear into a maw of government corruption. In general, we need the creation of economic institutions, investment, any mechanism to make sure that things of value get to the people who are in the most desperate economic circumstances, or even circumstances that distract them from playing roles as productive members of society.

Do you have policy recommendations to improve the middle class?

Tax policy: take less in taxes. I think supply-side economics has a good chance of success. From a prudential point of view, which is the starting point of my analysis, we should be very happy to have the middle class leading their prosperous and non-desperate lives. They are the backbone of any country.

James Wolfensohn
Chairman and CEO, Wolfensohn & Co.; Former President, The World Bank

"Most people don't have a clue about poverty outside their country. They understand inequality in their own country well. But when you're talking about global inequality, to convince the rich people in the U.S. and Europe that it is in their combined interest, and the interest of their kids, that they do something now to address the issue of potential global instability because of inequality, well that's very difficult."

James Wolfensohn was President of the World Bank from 1995 to 2005. Prior to becoming President, he owned his own investment firm with several partners, including the former chairman of the Federal Reserve and current Obama economic adviser Paul Volcker. During his tenure at the World Bank, Wolfensohn emphasized efforts to fight global poverty by addressing corruption, debt relief, building civil society and involving youth in development.

After leaving the World Bank in 2005, Wolfensohn worked briefly in the Bush administration as a Special Envoy for Gaza Disengagement before founding Wolfensohn & Company, a firm that invests in and consults to governments and corporations doing business in emerging markets. In 2006, Mr. Wolfensohn established the Wolfensohn Center for Development at The Brookings Institution to pursue his interest in lifting people out of poverty in the developing world.

He is Chairman Emeritus of the Board of Trustees of the John F. Kennedy Center for Performing Arts in Washington D.C. (1996) and of Carnegie Hall, and was Chairman of the Board of the Institute for Advanced Study at Princeton University (1986-2007). A Fellow of the American Academy of Arts and Sciences and the American Philosophical Society, he is the

R. Berger et al., *The Inequality Puzzle: European and US Leaders Discuss Rising Income Inequality*, DOI 10.1007/978-3-642-15804-9_13, © Springer-Verlag Berlin Heidelberg 2010

recipient of many national and international medals and awards recognizing his public service and his support for the arts.

How would you describe inequality in Europe and America?

I think the first thing which is evident from all the statistics is that inequality is increasing. If you look across the OECD countries over the past two decades or so, in a large majority you'll see that inequality has gone up. The gap between the top 10% – or even in fact just the top 1% – of the population and the remainder has grown by a substantial margin.

If you look at the United States, for example, during the Clinton expansion of 1993-2000, real average incomes grew by an annual rate of 3.7%, which on the surface sounds pretty good. But if you break it down it turns out that within the top 1% incomes grew by over 10% a year, while for the bottom 99% it was just 2.4%. And it got even worse during the Bush expansion of 2002-2006, when average annual income growth of 2.8% masked the fact that the top 1% of earners saw growth of 11%, and the bottom 99% just 0.9%. So this gives you an idea of how big these disparities are and how they're growing.

But for me, while this within-country inequality is undoubtedly a problem, the real pressing inequality question today is not about within-country inequality but rather between-country inequality: the gap between the rich countries and the poor countries. There are a billion people in the world living on less than 1.25 dollars a day, and 2.5 billion on less than 2 dollars, out of a global population of some 6.5 billion. This had been improving in recent years, but I think we've seen some backsliding under this recent cycle. The disconnect between these people living in abject poverty and us here in the West is the real inequality. The question is what will happen when the next 2.5 billion come on the planet, when we'll have nine billion people by the year 2050, and on current trends I fear such inequalities will become unsustainable.

If you take sub-Saharan Africa, depending on whose statistics you use – either purchasing-power-adjusted or not purchasing-power-adjusted, but if you take the straight numbers – the average per capita income is around one thousand dollars now, and it will probably grow to three thousand or so by mid-century. If you adjust for purchasing power, you can say 2,000 or so dollars today, growing to maybe 5,000. But India and China, representing as they do now 2.5 billion people, and over three billion people in 2050, will reach income levels of somewhere around 35,000 or 40,000 dollars per capita by mid-century, and Germany and the United States, and most other developed countries, will be around 95,000 to a 100,000 per capita. So the disparity between the rich and the poor, in a global sense, could become much greater.

Between now and 2050 Africa's population will nearly double, up to almost two billion people, with a standard of living only marginally better than it is today, while most of the rest of the world attains incredible riches. When Africans had no communications, back before the Internet and mobile phones, maybe this was easier to shrug off. But today Africa is linked to the world and can readily understand these inequalities. And you have groups like Al Qaeda, you have all sorts of people with less than positive ideas about what should happen in the world, and so income inequality at that level becomes a dramatic challenge, one which is wholly underestimated by the world.

For whatever reason, it is very difficult to get anyone excited about Africa. I tried to get money for Africa, [current World Bank President] Bob Zoellick is trying. The major industrialized nations piously say that they'll put more money in, and nominally appear to do so, but in terms of delivery it's not getting there.

Why is aid distribution so difficult?

The distribution of aid is a hugely inefficient enterprise. For every dollar announced, you'd be lucky to get thirty cents going to an actual project. And then even out of that thirty cents, there is some argument about how much of that then goes into overheads within the context of that project.

There are several reasons for it. One is you probably take a cut off the top for corruption, which is no less than 10% in most aid-recipient countries. But beyond that there are tremendous inefficiencies in delivery, primarily because there's very little coordination of effort between all of the various aid agencies – both official and private sector agencies – working in developing countries today. So you have incredible duplication of work, with official donor agencies, multilaterals, large NGOs, and religious agencies all essentially competing with each other.

If you get the leaders together, as I've tried to do over these last years and continue to do, there is now a willingness to recognize that this is an absolutely fundamental problem. You'll go to a little country in Africa and you'll have eight people trying to build schools, and they'll all want to do it in their own way, they'll all have their own plans, they'll all have their own timetables. They'll maybe end up building three schools, and then they'll go away and do something else, and then another eight people come along. There's just tremendous waste in the aid industry, and I think that's the quick answer for why distribution is so difficult.

Is the current crisis changing trends in inequality?

Well, the current crisis is most severely felt by people with high incomes and wealth, but frankly I'm not overly concerned by what happens to the top 1%, because they've got more than enough, you don't have to cry for them. What's more important is that the difference between the wealthy and the less wealthy has been increasing decade after decade in most developed countries, and in China, and in many African countries. In China, the Gini coefficient is now very high, as high as it is here in the U.S. Having just come back from China, it's pretty obvious, you can see the great concentration of wealth among a small elite. This is very different from when I first went there.

I think if you really want to see sustainable changes in inequality trends, that is, if we want to reverse this trend of increasing inequality, we need to focus on education. Without education, you're not going to see a change. The countries that do deal with education, that have strong education systems, have less inequality than the ones who do not. All of which I'm sure you've been told many times.

What are the reasons for the growing divide between the wealthy and very wealthy?

In this country, I think there are a number of reasons. One reason is the tax system, which is a system that encourages the creation of wealth. The tax system under President Bush, as I hardly need to tell you, awarded tax reductions that were not insubstantial. They followed a series of reductions before him and it stands to reason that those earning a substantial amount of money are now able to retain a very large absolute sum.

There are many other issues I could list. Technology has probably played a role, because with increased technology we're seeing machines replace low-skilled labor. You also have to look to weaker union power and changes in government policies on issues like the minimum wage and regulation.

What is stunning to me is the following. In 1980, the typical U.S. worker with a college degree earned about 50% more than a high school graduate.

By 1990, it was 73% more, by 2000, 85% more, and today, 97% more. So there's this great differential between the markets for skilled and unskilled labor, and I think it's being embedded in the system. It's a trend that I don't see reversing.

Has globalization also played a role?

It clearly has because those most vulnerable to globalization, in terms of labor, are those at the bottom end of the income spectrum. So if you have someone in this country that is manufacturing garments for you and is subject to trade union regulations and some form of minimum wage, you can produce it in any one of fifty other countries instead, where you could offer a wage that is half the wage in this country, and it would be a prince's salary. So you have this mobility of labor at the low end which keeps the price down. What you don't have is the same mobility in the upper 1%, and the same competition in the upper 1% to allow you to pay them less. The area where demand outstrips supply is the creative end of the spectrum. So the top 1% makes a hell of a lot, and the bottom 10% is subject to competition, significantly because of globalization. This is what ultimately leads to protectionism. If we want to fight back against protectionism – which I believe we must – we must fight back against inequality.

There's another interesting point on the globalization issue, however, which is that globalization appears to have helped lower the prices of goods the poor buy more than those the rich buy. So in this sense, if you're really looking at purchasing power, globalization has had some dampening effects on inequality, because as the prices for the rich continue to rise, the poor are relatively better off. This is a pretty marginal difference, and certainly doesn't outweigh the great increase in inequality in incomes that we've witnessed. But I mention it just as a side note to emphasize that the point here isn't to demonize globalization, because I think, all said, globalization is undoubtedly a good thing, and has produced lots of benefits, both in the U.S. and Europe and around the globe. But if we want to continue strengthening and deepening globalization, and want to have any kind of political support for it here at home, we need to address the inequality issue.

How will the level of inequality evolve over the next ten, fifteen years?

Well, I don't think the trends today are very promising. Unless we really decide to do something about it, I don't see any changes on the horizon. As I said earlier, if you look out over the next several decades to 2050, the forecast is really quite worrying, with the biggest worry being Africa. And the thing is, we don't have much time to waste if we want to change this. You can't wait until 2020 or 2030 to solve it, because there aren't any short-term, band-aid solutions that are really going to help.

What we need to be doing is addressing education. That's our best opportunity. If you're going to deal with education, it's a ten-year cycle, at least, to see meaningful results and help spur broad-based development. So we can't afford to wait.

I had lunch today with [former Mexican President] Ernesto Zedillo who's heading a group that's looking at exactly this question. I said, if you want to deal with inequality in these countries, we have to get back to education, health, and equal opportunity. If you don't, you can't fix it by saying we'll deal with it ten years from now. The problem that we have today is that there is a mechanical statement that goes into every G-7, G-8, G-20 communiqué, which addresses these development questions and says we're about to put in a billion dollars, or a 100 billion dollars, or even a trillion dollars. My experience has been that it very rarely materializes, and that the delivery mechanisms don't work.

What could international organizations do?

The international institutions are creations of individual governments. They have a certain momentum, which varies from time to time. If you take the Bank and the Fund, the Fund is in vogue at the moment because of the stability needs of the international financial system, and so Dominique Strauss-Kahn has had great success in recent meetings in getting funding support from the rich countries in order to ensure, as far as he can, stability in the international financial system. When it comes to the Bank, where you're dealing with poverty, Bob Zoellick has been pushing for more funding for the Bank and other development agencies, but so far as I can see, up to this point there's been no dramatic change.

To the extent that there has been more money provided during the crisis, 80 or 90% of it has been going outside Africa. It's been going primarily to Central and Eastern Europe. The amount of money that's going to what I regard as the trouble spots, in human terms, rather than financial terms, is small.

What we need are programs that are far-seeing, rather than only taking action on short-term crises. We should have thousands of Africans being financed to study abroad on a commitment that they would then go back and serve in government for three years, like the Singaporeans did. Lee

Kuan Yew had that brilliant idea forty years ago. If you go to Singapore, just about everybody you meet in government, or even outside government, has had the benefit of getting a top-notch honors degree somewhere. I'm not suggesting we do precisely the same in Africa, but the need for a core base of bright people, and trained people, is long overdue. You can take it right back to the early education systems. So it's not just picking a few people and taking them for post-graduate study. You really need to do it from top to bottom. And if you're going to really tackle education, you also need to deal with the question of health, and you need to deal with the question of gender equity. It's not one single shot that solves the problem. Education, health, and gender equity are all very important.

Could international institutions do more than they do now?

Yes, with more resources and with a better understanding from the governments of the countries in which they operate. Because it's important to remember you can't go into Guinea, Ghana, Botswana, or any other developing country, and get things done as the World Bank unless you have a counter-party who wants to work with you. You have to have a minister, you have to have somebody who's prepared to talk to you. The World Bank, or the African Development Bank, or the Asian Development Bank, they are not sovereign states, they are there to help.

But again, the delivery remains extremely difficult, and too often we don't have real coherence in our development policies. We'll spend five years trying to improve the school system, then we'll get bored of it and decide that what this country needs is not education but rather water, sewage, hospitals, roads, or an airport. And by then there's a new man or a new woman running the country, and they may have a commitment to education, but they also want to make a name for themselves in other things, and the government itself may say to these aid groups, look, we've done schools for a bit, you were very good, you gave us 50 million over five years for schools, now what we want your money for is a, b, and c.

So what you have is neither continuity at the level of individual organizations or at the country-wide, development strategy level. So you get tremendous wastage. You rarely get the churches, the international institutions, and the NGOs coming together regularly and saying, cumulatively, what can we accomplish in education over the next ten years in this country. But that's what's needed.

Might public-private partnerships help improve the situation?

Possibly. There are certainly some public-private partnerships that have been great successes, and I think there's potential to do more. But it's a challenge, because if you want to get the private sector more interested in dealing with governments, you really need to address corruption.

In the developed world, in the U.S., the U.K., and Germany, there are already mechanisms to address the problem of corruption. You have laws, you have supervision, you have regulation, you have agencies that are pretty well-developed, whether the SEC, the FBI, or whatever their equivalents are in other countries. They're by no means perfect, but broadly speaking, they work well. But when you go to the developing world, the people who are supervising and the people who are taking are very often the same people. That's not true universally. I mentioned I had lunch with Ernesto Zedillo, and he was a magnificent example of clean government: how you run a country and come out broke. But sadly this is an exception more than a rule.

When I first arrived at the Bank, I took off on the tenth day for Africa, visiting five countries. And I'll always remember, after touring one of these countries and seeing abject poverty for two days, the President comes to me and says (this is in French Africa), I'm really glad you could come because I stole my chef from the Elysée and the food is very good. I also get the wine from Paris and we're having a Lafitte whatever it was. I can tell you, all I wanted to do was be sick. I got madder, madder and madder, but realized I couldn't say anything in front of him. There are unfortunately too many countries in Africa where the leadership is on the take. Whether that is different from German princes, British kings or Spanish royalty, if you go back in history, there are probably a lot of similarities in how they accumulated their wealth. But in today's world, this surely isn't acceptable. I think the tools to unlock it are internal. You can't come in from the outside and tell the president in whatever country, shape up, because he won't do it.

You mentioned that inequality will be one of the defining issues in 2030, 2040, 2050. What can the World Bank and other institutions do to put that issue higher up on the agenda?

Well, they try to put it on the agenda. But I think it's very difficult. If you take someone as keenly interested in development as Gordon Brown, who has a passionate interest in development, it is extremely difficult for him, when his own country's economy is in need of great repair, to start talking about increases in development assistance. He's in fact doing it, but he's putting himself at risk – of that there's no doubt. At the meetings of the G-8 and G-20 that he's led, he put development centrally on the agenda.

The fact is, there isn't a leader who will say, not one that I have known or worked with – and I for years went to the G-8 and G-20 meetings, because they decided early on to bring the head of the World Bank and the Fund to these meetings – that what you're suggesting is not worthy. The plight of the poor will always be in the communiqué, there will always be a paragraph about the world's poor and the need to deal with impending disasters. But when you are a domestic leader and you're dealing with the problems in your own country; well, there aren't many Africans that vote here. Unfortunately the constituency for international aid requires a commitment and understanding that is not there in most countries. Most people don't have a clue about poverty outside their country. They understand inequality in their own country well. But when you're talking about global inequality, to convince the rich people in the U.S. and Europe that it is in their combined interest, and the interest of their kids, that they do something now to address the issue of potential global instability because of inequality, well that's very difficult.

But it's something we need to act on, because even though many in the West are largely ignorant of the enormous inequality that persists across the world, those in poor countries are well-informed. The unequal are no longer ignorant; they've all got radios and they've all got phones. The fastest growing market for phones is in Africa.

In my second year at the World Bank, I went to a village in Africa where I was honored to be made a chief. And I'm sitting there with my brother chiefs, and the chief chief says, "Do you want to see our computer?" We're sitting in a mud hut with a thatched roof. And we go into this room where there are two young Africans with two computers, one getting coffee prices from around the world and sending them out to the coffee farmers. The other guy was reading the *New York Times*. Here I am dressed as an African chief in a hut in the middle of Africa reading the *New York Times* on a computer. It just brought home to me in a way that is almost impossible to convey the realization that technology is challenging all the established differences.

But I don't think governments in the West think like this yet. If you try to convince your leadership that global inequality is something they need to deal with now, it's very difficult, because the instinct will typically be to leave it to the next government.

Has the focus been too much on fighting poverty than addressing inequality, or do they go hand-in hand?

I think they probably go hand-in-hand. When I was at the World Bank one of the most important policies I implemented was to shift our focus so that we concentrated our efforts on poverty reduction. With such great deprivation in the world, I think improving the absolute living standards for the poorest needs to be a priority. But at the same time addressing inequality should remain an important policy goal, both globally and within countries. I think in many developing countries, policies to fight poverty and lower inequality align very closely, most notably in the case of improving access to and quality of services.

What are possible trends for middle and lower-income earners in the U.S. and Europe?

Well, I'm not a great expert on that, but I can give you some thoughts. You can see in this country that President Obama has spoken of the injustice of existing income differentials and so he's going to cut them back, tax the rich a bit more. I don't know how much of an impact this will have; so, the rich pay x% or x plus 10% in terms of taxes, which will have some equalizing effect, but rich people typically are able to find ways to remain not poor. I don't think you'll have an egalitarian society in the United States any time soon.

I should add that I don't think we should be striving for a perfectly egalitarian society. I think that would be terrible, because one of this country's greatest attributes is its social mobility. Without glamorizing it, when I came to study here, I had two dollars and fifty cents every second night to buy a roast beef sandwich at the Harvard deli. I put half the sandwich in the fridge and I'd eat half that night. It never worried me; they were the happiest days that I ever had. But I borrowed all the money I used to get through Harvard, and the beauty of this country is that you can do that. Anyone can sit next to a billionaire's son. So even as the U.S. addresses inequality, what you hope is that this spirit is not going to disappear, and that there will be the mobility for the young individual like myself, who can still make it, lose it, give it away, waste it, or save it – whatever. For me, that's the great strength of this country, and in that sense, it's much stronger than many European countries. In terms of income mobility, this country is amazing, and it's built into the system so that those who have the ability to make money also give it away.

The tradition of private philanthropy in this country is incredible. I've always spent a minimum of 25% of my time and my income on non-business activities. I started this way because I thought it was the right thing to do. In the event, it was probably the best business strategy I possibly could have because I became engaged in society, I met people, and it's a sort of unwritten element that the best people are not there just to make a zillion dollars for themselves; they're also there to serve society. And it's an area in which, again, I think Europe is a long way behind.

Returning to the question of current trends, the economic downturn is having an effect – a significant one in terms of asset value losses for everybody's net worth but especially the rich. A lot of people have been hurt, including me and most of my friends. But for most of the well-off, it's not fundamentally affecting their way of life. Maybe houses in the Hamptons cost less, you probably can buy a second-hand Porsche cheaper or a Maserati or a Rolls-Royce. But if you're not interested in doing any of that anyway, happy to drive a Volvo, it doesn't make any difference. I think the upper crust is not suffering in a material way. Some people lost money with Madoff, and there are a number of horror stories there, but in general I don't think it makes much difference whether you've got x tens of millions in the bank or half x – it's still tens of millions.

What about the middle class?

I think that's much tougher. I think the rub is coming in the middle class, and in particular in this country, in those that have heavily borrowed. As you know, over the last several years, there were no savings in this country, with homes bought almost entirely on credit.

The middle class is currently under very serious pressure because, even though rates have been dropping, mortgage payments are becoming a higher and higher percentage of each family's income because their incomes are dropping. It is a very serious issue in this country when you have 10% unemployment, and on top of that, 6%, 7%, 8% underemployed, which are numbers that we've not seen for many years and are not likely to be reversed quickly. The average working family is having a tough time at the moment, a very tough time.

What is your opinion about executive and CEO compensation?

I think for many public companies it is too high – significantly too high. I think at the very least, it should be more closely tied to long-term company performance, with payouts depending on continuing performance at the institution, not just a good year or two. And I think that if the government is coming in now to put in money to keep companies afloat, it's only fair that they have the right to say something about salary levels.

Executive compensation went way over the top in many public companies over the past several years. It's changing a bit now, but only under pressure.

Where do you see pressure arising to adjust CEO salaries?

From the voters, from Obama, and from the Democratic administration. They can't take the heat on that. I think there will be big pressure for action from the public.

I saw in the press recently the total net worth of Ben Bernanke and Tim Geithner were reported, and the order of magnitude was something like one and a half million dollars. These are the two pillars upon which the recovery of the United States depends more than anyone else, and if you compare their compensation to what executives are making, there's a stark contrast.

Many years ago, Paul Volcker left the Fed to come work with me as Chairman of my firm. He was making something like one hundred thousand a year as Chairman of the Fed – easily one of the most important people in the economy. He smoked five cent cigars, and would always fly coach. I'm very glad he's made a few dollars since, but that inequity continues, and I think it puts a focus on executive compensation vis-à-vis public sector pay.

And I should add that there's also likely to be pressure on executive compensation coming from the average worker, particularly if he works for a company where the chief executive makes 25 million dollars a year and they're shedding hundreds of thousands of jobs. That kind of thing can't fly, and isn't flying. I think we'll see more pressure for change.

Jerry Yang
Co-Founder and Chief Yahoo, Yahoo!

"As the market becomes more global, the power of governments to lower inequality is reduced, indeed political leaders increasingly face a market rather than create it, just as managers increasingly face a market rather than create it. That may be the grand development of our time."

Jerry Yang is the co-founder of Yahoo!, the Internet indexing and portal company. In one of the most famous Silicon Valley start-up stories, Yang founded Yahoo! with David Filo while a Stanford student in 1994 as "Jerry and Dave's Guide to the World Wide Web," and renamed the company as Yahoo! in 1995. Initially built as a web portal indexing a range of online products and services, today the company is one of the most visited Internet brands. Jerry Yang is currently Chief Yahoo, a member of Yahoo!'s Board of Directors, and a prominent philanthropist pursuing a special interest in the environment.

There are long-standing debates about how much inequality is the right amount of inequality. How would you characterize the amount of inequality in the U.S. and Europe? Is there too much, too little, or about the right amount?

This question, which is a standard one, makes it appear as if inequality can be raised or lowered at will, whereas in fact the amount of inequality is to some extent beyond our control. Whenever you have a market-based system, you will have a bell curve with a few high performers, lots of middling performers, and a few poor performers. It's difficult to change the shape of that bell curve.

R. Berger et al., *The Inequality Puzzle: European and US Leaders Discuss Rising Income Inequality*, DOI 10.1007/978-3-642-15804-9_14, © Springer-Verlag Berlin Heidelberg 2010

Although our options in the context of a market may be limited, I think access to education is key here and can be manipulated. If education isn't widely available to all, then it's very hard to be successful in the marketplace, and it's very hard to end up at the top of the bell curve. We have to do better ensuring that everyone has access to education, not just because it's only fair that we live up to our commitment to equal opportunity, not just because education reduces poverty, but also because the U.S. and European economies depend on a highly educated labor force. It's commonplace to *talk* about equalizing access to education, but it's high time to live up to all that talk.

Even if access to education were equalized, this wouldn't of course generate equal outcomes. Some amount of inequality in outcomes is needed to motivate people to innovate and work hard. To be sure, top performers are motivated not just by money, but also by the challenge of succeeding, by camaraderie and teamwork, and by the idea of showing everyone what they can do. But money is clearly a main reason why people work hard and are driven to succeed, and that means some amount of inequality is necessary, at least if we want high performance.

At the same time, I don't want to overstate the case for inequality! The financial crisis has, reasonably enough, led some to question the assumption that inequality will generate high performance. As compensation packages are scrutinized, some people are wondering why top managers who seem to be making mistakes are still getting so much money, why managers whose firms are failing are still well-paid. We have to think more carefully about why inequality may not always do its job of generating high performance. It's a discussion we need to have.

Could you tell us more about the conditions under which the board of directors or top leadership could change the amount of inequality in their firm?

It's an interesting question. I do think there are limits to the amount of tinkering that's possible in a competitive market with a limited pool of available talent. The company's hands are often tied: The company's leaders are typically reacting to the market, not creating one. When it comes to recruiting great engineers, maybe there is a dozen possible recruits in the world. The great engineer is in a seller's market, that engineer can simply demand a price, and the company's leaders have to meet it or fail as a company. If, for example, you're one of the top five people in the search algorithm space, you can pretty much demand your pay. By contrast, if you're an entry-level engineer, then you're more driven by what everybody else is bidding, and it's more of a buyer's market. It's not like a bunch of managers are sitting around and saying, "Well, let's make it this way." This is a highly competitive, innovation-driven, mostly talent-driven industry. And it's the same with stock options. It's very much driven by people thinking, "Well, geez, if I work four years somewhere, what is my expected payout?" and if another company can deliver a better payout then they'll just go there. The company is in this sense reacting to the market, not really creating it.

Now governments have more power than companies in setting up the rules of the game and reducing or increasing the amount of inequality that is thereby generated. In Europe, the bell curve is a bit flatter, in part because labor laws tend to be more labor-friendly. This offers protection for workers, but at the same time presents challenges for businesses that need to move fast, that need to compete against businesses in other countries that haven't such protections. However desirable labor protection might be in the abstract, politicians must increasingly ask whether it makes their country's companies less competitive, thus reducing the total output. As the market becomes more global, the power of governments to lower inequality is reduced, indeed political leaders increasingly *face* a market rather than *create* it, just as managers increasingly face a market rather than create it. That may be the grand development of our time.

May I ask a follow-up? Let's say you happened to be educated in Europe, such that everything that you did, you did in Europe. Could Yahoo! have happened in Europe?

I'd like to think that there's something unique about the American system and Silicon Valley. There are venture capitalists, people who are willing to put risk dollars into small companies, students and professors and intellectual property people who understand what start-ups do, all of which allow a Yahoo!, a Google, a Sun to emerge. There are places in Europe with all that too, but of course the Silicon Valley was and remains special. And the complicated labor regulations that govern European labor markets aren't completely trivial. As a company scales into a 1,000 people, 10,000 people, a 100,000 people, then some of the labor protections in Europe can become a real constraint.

The ongoing debate about inequality has recently focused on issues of executive compensation. If executive compensation at Yahoo! were reduced slightly or substantially, would that likely affect executive performance and ultimately the profitability of Yahoo!?

This debate has indeed been ongoing. I think about it in a very simple way: The successful company has to compete successfully for top executives. Most of the top 300 people at Yahoo! could work anywhere they wanted, and if they are not compensated well perhaps a few of them would still choose to work at Yahoo! out of love for the work or their colleagues, but at the end of the day you'd have trouble attracting, maintaining, and retaining top employees if compensation at Yahoo! was below market.

Three or four years ago, the market was booming, and there was a shortage of skilled, highly talented executives. And so executive compensation went up because there was more of a demand for executives. Nowadays, some companies are shrinking or stable in size, so you're going to see more executives on the market, and you'll certainly not see an escalation in pay. It's simple market dynamics. The banking industry has of course come under increasing scrutiny. If, as a result of this scrutiny, reductions in executive salaries are mandated, I think you'll see people who are really talented decide not to enter the banking industry. They'll choose instead an industry where they can make more. How could it work any other way?

Recently, shareholders are starting to come out, saying, "Well, geez, top executives should not make that much money if the shareholders are not making any money." This is a very interesting debate. But I would say, when I look at executives both at Yahoo! and at other companies, almost everybody is being paid in line with what they could get on the outside market. Why would Yahoo! want to overpay? Why would anyone? Nobody wants to spend more than they have to. Sometimes, it almost seems as if people think companies *want* to pay all these people extra money, and it's just not the case. If you don't have to, you won't.

Have you seen recently much of a downward drift in executive compensation? Or is it too early to see that play out?

Because stock prices have gone down, bonuses are down. If companies perform, the people who helped make it happen ought to get compensated accordingly. The flip side has to hold too: If companies don't perform, the personnel just shouldn't get as much. And I think that is happening.

The media is much enamored these days with issues of executive compensation, yet one should also consider the entire spectrum of compensation at all levels within a firm. Do you think Yahoo! has about the right amount of inequality of compensation across its many categories of workers? Or would you favor making changes in compensation practices?

This is another big debate. When Yahoo! started out as a company with 50 to 100 people, the company was much less stratified, meaning that the functions were less distinct and people carried out multiple roles. If you were an engineer, for example, you could design a product, you could build a product, you could load the product on the servers. And that meant that compensation was more similar across workers. But now the scale has increased, functions are differentiated, and compensation is more differentiated too. The culture at Yahoo! is still the one-for-all, all-for-one style, but even so there's obviously more stratification in terms of grades of pay. This holds for equity in the firm too. In the past, Yahoo! could offer equity quite broadly, but now not everyone is receiving equity as compensation.

Why has economic inequality increased substantially in North America and many European countries over the past two decades? What role has globalization and other forces played?

This is a complicated question, and I don't *know* the answer, although I can offer a few observations. The high-tech industry is clearly becoming more global, meaning that we're not just competing with our neighbors down the street, but we're also competing with other companies in Europe, Asia, China, Japan, and everywhere else. In this global context, we need to search for talent at good value, just as all of our competitors are. Across our industry, the big firms have thousands of employees in India, in China, indeed in lots of overseas markets. We all travel to Kiev all the time!

This outsourcing does probably increase income inequality in the U.S. Because you can't outsource the top 1% of employees, the extremely high wages are still being paid out in the U.S., but we may start to see increasing outsourcing for the middle 20%, 30%, and 40% of the income distribution, and the resulting hollowing out of the middle class could lead to increased inequality in the U.S., at least in the high-tech industry.

The U.S. middle class is also suffering because our primary and secondary education continues to be subpar. This means that U.S. universities are increasingly educating students from other countries that do a better job preparing their students. If these students then return to their origin countries and work there for foreign companies like Yahoo!, there's yet more hollowing out of the U.S. middle class.

What role has the media played in either supporting inequality or fanning discontent?

By its very nature, the press always has the opportunity to look in the rear-view mirror and say, "Well, these people got paid lots and lots, and even so the company screwed up." It is clearly the case that people who were making the big decisions in the financial industry didn't always make good decisions. No doubt about that.

Here, however, is my concern. You want your business people to take risks. To some extent, inequality is the unfortunate price of relying on merit and supporting risk-taking, a price that companies in a competitive market have no choice but to pay. If you try to run a company by minimizing risk, in the end you run an even bigger risk, that of not innovating fast enough and therefore losing competitiveness. Historically, the legal community has protected the ability of business to take reasonable risks, knowing all the available facts.

I think the media will always try to side with what's going to sell papers or sell airtime. And so I don't think they're going to necessarily say, "Well, geez, AIG did okay, it's fine, what they did was fine." But don't get me wrong: I don't think it was fine. The public is worrying now, and rightly so, about the tremendous amount of job loss, the tremendous amount of suffering, the tremendous downturn in the economy. And the public doesn't know who to blame, and people are properly angry. It's just that the media is doing its historic job of playing to that sentiment. I wish instead it would dig a bit deeper.

What practical actions, if any, should the private sector undertake to address rising inequality?

The private sector has to help our future workforce emerge from the U.S. school system with a good education and thus be globally competitive. It's one thing for a company to say, "Hey, I'm just going to go hire the best people in the world, and the job of U.S. workers is to make the grade and compete successfully." Yes, that's true, they need to compete successfully, but it's also the obligation of our country to make that possible. We have to find a way to make sure our own educational system is competitive in the long term. It's not as if other countries are abandoning their educational systems in the way that the U.S. has. We have to compete with the educational investments that other countries are making, and there's a role for the private sector in making sure that this investment is made. The philanthropic arms of companies can and have made some headway on this issue.

What practical actions, if any, should the government undertake to address rising inequality?

The main short-term goal is obviously to restore the economy. If the economy continues to come back, ultimately poorer people will do better. We need therefore to continue to be in stimulus mode – stimulating job growth, stimulating job creation, incentivizing companies to hire, incentivizing companies to do business. I think the Obama administration is focused more on stimulation, on getting the economy back, than on any overt redistribution of income or wealth.

The question is to what degree do we want the market economy to operate. We all know the problems with a pure market, and we all know the problems with a very restrained market. What's key to the U.S. success story is that we're right in the middle on that fundamental freedom-regulation divide. We're a great capitalistic society with a tremendous amount of innovation, great entrepreneurial spirit, and, at least on the West Coast, we're relatively free of regulations when we create businesses. Although there have been problems of late with excessive deregulation, and we obviously must tend to them, it's good to bear in mind that in many important respects the market has worked spectacularly.

This means that major revisions should be carefully undertaken. We all know that's going to happen in the banking and financial industries, but how about elsewhere? I wouldn't try to change what's making Silicon Valley work, I wouldn't try to change what's making the IT business work, I wouldn't try to revamp in any fundamental way that economic engine that's been one of the most spectacular success stories of the late 20th century. There's just as much a danger of over-responding to the crisis as under-responding.

There is, however, one type of reform in which I believe very strongly, and that's making sure that the U.S. is living up to its commitment to equal opportunity. If everyone starts off at the same place, has an equal opportunity to get an education or start up a new company, then the resulting inequality is something we can believe in, something that can be justified as the outcome of a fair and equal race.

The big question of our time is, "How can you create a fair opportunity to get ahead for as many people as possible?" The main answer to this question: We need to have fair and equal access to high-quality education. This is the issue on which government can make a big difference. It's not easy to do, but we need to be very clear on the point that we should be all about creating opportunities, fair and equal opportunities.

And we're just not doing that now. The simple fact of the matter is that the California state system can't educate all qualified students. Because of that, we are killing off the next Yahoo!, the next Internet, the next environmental breakthrough. And, worse yet, we're not living up to our commitment to provide opportunities to all. This country has never been about a handout, but we've always been about creating opportunities for those who want to seize them. I don't know what the next generation will be doing, but it's clear that if they don't have the skills to do it, somebody else will do it. Because the world isn't going to stop.

Part 3: Summary

Trends and Topics from the Interviews

Tobias Raffel and Geoffrey Samuels, Roland Berger Foundation

The individuals interviewed in this book are all winners in life's competition. President, Prime Minister, CEO, Chairman, General Secretary, they speak from the pinnacle of their chosen profession. European and American, some come from families of means, others from modest backgrounds, some graduated from private universities, others from public institutions. They hold different opinions about rising income inequality, but all believe inequality deserves more thoughtful attention on the political agenda.

Rather than summarizing each individual's opinions, this overview discusses the major concepts, opinions, and recommendations in three sections: observations, causes, and remedies. In the interest of brevity, the following pages cannot even allude to nuances, anecdotes, and details the reader is encouraged to discover in the complete interviews.

Observations

Financial Crisis Draws Attention to Inequality

The financial crisis erupted in September 2008. One month later, the OECD issued a report, *Growing Unequal?*, to document rising income and wealth inequalities among many member countries. In the spreading economic crisis, the publication quickly slipped from view. When authoritative histories of the financial crisis arrive in bookstores a few decades from now, the growing gap between the rich and everyone else will likely stand out as a major contributing factor. This is because in countries most affected by the crisis, those in the highest income tax brackets had for some time captured a major portion of improved productivity's rewards, thereby reducing the middle and lower classes' ability either to consume without relying on debt or to service the debt.

Over the past ten years, polls have tracked rising public concern about the expanding gap between rich and poor in the United States and many Euro-

R. Berger et al., *The Inequality Puzzle: European and US Leaders Discuss Rising Income Inequality*, DOI 10.1007/978-3-642-15804-9_15, © Springer-Verlag Berlin Heidelberg 2010

pean countries.[1] By and large, favorable economies and easy credit muted calls for any political response. Indeed, no major political parties on either side of the Atlantic based election campaigns on income disparities and several countries even legislated declines in top marginal income tax rates. During good times the public remains relatively complacent about income inequalities, a view that is shared across the political aisles. However, "when people have to fear job losses or major salary reductions," as Josef Ackermann, Chairman of Deutsche Bank observes, income inequality is judged less dispassionately. The interviewees did not predict how the financial crisis may affect national politics, but some commented on public opinion. Maurice Lévy, for example, Chairman and CEO of Publicis, heads a consortium of advertising agencies whose success depends upon accurately assessing public preferences and he observes,

> *If you look at France, where President Sarkozy has asked for a report on how added value is shared, what this report – produced by independent economists – has demonstrated is that things have remained relatively stable during the last twenty years, with very small differences. Obviously inequalities in salaries remain. Where a huge difference is evident concerns in fact a very small number of people, 1%, maybe less, mostly CEOs. I believe this small number of people with huge revenue packages, particularly at a time when the economic situation has worsened, have fueled the feeling of inequality, and more importantly, of injustice. It is both a real problem and one of perception; people felt that there was unfairness in the way wealth is distributed.*

Social safety nets prevented a repeat of widespread 1930s street demonstrations protesting adverse economic conditions. Nonetheless, as Poul Rasmussen, President, Party of European Socialists, suggests, the "recession has opened the door for new thinking in governments, in universities, and among the general public. There's a potential for reforming our economies." Gabriele Galateri, Chairman of Telecom Italia, also sees opportunity for reform,

> *The economic crisis has produced an enormous disruption that forces people to act. Therefore I think, at least I hope, that there*

---

[1] "Overall, over the entire period from the mid-1980s to the mid-2000s, the dominant pattern is one of a fairly widespread increase in inequality (in two-thirds of all countries)...", *Growing Unequal? Income Distribution and Poverty in OECD Countries*, OECD, 2008, p. 27.

is an in-built mechanism which corrects imbalances. The world has survived ages of tragedies and disasters and of confidence and development, because every action produces a reaction that tends to stabilize or recreate equilibrium. So even in this field I think that what has happened will create a better equilibrium in terms of speculation and remunerations, and more generally in terms of diminishing inequalities.

Excess, Not Inequality, Is the Concern

I think the excesses of capitalism are the biggest threat to capitalism. (John Monks)

Inequality is a perennial issue. Ancient Greece heard popular rallying cries for land redistribution and capitalism continues the drama because nature distributes abilities, ambition and chance unequally. All interviewees believe some inequality is healthy, natural, and stimulating. "Competition promotes diversity and creativity, and the results of such competition are unequal per se. Inequality is thus part and parcel of any democratic society," notes Jürgen Hambrecht, Chairman of BASF. "We should do our best to reduce inequality, but we should do so by working to ensure that opportunities are fairly distributed, and we should avoid extremes of inequality."

Everyone warns about excess, yet one person's excess can be another's thrill. Prudent politicians hope to prevent protest marches, vandalism, and other forms of discontent spinning into social unrest, but this is easier said than done and all agree there are no formulas or guidelines to identify dangerous excess. Cultural traits differ and some societies are simply more comfortable tolerating higher levels of inequality. A frequent example contrasts entrepreneurial America with equality-minded Scandinavia. Nonetheless, today's income disparities, considerably higher in the U.S. and U.K. than other European countries, gives some interviewees concern about potentially adverse social consequences. Sir Mark Moody-Stuart, former Chairman, Anglo American, comments, "I think that the divergence of remuneration between the top and bottom of an organization is now causing strain in society." William Weld, a former Republican Governor in famously liberal Massachusetts, refers to the social stability created by a confident middle class and argues that prudence would suggest some spreading out and flattening of income curves.

The guiding hand of religion which sometimes curbed excess has largely faded from secular Western countries to be replaced by invisible hands of globalized markets. "What is fair?" Maurice Lévy asks, "Today we are in a situation where all this is decided by what we call *les forces du marché*, the market conditions. So I'm not sure that someone can say from any standpoint – could be a philosopher, a sociologist, a politician, or a man in the street – what is equal, what is not?"

Concerns about rising inequality are not restricted to Europe and North America. "I believe the level of inequality that has developed over the last twenty years is probably excessive," observes Bertrand Collomb, former Chairman of Lafarge. "This is true in western countries like the U.S. or Europe, but even more in emerging countries. It is also true between countries, with the poorest countries being unable – more for social reasons than economic reasons – to catch up with economic development." James Wolfensohn, former president of the World Bank, wholeheartedly agrees:

> *But for me, while this within-country inequality is undoubtedly a problem, the real pressing inequality question today is not about within-country inequality but rather between-country inequality: the gap between the rich countries and the poor countries. There are a billion people in the world living on less than 1.25 dollars a day, and 2.5 billion on less than 2 dollars, out of a global population of some 6.5 billion. This had been improving in recent years, but I think we've seen some backsliding under this recent cycle. The disconnect between these people living in abject poverty and us here in the West is the real inequality. The question is what will happen when the next 2.5 billion come on the planet, when we'll have 9 billion people by the year 2050, and on current trends I fear such inequalities will become unsustainable.*

Many Europeans and Americans consider CEO pay to be the most visible sign of inequality. A later section will discuss the interviewees' recommendations about CEO compensation, but here it is relevant to note that mathematics threaten ever-expanding CEO-worker pay ratios. Sir Mark notes that over the past ten to fifteen years, senior executive salaries increased annually in the 5 to 10% range, while wages kept pace with inflation or climbed a few percentage points higher. "It is clearly unsustainable that the differential should keep on growing as it has done for ten years or more," says Sir Mark. "Certainly the growth in disparity between top and bottom has to stop, but reversing or switching back will be very difficult."

"Executive compensation went way over the top in many public companies over the past several years," says Wolfensohn, "It's changing a bit now, but only under pressure." Asked whether he recommended a method to adjust CEO-worker salary ratios, John Monks says, "There is no rigid formula. We used to talk in the 1970s, when a Swedish economist proposed that chief executives should get no more than five times what the lowest paid employee in his company should get. Well, multiply that now by hundreds. But let me make clear – I'm not trying to remake East Germany, I'm not trying to restore the Soviet economy."

A solution lies in raising worker and employee compensation, leading Fred Smith, Chairman, President and CEO of FedEx, to emphasize the challenge of improving incomes for the bottom half in a globalized world of fast-changing technology and markets.

> *I think that's at the heart of income inequality, our inability to improve the earnings of the bottom half of the income distribution curve. I personally think it doesn't make any difference what they do in terms of trying to limit compensation at the top, because the key is how you increase compensation at the bottom. Nobody's talking about that.*

The Public, Perception, and the Media

> *So while there is a great amount of inequality and CEO compensation packages undoubtedly did get too high relative to societal norms, the reality is quite a bit different than the popular press would make it out to be. (Fred Smith)*

The Gini coefficient, the most commonly cited index to rate a country's overall income inequality, is an invisible number. Most people assess inequality by what they see in daily life and what the media shows. Several interviewees disapproved of the media's distorting influence. Celebrity profiles and exposés about income extremes may sell copies and attract viewers, but they convey inaccurate pictures of social and economic realities. Jürgen Hambrecht suggests such media coverage may also project inappropriate values. "I believe that people are more willing to tolerate differences in wealth if they can see a correlation between what a person earns and what they contribute to society. The mass media, however, show us a world in which there is no longer a link between performance and status, prestige and income." Jerry Yang, founder and Chief Yahoo, Yahoo!, notes the tendency of mass media to eschew thoughtful analysis,

> *I think the media will always try to side with what's going to sell papers or sell airtime. ... The public is worrying now, and rightly so, about the tremendous amount of job loss, the tremendous amount of suffering, the tremendous downturn in the*

> *economy. And the public doesn't know who to blame, and people are properly angry. It's just that the media is doing its historic job of playing to that sentiment. I wish instead it would dig a bit deeper.*

France presents an apt example of how the media can shape public perceptions. A country that hosted a major and several minor revolutions is obviously sensitive to inequality, and recent polls indeed report the French public's growing disapproval of rising income inequality. However, the statistical facts are starkly different. The French Gini coefficient, with minor variations, has been stable over the past two decades. The "bling" effect of media stories about a tiny minority's antics and extravagances have undoubtedly influenced public opinion. But there are other factors at work to create misperceptions. For example, changing technology, social and business patterns also affect public impressions. Available cash at an ATM is no longer a reliable guide to one's standard of living because many expenses are now deducted automatically. Consumption priorities change, such as expensive monthly mobile phone bills, and the price of goods in the supermarket fluctuates more than in the "good old days," which contributes to worries about diminished purchasing power. Observing the discrepancy between statistics and popular impressions, Lévy notes,

> *If we look at things statistically, as we should when we are doing a survey on macroeconomics – obviously I can speak only for France – there is certainly a relatively stable situation and in some areas a small improvement. But we cannot ignore that despite what statistics tell us the feeling of injustice and inequality has increased. Clearly there are some elements that have given the idea of a worse situation.*

Categories of Wealth (Not All Money Is Equal)

Banker and public company CEO compensation is a lightning rod for negative public opinion on both sides of the Atlantic. The *Economist* advocates a liberal view toward executive pay, yet during an October 2009 online debate proposing that senior executives are worth their pay, *Economist* readers voted four-to-one against the proposition. However, despite their publicity, CEOs only represent a minority of those in the top earning league and the public does discriminate among different methods to acquire wealth. By and large, as Sir Mark observes, the public approves of inherited, old money, highly talented athletic, entertainment, and artistic performers, and successful entrepreneurs. He considers "the current issue has arisen because in the last ten or fifteen years there has been a growth in the differential between these people at the top of major public companies and those within the company or in society at large. I think that is where the strains begin to grow."

Pending and enacted financial reforms in America and Europe, a U.S. pay czar, and EU initiatives on salaries and bonuses will keep financial executive and CEO pay in the spotlight for some time. Coincidentally, no other group of high-income earners attracted as much attention in the interviews.

Causes

Ethics

> *There are only three fundamental questions in life, as best I can tell at age sixty-five. Number one, what does one person owe to another? The whole issue of envy and equity has been a driving force since the time people first put pen to papyrus, or whatever. The second, is there a God and what does God want? People have been fighting over that since the beginning of time. And the third, how are we as a society going to organize to deal with the first two questions? Everything goes back to those three points. So anybody who says that inequality isn't a big issue for the effective functioning of a society, is simply ignorant of the record of humanity. It's a huge issue. (Fred Smith)*

The obligations of the wealthy to the less fortunate preoccupies all religions. For the secularly minded, ethics define good and bad, rights and duties, and several interviewees commented on a general value shift away from duties toward rights or freedoms. Over the past thirty years, liberalized markets, lower trade barriers and deregulation helped economies transform, asset values increase, and the mantra of enhancing shareholder value almost won universal approval. Gabriele Galateri, Chairman of Telecom Italia, notes how a corresponding ideological shift toward pursuing great wealth overran earlier ethical constraints limiting compensation.

> *I think it reflects a much wider problem than corporate governance. There was an overall worldwide cultural movement that has slowly taken over and reduced the importance of many rules, legal or natural, that kept people on track. Why do morals*

> *matter, if growth, profits, and jobs are assured? It was all fine, having the "huge air of the world" rush through without real limitations, except of course the legal order, it was a fantastic period of anyone's life, but I don't think it really was the right way.*

John Sweeney, President Emeritus of the AFL-CIO, has a short word to describe this movement – greed. "Workers have not been receiving their fair share of the wealth they create, and the gap has gotten wider and wider with the greed of the highest paid."

John Monks observes that after the Second World War there was a "sense of greater mutual obligation" as countries worked to repair the damage. The eighties saw the start of a move away from these implicit bonds.

> *Since financial market deregulation in the mid-1980s, the gaps between rich and poor have widened dramatically. I believe too that the concern the people at the top have for the wider society has also become correspondingly less. They're in a bubble. ... It is not the politics of envy. The rich, super-rich, not all of them, but too many of them, have completely forgotten those responsibilities and obligations.*

Globalization and liberalized markets ushered in greater executive mobility, loosening an individual's ties to a company or community. Executive suite migrants searching for better paying contracts may also have diminished loyalties and sense of obligations. While it is difficult to generalize across one society, let alone two continents, many countries have seen a rollback of the state in the economy and less public regard for public institutions, suggested by such statistics as falling voter participation. When economic power moves into the private sector, wealth becomes the principal way to gain honor, status, and prestige. Conspicuous consumption, and other self-indulgent behaviors evident among all classes, are viewed differently when practiced by the wealthy.

Sir Mark notes, "I think people are much more tolerant of high remuneration if they feel the person earning it actually does something with it other than just spending it. Behavior, of course, makes a difference." European philanthropy has been considerably lower than in the United States, whether due to stronger welfare societies, higher taxes, or other cultural differences, although there are signs of change as European wealthy begin to establish foundations. "With its many private foundations, the U.S. is clearly doing a lot to help the disadvantaged," observes Ackermann, "We are just now learning from this in Europe, which is a good thing."

Psychology, Peer Groups, and Pay

The standard model to explain the rise of executive pay is well known. Incentivizing senior managers through a complex array of salary, bonus, and stock options began in the United States in the early eighties as an attempt to correct the agent phenomenon where managers did not advance the shareholders' best interests. Pay awards for CEOs who could increase shareholder value rose at the same time many companies considerably expanded to compete across globalized markets. Many corporations recorded substantial increases in revenues. Financial intermediaries were the initial beneficiaries and Wall Street pay packages climbed to set new compensation benchmarks. Despite calls for long-term thinking, quarterly performance became a preoccupation, CEO turnover accelerated, and pay transparency stimulated Boards to increase pay to attract and retain talent. An inflationary pay spiral evolved, fueled by easy credit, rising markets, and asset inflation. While European senior executive compensation has not matched the highest American levels, the international market for executives has nonetheless stimulated substantial jumps in European CEO pay. In this context, the interviewees drew particular attention to pay transparency, executive mobility, and financial incentives.

Pay Transparency

Initiated as a reform to discourage egregious compensation, the practical effect was more pay competition. As Maurice Lévy observes,

> *In Europe, and particularly in France, we have been faced with the consequences of transparency. What happened was that salaries or compensation were benchmarked and adjusted to the highest-paid person. New experts appeared whose analysis was that if you wanted to keep your people, you had to be in top quartile, etc. ... The transparency which was meant to moderate has in fact created a serious inflation.*

Mobility and Reduced Loyalty

Long-term strategies obviously need executive continuity to lead the company through inevitable market and development cycles. However, when investors seek short-term financial gains, it becomes more acceptable to change leaders to focus on improving quarterly earnings rather than longer-term issues. "While mobility is in principle a good thing, in many corporations I think there has also been a decrease on both sides in long-term commitment and loyalty," notes Sir Mark. "Companies became more focused on financial returns and forgot about all the other issues. I think that was another aspect influencing changing attitudes toward pay."

Limitations of Financial Incentives

"Financial incentives are important," observes Jürgen Hambrecht, "But money is not the prime motivator. The motivation it provides fades fastest. In my experience, the most important source of motivation comes from within – our 'inner spark, ' so to speak." Gabriele Galateri agrees, "I think that money is not the only way to motivate performance, which depends very much on your culture, your past, your future, your age, your experience, and so on. ... Today, I don't think that I would move from my position to another company just for the sake of making twice the salary." "You could pay the CEO ten times less," observes Collomb, "he would still do his job, provided no peer was paid more. You don't do that job for money."

Relying on financial rewards to improve performance risks diminishing priorities and encourages both executives and employees to view work primarily as a pay check. A financial matrix can neglect the drives and allegiances that help individuals cooperate to overcome challenging conditions. Sir Mark advises,

> *... the real problem with all of these measures is that you can start to look at them as if they are the controlling mechanism, and that the whole thing is driven by remuneration. Because when you start to treat people like a financial investment – if you just add some more money here, the following happens – that's exactly what you don't want. The more you devise these crafty mechanisms, the more you forget that pay is only a little piece of the whole motivation of people. The really important bit is how you build the spirit and the ethos of the company. And it's as companies began to lose that spirit and ethos that the unwelcome bits of mobility, the weakening of loyalty, increased.*

Pay Conflated with Status

Soaring compensation can reach levels that bear no relation to needs. "Candidly, I don't see how someone can spend responsibly more than five million dollars a year," comments William Weld, "but at least until quite recently, on Wall Street that amount was considered an odd lot. That sort of brings the issue home." Higher pay to win 'bragging rights' stimulates competition to win the highest compensation. Observing the trend toward increasing senior pay, Sir Mark notes, "the size of remuneration at the top of major corporations is such that you could live a perfectly happy, comfortable, affluent life on significantly less. So the root of it has been this competitive relative growth. That's very difficult to deal with."

Historically, Western culture once recognized other established ways to win status, such as priestly castes, military rank, aristocracy, where wealth and income could be relatively less important. In today's market culture, money carries more social cachet, and John Monks agrees that the pursuit of status through pay complicates tamping inequality excess.

> *I think we know that pay levels are not just about how much you get, but about how much you get relative to what other people get. The level of dissatisfaction is relative. Seeing people in financial services, and seeing people at the top of other organizations who want the same as the people at the top in financial services, people in the public sector want the same as people at the top in the private sector, who want the same as the top in the banks, has led to this widening of the gap. I think it's very divisive.*

Equal Opportunity Failings

Equal opportunity is a bedrock principle to stimulate competition by rewarding merit. The United States, despite a long and difficult campaign to overcome racial prejudice, is famous for the American Dream, the opportunity to improve one's station in life. Today, John Sweeney observes that inequalities may threaten this iconic American emblem.

> *I don't think that attitude is as prevalent as it was years ago. People today are not confident that their son or daughter will automatically experience the American Dream. Based upon the experiences that workers are going through, or have gone through, they're fearful that their children are not going to enjoy life as well as they were enjoying it for a while. But there is a complete frustration with what has happened and there is a sense of bitterness over what the extreme has gone to in terms of the haves and have nots.*

Post-war European societies made considerable progress trying to overcome centuries of established privileges, but improvements may be slowing. "I strongly believe in equality of opportunity and social mobility," says Josef Ackermann, and he worries that there is growing public concern on both sides of the Atlantic that individuals from a modest background do not enjoy the same opportunities as those from wealthier families. Poul Rasmussen concurs, noting the difficulties many young people face even to enter the job market.

> *Another aspect of inequality is what I would call those who are excluded from society, not least those who are excluded from the labor market. Increasing numbers of the young generation have found it extremely difficult to enter the job market, resulting in them being marginalized, dropping out of their educational system, and not managing to reintegrate. The barriers preventing young people from getting this crucial first foothold are significant.*

There has never been a year without calls to improve and invest in education, but educational reform today is a higher priority because the consequences of school and university deficiencies are judged to be much more costly in a global knowledge-based economy. Sir Mark notes that the United Kingdom's earlier efforts to promote equality by aggressively pursuing comprehensive education simply failed, either through flawed execution or design. "So here was an effort at increasing equality, which has actually in my opinion damaged social mobility, which is a huge tragedy. ... Unfortunately around the world we see that when you do something and damage the education system, you can damage it extremely quickly and it takes decades to recover."

Bertrand Collomb cites the failure to give blue-collar workers the skills they need to compete in a globalized economy.

> *I go back to my initial answer to inequality, which is social mobility. If we were able to develop social mobility, it would make inequality more acceptable. The problem is we've had more inequality and less social mobility, at least that's the feeling people have in France. Even in the U.S., I'm not sure that the blue-collar worker feels he has the potential for social mobility. Probably less now than before, because they are disenfranchised from the rest of the country. You have pockets in the U.S. of people who are living by their own standards, the skill level of the blue-collar labor force is not very good.*

Fred Smith emphasizes the need to raise incomes for the bottom half and questions American educational priorities. Significant amounts of federal funding also flow into educational areas which are not economically productive. Furthermore, excessive regard for degrees from prestigious universities has tended to diminish support for community colleges and vocational schools, the very institutions that provide the type of practical education and instruction so necessary to improve blue-collar skills.

Remedies

Ethical Reform

> *... inequality has arisen not only from the lack of rules, as many people suggest, but also and mostly by a reduction of what is called, unfortunately in too generic terms, a sense of ethics. Undoubtedly further regulation in certain areas would have helped and will help. But I don't think that the basic situation can be changed unless we restore an ethical sense, a commitment of the human being toward a correct behavior that otherwise would be very difficult to promote strictly by regulation. (Gabriele Galateri)*

> *Not only cleaners, taxi drivers and unskilled workers have rights and duties; this also applies to CEOs, the bankers and hedge fund managers. We should introduce new ethics based on rights and duties. ... (Poul Rasmussen)*

The scale of the financial crisis leads several interviewees to suggest it is time to examine society's ethics, values, and priorities. Should the public and leaders recognize the need for change, ethical reform requires patient efforts by families, educational institutions, the media, and governments. Noting that at one time civics and basic ethical instruction was a standard class in many primary schools but now such classes are uncommon, Galateri judges their absence a mistake. Reflecting upon the many ways to advance ethical reform, Jürgen Hambrecht observes, "A good education is only one side of the coin, however. The other side is discipline and hard work, unpleasant as those terms might sound. And that is why I wish governments would place more emphasis on the importance of a positive work ethic."

The past three decades have seen an extraordinary increase in wealthy families. However, individuals who do not acknowledge the greater responsibility money brings and how their personal conduct might influence public opinion, led Sir Mark to advise, "for people who earn a lot, what they do with the money is important. It's an entirely private matter, but I think it's nonetheless socially important." James Wolfensohn also emphasizes the need for philanthropy, noting that many European wealthy do not share the enthusiasm of some rich Americans.

> *The tradition of private philanthropy in this country [United States] is incredible. I've always spent a minimum of 25% of my time and my income on non-business activities. I started this way because I thought it was the right thing to do. In the event, it was probably the best business strategy I possibly could have because I became engaged in society, I met people, and it's a sort of unwritten element that the best people are not there just to make a zillion dollars for themselves; they're also there to serve society. And it's an area in which, again, I think Europe is a long way behind.*

Andrew Carnegie's most lasting legacy is likely not steel rails crossing the country, but the public libraries he endowed in many cities and his essay, the *Gospel of Wealth*, which influenced wealthy Americans to found colleges and universities. Today, Bill Gates has committed himself to philanthropy, and he may eventually be viewed as a latter-day Andrew Carnegie. Whether substantial numbers of wealthy families follow his lead remains to be seen, but William Weld counsels that the scale of the inequality challenge will require even more than donations. "People say, what should the private sector do, what should the public sector do? I think this is not going to be solved by charity, it will be solved through the public sector."

Improve Equal Opportunity

> *Above all, governments should address the subject of equal opportunity. I believe this is key. To some extent, of course, this also means fighting the root causes of poverty, but it is just as important for people to have the feeling that they have the same opportunity to succeed if they are talented. If that is the case, inequality of wealth and income distribution will be much more widely accepted. ... The government should invest as much as possible in education. This makes a country more competitive on a global scale, but it also gives its citizens the feeling they have opportunities in life. (Josef Ackermann)*

Education

European interviewees across the political aisles agree that the government should invest more in education. "In my view, the role of government should be to promote opportunities for social mobility and provide incentives to perform at all levels in society," says Jürgen Hambrecht, "I would therefore like to see much, much more spending on education." Poul Rasmussen agrees, "Improving the mobility in education systems must be a priority."

Hambrecht and Ackermann recommend programs to improve early education where numerous studies have documented highly favorable results. Galateri expands upon the need for early education by advising "rebuilding the parents' sense of responsibility along all the course of life of their children from childhood to adulthood, and restoring the key social role of teachers."

Sir Mark suggests that a solid education must also encourage the creativity that diversity brings, "you need to make sure the education system gets everyone properly educated, but paradoxically also allows for differentiation, because people are not all the same. We need a system which allows people to develop their talents. Because what's extremely disruptive in inequality is not just inequality itself, it's when individuals feel that they are trapped in the unequal half of the equation. If they feel they have an opportunity to achieve, then I think it causes less stress."

Across the Atlantic, Wolfensohn links educational reform to improving health and equal rights for women.

> *What we need to be doing is addressing education. That's our best opportunity. If you're going to deal with education, it's a ten year cycle, at least, to see meaningful results and help spur broad-based development. So we can't afford to wait. ... And if you're going to really tackle education, you also need to deal with the question of health, and you need to deal with the question of gender equity. It's not one single shot that solves the problem. Education, health, and gender equity are all very important.*

Fred Smith suggests American priorities do not emphasize improving blue-collar prospects. Taking issue with the goal that everyone should get a college degree, especially from a prominent university, he advocates more support for community colleges and vocational training to give high school graduates the skills to find jobs. He also recommends more economically-focused Federal funding and "the government should phase out Federal loans and support of higher education, except in the scientific disciplines where it can be justified on the basis of national security and economic wealth generation."

Mentoring

Corporate Social Responsibility's reputation has suffered the fate of many buzz words, more often honored in the breach, but some corporate mentoring programs have demonstrated effectiveness in reaching out to disadvantaged students of ability. "Money is not everything," notes Ackermann, "you can and should, of course, invest time and talent, for example, in mentoring programs." In 2005, BASF was a founding member of the Knowledge Factory that has expanded to sixty-five German companies supporting educational projects at the preschool, kindergarten, and elementary levels. "It's also important for businesses to live up fully to their social responsibility," advises Hambrecht. "Initiatives related to education have long been part of BASF's social responsibility efforts and go back far longer than the term social responsibility!"

Corporate Equal Opportunity

Diversity and promotion by merit need more than lip service. Corporate politics will certainly not disappear, but, "Within companies we need to work carefully on diversity, making sure that there are no hidden barriers, that there are not people with advantages because of who they are or where they came from," advises Sir Mark. "That's hugely important in a corporation."

Targeted Investment

> *The question is how to enable prosperity to penetrate. People often talk about it in terms of creating equality of opportunity. I'm not sure that's concrete enough. I like the example of a category of infrastructure which if constructed could have a real economic impact. (William Weld)*

Public infrastructure projects that attract substantial private investment is another way governments can increase opportunities. Road building, railroads, and other transportation projects have been abused to 'make work' or benefit special interests, but if properly planned they could increase economic opportunities. Former Governor Weld contrasts flourishing Mexican maquiladoras free-enterprise sites located near the U.S. border with under-employed labor housed further south in areas lacking adequate roads or efficient access to markets.

Compensation Reform and Corporate Governance

> *Executive compensation is a very big issue. I think that meritocracy should be reflected in remuneration, and this is an instrument of capitalism which I fully support. You cannot pay everyone the same amount because you would never have the right incentives. I'm not shocked by the fact that there is a strong level of remuneration for some executives, as long as this is clearly tied to medium and long-term results and makes a minimum of sense. I don't know if the top manager remuneration has to be a maximum of 20, 50, 100 times the lowest level of remuneration, but there has to be some logic in the level of compensation. (Gabriele Galateri)*

CEO employment contract clauses once cached from public scrutiny in remuneration committee memos now take the spotlight at Congressional committee hearings. The general consensus of the interviewees is that executive pay should be addressed because public concern, criticism, or confusion is understandable and if not dealt with properly, events could evolve in unanticipated directions. "Public outrage is not a very pleasant sight," says Sir Mark, "and has unintended consequences because it operates in a capricious way and often hits people and organizations who are not the most guilty of the egregious offences, but who are merely most visible."

The interviewees recommend a broad framework to review and reform executive compensation:

Transparency

"For CEO bonuses and salaries, level and methods, I would say that the number one aim is transparency," advises Rasmussen. Ackermann concurs, "let me speak about my own industry: The financial industry is particularly dependent on trust. For this, transparency is key." Several industry associations and government agencies have proposed definitions of transparency, and standards will certainly evolve, but good faith efforts to show transparency are critical to restoring public confidence.

Principles and Guidelines – Moderation

Competitive CEO markets, rising stock markets and asset bubbles, and compliant Boards have lifted senior executive compensation inexorably over the past couple decades. New pay principles promoting moderation should be instituted. "The pay and bonus level has to be negotiated on some ethical level. Having finance executives earning 22,000 times the average wage of a hard-working American industrial worker is obviously disproportionate," advises Rasmussen. Bertrand Collomb observes:

> *The current focus on executive compensation is not totally logical. The main reason why people focus on it is because it is known, public, and probably because they don't understand why there should be so much difference between the boss and the rest of the people in the company. On that, I agree with them. I don't understand why the boss should have a remuneration so completely out of line. Personally I believe there is probably an ethical problem when you see a CEO who's paid ten times more than the number two, and I can understand the negative reaction. In a situation where the whole scale of salaries has been extended, but in a reasonable way, which means if the CEO is within an acceptable system, like maybe twice the number two, something like that, even three times if you add long-term incentives, I would consider that as acceptable. I think that people would probably accept that better.*

Calls for self-restraint and moderation are also prudent because they could defuse pressure to enact government imposed limits. "I don't think we have to have a national solution about how do you organize compensation within a corporation," observes William Weld. "But should people be making a hundred million dollars a year in salary? I don't think so. That wealth would belong to the corporation if it didn't go to the CEO. Does that have to be legislated? I would hope not."

Limits on Pay Not Recommended

The interviewees recommend against setting strict limits for pay. "Legally imposed limits for compensation are diametrically opposed to the principles of a free-market economy," states Jürgen Hambrecht. The historical record suggests that legislated pay caps merely divert energies into efforts to find other methods to award higher pay packages. Reflecting on earlier attempts to cap compensation, Sir Mark observes, "I do not support [legal limits] because I think it would result in an enormous amount of effort being put into devising ways to get around the legislation. When we had so-called pay restraint in the seventies in the U.K., it resulted in very complex pay packages, benefits-in-kind and all sorts of stuff which took years to remove."

Doubts about how to restrict compensation are not only expressed in corporate executive suites. When asked about setting limits on executive pay, John Monks replied,

> *It's hard, isn't it, I don't know how you do that. If you were in the Gates position and you had a fantastic product that the whole world wanted and was virtually unchallenged, and you make an absolute fortune, what can you do about that? I don't think you can do anything about that. But in a way, this is a weakness of our position, we try to divide the ones who've done something from the ones who've done nothing, apart from improve the returns for their bank or whatever, often by rearranging their tax affairs.*

Taxation to Control Excess Compensation

Several interviewees suggest taxation is a more appropriate and efficient way to influence pay restraint. "I don't think the government should regulate compensation packages," notes Fred Smith, suggesting instead that if the government wants to moderate compensation it should increase the marginal personal income tax for higher earners. However, international markets can impose an upper limit on tax rates which in turn will restrict the potential of higher marginal income taxes to redistribute wealth. Bertrand Collomb sounds a cautionary note.

> *If your marginal income tax rate doesn't go above 50% altogether, it's probably acceptable in terms of economic value creation. People will not probably leave the country because they're taxed at 50 and they could be taxed at 40 somewhere else. But if you go to 70 or 80, clearly they will leave. And if you go to 50% total, which means 45 federal, that doesn't give you a lot of potential for redistribution if the system still creates a lot of inequality at the source of income. So I don't know whether that will solve the problem.*

Variable Long-Term Pay Based on Real Results

A general consensus agrees with Ackermann's recommendation that "we must take a long-term perspective, remuneration must be based on real, bottom-line contributions to earnings, not on revenues, with vesting over several years." To ensure that pay is based on solid earnings, he suggests it is especially important to introduce effective claw-back mechanisms to recoup bonuses if the award benefits from transitory market movements. Sir Mark advocates that a large portion of an executive's wealth should be "tied up in the fortunes of the company. I think that would be the key and that's the principle I have always worked on, that as an executive one's variable remuneration becomes an investment in the company."

Shareholder Participation

Enhancing shareholder value is frequently cited to justify higher senior executive pay incentives, yet if shareholders are unhappy with company performance their practical ability to influence policies has often meant selling shares. Non-binding 'say on pay' is a step toward letting shareholders participate in important corporate decisions. Commenting on the U.K. experience, Sir Mark notes, "What shareholder pressure has clearly done is to help ensure that the variable elements are reasonable and generally have sensible performance conditions. There is no doubt that this could be made more active and effective, but it has had an effect." Gabriel Galateri suggests strengthening "say on pay" to make it more robust, "if only top management remuneration will have to pass through the shareholders' meeting and be approved by the shareholders, not just by the remuneration committee, this simple act might improve the situation." Bertrand Collomb agrees:

> *I think executive compensation has to be more streamlined in terms of process, and we need some type of "say on pay" for the shareholders. What I would like is to go back to the situation where the CEO is not paid ten times, fifteen times the number two of the company. I think the range of remuneration within the company will probably remain open, because that's part of the overall inequality system, but to treat the CEO as a special case outside of a normal compensation scheme has always shocked me.*

However, both labor leaders express concern that shareholders may lack the will or the long-term perspective to manage their responsibilities as owners. Commenting about efforts to regulate pay, John Sweeney notes,

> *That remains to be seen what we can do about it, and whether we have the will to be aggressive enough. It's not just what can be done legislatively, but what are the shareholders going to do, how are the stockholders of these companies going to hold their CEOs accountable and restrict CEO compensation, how are they going to relate these salaries to the performance of the CEO, and the performance of the company.*

Level Playing Field

Governments and regional bodies could devote more attention to the international implications of regulations. The financial industry is on the front lines. "There is a war for talent out there," Ackermann observes, "and we see that some banks are losing good people to non-regulated institutions that do not have to disclose compensation packages. That is why regulation has to be industry-wide in order to avoid competitor distortions." John Monks supports international coordination. "I think much of this lies in corporate governance. It's very difficult for one company to take action in isolation from the others, which is where I think the state, and perhaps beyond the state, Europe and North America, have to do something concerted. But I do think it helps having shareholder organizations demanding that pay is more long-term related."

Government Policy, Tax, and Regulatory Reform

The trend toward services to the detriment of the industrial sector concerned several interviewees. "We have become dominated too much by services, particularly by financial services, and we have forgotten too quickly the real economy," says Galateri. "I think that bringing back a different concept of the real economy and financial services is advisable." Fred Smith, a noted entrepreneur in the service sector, agrees that the American economy has become unbalanced.

> *There is a complete mismatch between the needs of the blue-collar sector for the kinds of government policies that create investment and skill sets to increase their earning power relative to government policies that prejudice the system toward government and the financial sector. ... I am pessimistic so long as the government is so focused on the financial sector to the detriment of the industrial sector. Eisenhower used to talk about a military-industrial complex. We have a Washington-Wall Street complex, and it is at the heart of a lot of the problems.*

The tax code favors the financial sector and Smith recommends reforms to promote industrial investments. Specifically, he advocates that capital equipment should be expensed immediately and the corporate tax rate lowered to 25% to be globally competitive because "what makes blue-collar people able to sustain a reasonable standard of living, the investment in the industrial sector, and that is treated poorly by our tax code and our government policy."

Deficit reduction has motivated Western governments to tackle tax havens, which coincidentally may help address wealth inequalities when stricter tax enforcement captures more unreported earnings. Monks and Rasmussen advocate stronger tax regimes and higher progressive income taxes in countries with comparatively lower rates. "We need to solve the tax haven problem and taxation problem," advises Rasmussen. "We need to ensure that capital income is treated in principle the same way as labor income, which will mean an increase in taxation, I admit that. But could you explain to me, why not? Why should the CEO be taxed more lightly than the hard-working industrial worker, why? I don't understand that."

Rebuilding middle class finances is a priority for William Weld, who, as Governor of Massachusetts, scrupulously followed tax reduction policies. To improve middle class financial security he recommends to "take less in taxes. I think supply-side economics has a good chance of success. From a prudential point of view, which is the starting point of my analysis, we should be very happy to have the middle class leading their prosperous and non-desperate lives. They are the backbone of any country."

Other Suggestions to Strengthen the Disadvantaged

Monks, Sweeney, and Rasmussen suggest measures to enhance labor's ability to negotiate for higher wages. Sweeney calls for passage of the Employee Free Choice Act to give American workers organizing rights widely recognized in Europe, while Rasmussen supports measures to encourage EU labor mobility, notably "equal pay for equal work" when companies hire foreign workers.

Jürgen Hambrecht would like to see more EU commitment for the Lisbon Strategy, especially measures to promote innovation and a learning economy. Rasmussen concurs and suggests expanding the brief and use of European-wide funding to promote job creation. For example, the European Social Fund should expand to support more education and training projects beyond its successful Erasmus project. He also recommends changing the Cohesion Fund and the Globalization Funds to help marginal workers and immigrants enter the economy. Lastly, flexicurity, introduced in Denmark when Rasmussen was Prime Minister, could serve as a model to help workers retrain and acquire new skills.

A View from the Top

David B. Grusky and Christopher Wimer,
Stanford Center for the Study of Poverty and Inequality

The preceding chapter provides a comprehensive summary of the many issues addressed by our contributors. In this chapter, we provide yet another summary, but now one that is oriented to a more delimited set of themes. We present such themes in the form of answers to three questions: (a) Is rising inequality a problem?; (b) What are the causes of rising inequality?; and (c) How, if at all, should inequality be reduced? These questions, which are addressed in turn below, merit a special chapter because they are so central to public debates about inequality.

Is Rising Inequality a Problem?

We led off the first chapter by noting that unusually high levels of inequality, such as those observed in the U.S. or Italy, are typically deemed acceptable when (a) the population is convinced that rewards are fairly allocated, and (b) the opportunity for a comfortable working-class or middle-class life is quite widely available. We referred to this two-pronged formula for justifying and legitimating inequality as a fundamental "social compact" that has generated widespread buy-in and stability even as inequality took off. We further suggested that the combination of the financial crisis and recession may be calling this compact partly into question. That is, insofar as compensation practices at the very top are not as tightly tied to merit as was previously assumed, then the public may be less willing to tolerate high pay at the top. Obversely, insofar as hard-working employees are laid off during the recession and cannot find new jobs, it's again more difficult to argue that the treatment they're receiving is just or merited.

Do concerns of this sort appear among the business, labor, and political leaders interviewed here? Although their views are subtle and diverse, it is notable that several commentators suggested that the public is indeed increasingly questioning whether rewards at the top of the class structure are always closely tied to merit. The merit-reward connection, which is of course the core of the social compact, may be called into question insofar

R. Berger et al., *The Inequality Puzzle: European and US Leaders Discuss Rising Income Inequality*, DOI 10.1007/978-3-642-15804-9_16, © Springer-Verlag Berlin Heidelberg 2010

as top executives, financiers, and bankers were understood to be securing substantial compensation even as their companies were failing and even though their financial maneuverings may have precipitated the economic crisis. The CEO of Publicis, Maurice Lévy, comments on the likely fallout when compensation practices are perceived as unfair:

> *Lots of people are having a tough time and live with revenues which are insufficient. This is a reality and is exacerbated by the fact that they don't see how their life can improve with the current state of the economy. It can only get worse. It is also exacerbated when they see in the press the millions that executives are making, including when they fail. And it is normal that they have this feeling of "injustice" and get angry.*

The same concern is expressed, now in more strident tones, by John Monks, the General Secretary of the European Trade Union Confederation:

> *I can acknowledge a deserving rich, and I'd like to find some way to separate them from the undeserving rich, many of whom are fairly ordinary people who happen to be working in certain areas and do what everybody else does, and make a fortune. I don't think in a period when living standards were generally going up, people noticed [that top pay was going up]. I think they're noticing now what has happened to top wages when the economy's gone down. And who are the people responsible for the collapse? ... Certainly it hasn't been the shareholders, it hasn't been the workers, it hasn't been the customers, it has been the executives. Outside people have been noticing, and if I can do anything to help them notice more, I shall certainly do so.*

In our interview with Jerry Yang, the co-Founder of Yahoo!, we find yet another explicit reference to issues of fairness, the concern again being that seemingly undeserving executives have been paid far more than was warranted:

> *The financial crisis has, reasonably enough, led some to question the assumption that inequality will generate high performance. With the financial crisis, some people are wondering why top managers who seem to be making mistakes are still getting so much money, why managers whose firms are failing are still well paid.*

The presumption here is that those at the top were sometimes paid excessively and without much justification in terms of underlying merit, talent, or effort. This sentiment reappeared more or less forcefully in other interviews as well. The Chairman of Deutsche Bank, Josef Ackermann, insisted that "we in the financial industry have to make sure remuneration is well-deserved and based on proven and solid lasting performance," while the Honorary Chairman of Lafarge, Bertrand Collomb, stated quite frankly that the practice of treating CEO pay as a "special case outside of a normal compensation scheme has always shocked me."

There is some concern, then, that the connection between merit and reward may not be as strong as it should be at the very top of the income distribution. If one considers next the middle and bottom of the distribution, here again some of our commentators express concern that the merit-reward connection is not strong enough, although the problem in this case is not that rewards exceed merit (i.e., excessive CEO pay) but that merit exceeds rewards (i.e., laid-off or underpaid workers). It has long been noted that workers born into poor families or neighborhoods may suffer disadvantages (e.g., poor schooling) that are inconsistent with a commitment to equal opportunity. The former President of the AFL-CIO, John Sweeney, concludes that "people today are not confident that their son or daughter will automatically experience the American Dream." Outside the U.S., there seems to be even more concern that opportunities to get ahead are closing off, with the presumed psychological consequence being a burgeoning frustration at the bottom of the income hierarchy:

> *I strongly believe in equality of opportunity and social mobility. ... The feeling is growing, especially in Germany and other European countries, but probably less so in the United States, that people with a modest social background don't have the same opportunities. This is creating a tremendous amount of frustration. (Josef Ackermann)*

The underlying worry expressed in this passage is that the run-up in inequality won't long be tolerated if it's understood as an inside game in which only those from more privileged backgrounds have the means with which to get ahead.

The social compact, as we've described it here, rests not only on the fairness with which rewards are allocated but also on the market's ability to "deliver the goods" to everyone who works hard and plays by the rules. The runup in inequality presumably becomes more tolerable when most workers are at least able to get a job, earn a decent living, and otherwise get by. As Josef Ackermann observes, "when you are in a stagnant or recessionary environment, when people have to fear job losses or major salary reductions, inequality is perceived much more clearly." Likewise, John Monks suggests that, when living standards were going up and people were doing well, they didn't "really notice or care" about rising inequality. However, now that living standards are "going down," he suggests that they're definitely "noticing now." These comments, if an accurate barometer of public mood, suggest that the two-pronged social compact may be doubly vulnerable. That is, there may be a growing tendency to question (a) whether those at the top truly merit their increasingly high pay, and (b) whether those at the bottom truly merit their fate of increasing unemployment and financial distress.

But how problematic is this fraying of the social compact? The interviews reveal a wide gamut of views on this question, with a few commentators adopting an almost alarmist rhetoric, and the majority adopting a more measured tone. On the alarmist side of the continuum, one finds John Monks suggesting that "the excesses of capitalism are the biggest threat to capitalism," while the President of the Party of European Socialists, Poul Rasmussen, stresses that a sea change in attitudes may be underway:

> *The U.S. is probably the part of the world where the anger is not only most visible, but also most widespread among the population. Ordinary American working families, the mainstream, feel that Wall Street has simply been too greedy. You cannot expect these workers to go to work and forget all about it – that will not happen. ... Anger is very high, and it will not go away.*

The foregoing sentiment is by no means an exclusively socialist one. Although many commentators agreed with Monks and Rasmussen that high and increasing inequality is problematic, they often did so in more muted tones and with greater appreciation of the possibility that some of the public anger is misplaced. The former Chairman of Anglo American, Sir Mark Moody-Stuart, comments that "the divergence of remuneration between the top and bottom of an organization is now causing strain in society," while the Chairman and CEO of Publicis, Maurice Lévy, refers to the growing "angst," "bitterness," and "anger" within the population, and the former Republican Governor of Massachusetts, William Weld, advises, "If you don't have some spreading out, some flattening of these curves, you're going to have sufficient disquiet so that sand will be thrown in the gears of commerce." For these commentators, the possibility is raised that the public may be making too much of the most egregious and highly publicized cases of excessive compensation, but even so such changes in public perception are clearly regarded as worrying and worth addressing.

What Caused the Rise in Inequality?

We turn next to the causes of the takeoff in income inequality that has played out in many (but not all) OECD countries. Although the takeoff has been the focus of much scholarly discussion and research, it is striking that this discussion has not been well informed by the views of CEOs and other elites who can offer that rare behind-the-scenes account of how inequality is generated. How *do* elites account for the increase in inequality?

The prevailing view among scholars of inequality has the takeoff arising from a historic increase in the demand for skilled labor (i.e., skill-biased technological change), a resulting shortage in the number of skilled and educated laborers who might meet this new demand, and a consequent bidding-up of the price for skilled labor. The growing divide between the earnings of skilled and unskilled labor is interpreted under this account as an important source of rising inequality. When our commentators did take on this standard account, they tended to do so with some sympathy, although they were typically more focused on the short supply of skilled labor than on the ramped-up demand for such labor.[1] This shortage was in turn typically attributed to deficiencies in the educational system. For example, Bertrand Collomb argues that, because educational institutions haven't been doing their job well, much of the population remains "under-educated, underskilled, and ... paid at the level influenced by competition from the emerging markets workforce." The Chairman, President, and CEO of FedEx, Fred Smith, provides an insightful elaboration of this account, his claim being that the real problem is not so much a shortage of educated labor as a shortage of the *right type* of educated labor:

> *I think our society has become so enamored of getting that degree from a prestigious institution, regardless of what type of degree, that we have a complete mismatch between what the educational structure is producing relative to what society needs and will compensate. Building new sources of wealth in the future will be basically focused on scientific, engineering, and managerial disciplines.*

If this account is on the mark, it implies that students are too often investing in the wrong fields, with the result being a mismatch between the type of skills the labor market is supplying and the type of work the economy is demanding.

---

1 Goldin, Claudia, and Lawrence Katz. 2008. *The Race Between Education and Technology*. Cambridge: Harvard University Press.

The interviews also addressed the causes of rising executive pay. The conventional approach among scholars has been to explain the increase in executive pay in terms of some corresponding increase in the marginal product of executives.[2] If, for example, globalization means that executives are making decisions involving ever-larger global markets, then good decisions will be worth more because they can pay off globally; and executives can reasonably expect to be paid in keeping with their growing marginal product. This type of account did occasionally come up in our interviews, but it was not featured all that much. Instead, many of our business leaders drew on more subtle sociological mechanisms to explain rising pay, mechanisms that are closely related to one another and thus emerge from the transcripts as a coherent, integrated, and almost seamless whole. We review these various mechanisms below.

The transparency movement plays a featured and fascinating role in this narrative. It is fascinating because its main rationale, which was to discourage egregious compensation by openly and fully revealing pay packages, appears not to have been realized very successfully. As Maurice Lévy so engagingly relates, the actual affect of transparency was to make pay comparisons possible and to ratchet up competition between executives, a type of competition that had long been suppressed because executives simply didn't know how much their peers were paid.

> *In Europe, and particularly in France, we have been faced with the consequences of transparency. What happened was that salaries or compensation were benchmarked and adjusted to the highest-paid person. New experts appeared whose analysis was that if you wanted to keep your people, you had to be in top quartile. ... The transparency which was meant to moderate has in fact created a serious inflation.*

The main effect of the transparency movement was to set in motion a race to the top by engendering competition rather than self-limitation. Once the possibility of comparison is unleashed, Bertrand Collomb argues that status competition among peers will instantly emerge, a competition that in turn precipitates an inflationary pay spiral:

---

2 Gabaix, X., and A. Landier. 2008. "Why Has CEO Pay Increased so Much?" *Quarterly Journal of Economics* 123, pp. 49–100. For a review of relevant evidence, see Bebchuk, Lucian A., and Michael S. Wiesbach. 2009. "The State of Corporate Governance Research." Dice Center Working Paper 2009-21.

> *If I look at the view of the executives, they live in an unequal world and they've seen inequality rising. They know what public opinion doesn't know, that their investment banker is making millions, that their lawyer is making millions, that the fund managers are making millions. They generally work in a world where their Brazilian partner belongs to a very wealthy Brazilian family. When they are French, they see their American colleagues making ten times what they are making, so they don't feel rich and they don't feel overpaid. They feel that, given the amount of responsibility they have, it's not abnormal to be among the people who have high compensation, not necessarily the highest, because a lot of people are paid more, but in that league. So I feel many mistakes made in executive compensation are rooted in the feeling that they don't feel overpaid by comparison.*

These comparisons were of course prosecuted in terms of the only shared metric that was available (i.e., money). It follows that everyone's focus shifted laser-like to the monetary side of the employment relationship.

This is a crucial shift. As many commentators noted, the CEO job has not historically been just about money, rather it's also been about the intrinsic satisfaction and sense of accomplishment that comes from building something. These intrinsic incentives are undermined, however, when CEOs become more focused on immediate economic payout. If companies are ruthlessly focused on the marginal product of their executives, then executives will likewise come to view their worth in terms of a compensation package that's assumed to equal their marginal product. The result, as Sir Mark stresses, is that companies begin to treat executives as a simple "financial investment" in which the desired behavior has to be elicited by building financial mechanisms directly into the compensation package. "The more you devise these crafty mechanisms," Sir Mark notes, "the more you forget that pay is only a little piece of the whole motivation of people."

The extrinsically motivated executive will also feel less loyal to her or his company and be more likely to consider moving to a new one. Here again, if the executive is reduced to a "financial investment" on the part of the company, then that executive will naturally in turn become committed mainly to the compensation itself, and any residual interest in the company itself is quite reduced. Moreover, insofar as investors and companies emphasize short-term financial returns, it becomes acceptable to frequently replace executives as a means of improving such returns. "While mobility is in principle a good thing," notes Sir Mark, "in many corporations I think there has been a decrease on both sides in long-term commitment and loyalty." Although our commentators left the connection between mobility and pay implicit, the standard academic account on this point is that mobility increases efficiency by imposing a more frequent market test on compensation, a market test that then moves pay ever closer to true marginal product. If the loyal executives of the past were typically underpaid relative to their product, then a reduction in loyalty will serve to increase pay.

The new brand of CEO that emerges from these accounts is increasingly mobile, status-competitive, and compensation-oriented. This CEO is less committed to the firm's welfare, less committed to any larger societal welfare, and less committed to any ethical framework that might mitigate against the pursuit of ever-higher income. The Chairman of Telecom Italia, Gabriele Galateri, discusses quite explicitly this cultural shift:

> *Guys of forty, forty-five years old, who were earning as much as 20 or 30 million euro in one year, went completely unnoticed and did not give rise to perplexity in anyone. ... If you work in a normal company then it doesn't make any sense. But there has been a sort of addiction that made us accept this as a fact of life, instead of saying that there was something wrong going on. I think it reflects a much wider problem than corporate governance. There was an overall worldwide cultural movement that has slowly taken over and reduced the importance of many rules, legal or natural, that kept people on track.*

The claim, in short, is that narrowly self-interested behavior has come to be viewed as ever more acceptable, indeed any deviations from such behavior are understood as pathological, perhaps even a signal of weakness. The same idea shows up in various forms in many of the transcripts. For example, John Sweeney refers to the growing "greed of the highest paid," while John Monks suggests that an earlier sense of "mutual obligation" has gradually weakened and that the rich have "forgotten those responsibilities and obligations."

There is, then, a novel line of argumentation running through much of the commentary on executive compensation. We do not mean to suggest that all of our commentators adopted this particular account or that it was presented by any of them in the especially simplified form rendered here. There was, however, a shared kernel to the commentary on executive compensation that is quite striking and would be intriguing to explore further.

How Might Inequality Be Remedied?

We will close off our review by briefly rehearsing the various remedies for inequality that our commentators have advanced. It is sensible to treat the topic in short order because our two concluding essays will engage at length with our commentators on the matter of remedies.

We have already noted that the prevailing account of the takeoff emphasizes that the supply of skilled labor has not kept pace with the demand for such labor. Under this formulation, inequality is delivering a simple message to the workforce, a message to the effect that money can be made by acquiring those skills that are in short supply. The obvious role for policy here is to assist workers in responding to this message by improving access to and the quality of education. And indeed many of our commentators suggested just such an approach. For example, the Chairman of BASF, Jürgen Hambrecht, advocates "much, much more spending on education," while Poul Rasmussen argues for improved "education and training projects," and Jerry Yang stresses the need for "fair and equal access to high-quality education." For many of our commentators, including Hambrecht, Ackermann, and Galateri, early education is especially important because it's been shown to yield an attractive cost-benefit ratio. It bears noting, however, that Fred Smith takes a rather different tack in arguing that the conventional four-year college is too often oriented toward building skills for which there isn't much of an economic payoff. This line of reasoning implies that federal funding should instead target vocational skills of the sort that the economy is actually demanding.

If we turn to the matter of executive compensation, here the commentaries become more detailed and energized, and indeed some fascinating dilemmas are revealed. It bears recalling that many of our commentators understood the upward spirals in compensation as a consequence of fierce status competition that in turn was engendered by transparency reforms. Although such reforms may well be the smoking gun, none of our commentators suggested that they can or should be rolled back. To the contrary, Rasmussen suggests that the "number one" reform should be effecting *yet more* transparency, while Ackermann likewise notes that "transparency is key" insofar as public confidence is to be restored. The quite reasonable logic here seems to be that one can't possibly roll back on transparency in light of the now very public concerns about pay. The effect, however, of maintaining transparency is that the market is accordingly trapped in a high-competition system that then complicates any efforts to reign in pay. That is, insofar as compensation packages are inevitably a matter of public record, any remedies must now be focused on preventing transparency from generating the spiraling increases of the past.

How, then, are our commentators suggesting that such containment might be secured? Not surprisingly, there's rather little support for legally imposed limits on compensation, and not just because, as Hambrecht notes, such limits would be "diametrically opposed to the principles of a free-market economy." The further purely practical point made by Sir Mark is that legal limits "result in an enormous amount of effort being put into devising ways to get around the legislation." If legally imposed limits are rejected, then some form of self-regulation is of course required. It's useful in this regard to distinguish between three classes of self-regulation that could, according to our commentators, be deployed: (a) moral regulation, (b) stockholder regulation, and (c) performance regulation. We review each in turn.

The first approach, that of moral regulation, recognizes that excessive compensation packages offend the public and may be counterproductive from the firm's point of view because public hostility can exact a public relations toll or generate support for legally mandated limits on pay. How might such a moral cap in practice be set? The guiding principle, it would seem, is simply to be sensitive to the public's view of what's fair and reasonable. As Rasmussen puts it, the pay level has to be "negotiated on some ethical level," as it's simply disproportionate to have "finance executives earning 22,000 times the average wage of a hard-working American industrial worker." The case for moral regulation emerges even more clearly in Maurice Lévy's interview:

> *I think that it is very important to act reasonably,* avec mesure *as we say in France. It is clear that we have seen an escalation and it would be a good thing to bring compensation to more moderate levels ... I am of the opinion that the years to come will see the return of great values like ethics and the fading away of cynicism. I believe that this would help change behaviors particularly if appropriate didactic communication is applied. The effect on moderation of compensation would be much more important than any regulation.*

The idea of injecting moral sensibilities into the pay-setting exercise may be contrasted with the alternative view that such sensibilities are better expressed at the point of taxation. For example, Fred Smith suggests that, insofar as pay restraint is desired, it would be straightforward to "increase the marginal personal tax rate as [one goes] up the income scale."

The second approach, that of stockholder regulation, is well known and probably does not require much discussion. The logic behind the regulative approach is that stockholders are necessarily focused on bottom-line results and will accordingly be disinclined to approve any compensation package that can't be defended in such terms. As Sir Mark notes, shareholders tend to ensure that compensation packages have "sensible performance conditions," although he adds that such conditions could usefully be strengthened and made "more active and effective." Similarly, Galateri questions whether shareholder remuneration committees provide sufficiently active oversight, and he suggests that remuneration packages for top management should instead "pass through the shareholders' meeting and be approved by the shareholders, not just by the remuneration committee."

It's worth noting that our two labor leaders, Sweeney and Monks, are less enthusiastic about shareholder oversight. As Monks sees it, because shareholders have historically been focused on short-term stock appreciation, any performance conditions they might impose will likely be short term in form:

> *I don't think shareholders are long-termist. How do you get people to think more long term, about the growth of the business over a period? I posed these questions at a seminar in the City of London and some bright spark put his hand up and said, "I've got some long-term investments, Mr. Monks. They're short-term investments I can't get rid of."*

Although Sweeney is likewise skeptical, his main concern is that shareholders haven't "the will to be aggressive enough" and can't be counted upon for any serious oversight.

If shareholders won't reliably hold the line on pay, some companies could instead proceed by insisting that all contracts for top executives must have standardized performance incentives. This third approach, which in effect makes performance contracts a matter of company policy, focuses on bolstering the connection between merit and pay rather than on simply capping pay. There is a general consensus among our commentators in favor of Ackermann's recommendation that contracts "must take a long-term perspective and remuneration must be based on real, bottom-line contributions to earnings, not on revenues, with vesting over several years." These contracts should further have a "claw-back mechanism" to recoup bonuses whenever they're driven by transitory market events. The obvious difficulty with this approach, a difficulty that our commentators well appreciate, is that one cannot easily ensure that pay will exactly equal "bottom-line contributions to earnings."

Conclusions

We are in the midst of a special moment in history in which inequality has become an unusually prominent matter of public discussion. To date, our understanding of the views of business, political, or labor leaders has rested on the occasional brief interview or yet shallower sound bite, and rather little is therefore known about how elites are actually thinking about rising inequality during this unique period in history. The transcripts provided here allow for an unusually detailed accounting of how elites are making sense of rising inequality and the various proposals to address it.

It's rather surprising that scholarship on inequality is practiced with so little evidence from those at the top of the class structure. We routinely interview and study the poor; we routinely interview and study the middle class; we routinely poll and survey the general population. And yet we too often ignore those at the very top. Although sometimes it's claimed that elites will at all costs avoid the interview, we have found that access was often gladly provided and that, in most cases, our participants quickly warmed to the topic.

The case for interviewing elites rests in part on their familiarity with the processes by which inequality is generated. If we want to understand how CEO compensation works, it cannot hurt to talk to those who have been compensated as CEOs and who have sat on boards that decide on the compensation of other CEOs. If we want to understand why and how skill is remunerated, it cannot hurt to talk to those who have established the compensation schemes that implement those skill distinctions. If we want to know how skill deficiencies and mismatch play out in the labor market, it cannot hurt to talk with those who confront these deficiencies on a daily basis. The views of CEOs and other elites provide, then, an important window into the sources of changing inequality.

It's no less useful, however, to turn the microscope away from the labor market and wage-setting practices and onto elites themselves. We of course care about what elites are saying and thinking because their ideas are behind so much corporate and government policy. The transcripts provided here can therefore be doubly mined for the window they provide into the dynamics of inequality as well as for the window they provide into the minds of elites themselves.

We can't pretend to have reviewed here anything but a sampling of the themes that surfaced in the interviews. If only to keep our review tractable, we have focused on commentary addressing (a) the effects of the financial crisis on how inequality is viewed and explained, (b) the causes of the long-term increase in income inequality and executive compensation, and (c) the merits of various approaches to reducing inequality. The interviews themselves take on these and other questions in far more detail than can possibly be commented upon in this chapter. We encourage our readers to mine these transcripts as a fascinating commentary on this very special moment in the history of inequality.

Part 4: Commentary

Five Principles for Moving Forward

Roland Berger, Roland Berger Foundation

1. Inequality: General Observations

I would like to present first a few general observations about inequality before turning to some recommendations.

Statistics

The introduction gives a statistical overview of inequality and some related aspects in Europe and the United States over the past couple decades. As might be expected in dynamic economies, inequality levels have fluctuated and these changes are primarily the result of long and short-term trends within a country. Furthermore, the Gini coefficient and the P90/P10 index are measures, not diagnostic tools, and while they are useful indicators of a country's inequality level, they of course cannot reveal underlying causes which are complex and vary across countries and time.

A few examples will suggest the complexities underlying statistical snapshots of inequality. The Nordic countries are well known for their more egalitarian societies and their Gini scores are indeed correspondingly below the OECD Gini average. However, since the mid-1980s, with the exception of Denmark, they have recorded among the highest increases in Gini coefficients among all OECD countries. Until the financial crisis, Ireland's rapid growth, more akin to a developing country, earned it the Celtic Tiger moniker. Rapidly developing countries typically experience rising inequality, yet over the same period when all Scandinavian countries saw increasing inequality, Ireland experienced decreasing inequality despite high growth.

However, we should be quite cautious when comparing country performances in areas such as inequality because we need more consistent information to make appropriate comparisons. Despite indisputable advances in ICT power and techniques to collect and store information over the past twenty years, there are significant issues with regard to data collection concepts that affect cross-country comparisons. For example, countries choose among an array of income statistics, such as those derived from

R. Berger et al., *The Inequality Puzzle: European and US Leaders Discuss Rising Income Inequality*, DOI 10.1007/978-3-642-15804-9_17, © Springer-Verlag Berlin Heidelberg 2010

income, expenditure, gross income, or income net of taxes, just to give a few variations, to calculate Gini coefficients. Regardless of the merits of these choices, these diverse methods complicate comparing performance across countries.

Compounding these methodological issues is that different inequality measures can detect contrasting trends. Since the 1980s, there has been a moderate decline in inequality among countries, as measured by mean or median income, while at the same time within a country's borders, inequality in most countries has increased, though at varying rates and phases. The point is not to dispute a trend over the past couple of decades toward rising income inequality in many countries, but rather to emphasize the dangers of generalizing, trying to find standardized approaches, and the risk of inaccurate analysis due to complex, multifaceted, and idiosyncratic data.

Culture

Countries also tolerate different levels of inequality for complex reasons reflecting their culture, history, social values, economy, and politics. Despite the urgings of philosophers, politicians, economists, and pundits, these core traits and qualities, in the aggregate, change slowly. The French saying *plus ça change ...* gives pithy expression to the conservatism in most societies, the way fundamental cultural traits and attitudes tend to perpetuate over generations.

No country exhibits perfect egalitarianism where each percentile of the population commands an equal share of national income. Not only is this contrary to human nature, it does not promote a vibrant economy where a portion of the population using competitive skills and higher productivity creates a more active, innovative economy, as well as greater inequality. Skewed income distribution is not necessarily a sign of cronyism, rent seeking, or predatory practices. Indeed, some scholars suggest that an "efficient inequality range," between a Gini of .25 and .40, creates economic efficiency, in which case almost all OECD countries fit within an efficient range.[1] Again, the point is not to contest the need to reduce exces-

---

[1] Giovanni Andrea Cornia, and Julius Court, *Inequality, Growth and Poverty in the Era of Liberalization and Globalization*, UNU World Institute for Development Economics Research, 2001.

sive inequality, but to emphasize the need to examine the particular issues in a country within the context of its social norms and values. Cross-country comparisons are very useful to suggest areas for inquiry and improvement, but there is no ideal template to apply to all countries at a particular development phase.

Globalization and Economic Growth

This is particularly true with regard to globalization. Politicians, pundits, and the public have praised or pilloried globalization depending upon their ideological persuasion, and many cite globalization as a major contributing factor for rising inequality. What is often missed in these debates is that since 1980 the world population has increased by almost 2.5 billion, yet 500 million fewer people now live in extreme poverty. According to the World Bank, in 1981 one out of two individuals in the developing world survived on less than 1.25 dollars, while today it is one out of four. Extreme poverty in East Asia has seen even more eradication, falling from 80% in 1981 to 18% in 2005.[2] As the World Bank observed, "the long trend of rising global inequality and rising numbers of people in absolute poverty has been halted and even reversed."

Since the 1980s, when a series of international agreements and policies worked to reduce tariffs, liberalize and open markets, and the revolution in ICT infrastructure and logistics created new methods of production, service, and distribution, no country that had embraced more open trade subsequently raised barriers or retreated from global markets. There have been disputes and disagreements in practice, but no fundamental changes in policy. Freer international trade has lifted millions out of extreme poverty and benefited many more in less abject conditions through reduced prices for a greater variety of goods and services.

Adjustments in the advanced economies have been difficult and wide-ranging, but not nearly as much as for the developing economies, many of whom have seen a train of major reforms follow more liberalized trade, such as strengthened respect for laws, improved product standards, infrastructure investments, reform of state companies, etc. These changes differ

---

2 "New Data Show 1.4 Billion Live On Less Than US$1.25 A Day, But Progress Against Poverty Remains Strong," Press Release No:2009/065/DEC, World Bank, August 26, 2008.

across countries, but in the aggregate have contributed to more global economic activity. Since 1980, world trade in goods has expanded almost sixfold in under a generation and less developed economies increased their share of global exports of goods by more than a quarter from 29.4% to 36.8%. World trade in services grew even faster than goods and is seven times higher today than in 1980.[3]

Many developing countries show high levels of inequality, which was also true for the United States and Europe in the 19th century. The inequalities, disparities, and dislocations in rapidly industrializing Germany convinced Bismarck to introduce social security to help alleviate social and personal stress. These welfare principles, now solidly ensconced in advanced economies, will eventually adhere in developing economies as their economies mature. And as with contemporary welfare societies, there will be continuing debates about methods to balance social protections and competitive markets. Likewise, the progressive income tax, poverty assistance programs, inheritance tax, as well as other income and benefit transfer techniques will proliferate across more countries as they climb the development ladder.

Economic growth, therefore, is a prerequisite for an eventual lessening of inequality, for without growth there are neither the means nor the flexibility to change existing patterns. The principles for a resilient economy are well known, such as open goods, services and capital markets, appropriately skilled and flexible labor force, and competitive tax policies. The financial crisis and its aftermath will test these principles, but we should not lose sight of some of the deeper fundamental trends affecting many advanced economies. Aging populations, more females in the workforce, fewer children, more students in college and advanced study, and smaller households. These structural changes, in addition to labor dislocations as companies embrace global distribution and manufacturing opportunities, would by themselves require major adjustments in how work is structured and labor compensated, and countries will continue to respond in different ways.

For example, in Germany, following the principle that a job is the best route out of poverty, Agenda 2010 reforms made it possible for more people to enter the job market through low-paid jobs supplemented by government financial support. The new employees acquire job skills and a work ethic, which gives them an opportunity to improve their prospects,

---

[3] *Globalisation and Distribution, Industrial Countries Also Face the Challenge*, Deutsche Bank Research, November 21, 2007.

which they would otherwise not have had by remaining unemployed. Between 2001 and 2008, job market participation rates have increased from 65.8% to 70.2%.[4] While these new workers do not alleviate, and indeed may factor in rising income inequality statistics, they are now in the job market. Inequality is not static and they have the potential for advancement they did not previously enjoy.

Democracy and Fairness

The possibility to improve one's condition is a major incentive and just as too much inequality is debilitating for a society, too narrow a range of inequality compromises motivation and often compels high performers and risk-takers to emigrate. The 20th century experiment with Communism is proof enough that rigid economic systems are inefficient, not to speak of the human cost in stunted lives. Despite its flaws, a market economy has the flexibility to let individuals and resources adapt to changing conditions. This flexibility is enhanced by a democratic government, respect for personal liberties, and open political processes which can also help reduce inequality. A recent World Bank review of academic literature found that "restrictions on the voting franchise appear to have caused a high degree of economic inequality and ... recent evidence indicates an inverse relationship between other measures of democracy, based on civil liberties and political rights, and inequality."[5] Furthermore, the beneficial tendencies of democracies to ameliorate inequality strengthen over time.

One of the reasons democracy is so effective in lessening inequality is that it gives voice to frustrations when a significant percentage of the population considers economic relations to be unfair. The decision of the British government to impose a special tax on bankers' bonuses, despite its potential to convince some financial executives or firms to leave the City, is the most recent indication of how democracies adjust to address inequality. Whether the level of additional taxation is an appropriate governmental

---

4 Bertelsmann Foundation, *Arbeitsmarkt und Beschäftigung in Deutschland 2000-2009*, 2009, p. 10.

5 "Does Liberté = Egalité? A Survey of the Empirical Links Between Democracy and Inequality with some Evidence on the Transition Economies," Mark Gradstein (Ben Gurion University), Branko Milanovic (The World Bank), *Journal of Economic Surveys,* Vol. 18, No. 4, 2004.

response is an entirely separate issue from how robust democracies respond to public concerns.

Indeed, a sense of fairness and just process is more important than inequality, because when the public believes the system unfairly rewards individuals or opportunities for advancement are blocked, severe social stress can appear. Opinions about fairness differ across cultures and, aside from the Ten Commandments, societies show considerable variation in how to interpret just and fair processes. Nonetheless, popular views about acceptable levels of inequality are closely linked to standards of fairness and appropriateness.

For example, compensation ratios have historically ranged considerably wider in the United States than in Europe, and the American public until very recently has not been particularly concerned whether compensation structures are unfair. Despite rising levels of executive compensation over the past couple of decades, no political party has campaigned on the issue. The financial crisis has brought executive compensation under the spotlight, but whether it becomes a lasting issue will likely depend upon how the recession evolves and whether the public believes corrections already underway are considered adequate. Americans also view bankruptcy and business failure quite differently from most Europeans and would consider it unfair to permanently stigmatize an individual because of a failure.

We should be wary about populist measures than can potentially sacrifice longer-term benefits for short-term satisfactions. The mass media, almost by definition, is not inclined to present a nuanced picture of the issues. Surveys have become ubiquitous, but unfortunately they are prone to substantial abuse because many are poorly designed or executed, yet offer seemingly legitimate cover to advance a particular point of view. Misleading or sensational reporting can lead to unintended consequences. Because these are outside the "remit" of the media, the penalties for inaccurate, incomplete, and slanted reporting are not borne by the media, but by the public when legislation or regulations are rushed. The 2002 Sarbanes-Oakley legislation in response to the Enron crisis is a case in point, for while its intention is to prevent a repeat of fraudulent practices, the remedies were more onerous and less efficient than desired.

2. What to Do: Recommendations

Provided inequality is viewed in the context I have outlined, I would like to suggest some possible ways to address inequality. I agree with our interview partners that:

Inequality is a major problem of our time: "So anybody who says that inequality isn't a big issue for the effective functioning of a society is simply ignorant of the record of humanity. It's a huge issue." (Fred Smith)

We have to reduce the level of inequality: "In the current socio-economic environment, there seems to be a broad consensus that the present level of inequality is too high, not so much in terms of wealth, but in terms of compensation." (Josef Ackermann)

Excess is the principal concern: "We should do our best to reduce inequality, but we should do so by working to ensure that opportunities are fairly distributed, and we should avoid extremes of inequality."
(Jürgen Hambrecht)

Our interview partners have suggested a number of options and remedies, and without in any way diminishing their priorities or approaches, I would like to make some recommendations that particularly resonate with my experience. In my opinion we should be guided by five principles:

1. Ensure equality of opportunity (equal opportunities, not equality of outcome)
2. Improve social mobility
3. Advocate ethical behavior
4. Rethink compensation in terms of corporate governance
5. Balance taxation intelligently

I will discuss these briefly in turn.

Ensure Equality of Opportunity (Equal Opportunities, Not Equality of Outcome)

Globalization has changed the rules for the advanced economies. The well-paying industrial jobs which helped millions move into the middle class have been superseded by work requiring a broader span of trade, technical and professional skills, specialized training, or a university degree. Education is a potent mechanism to make society more equitable, and beyond the economic advantages earned through better education, studies show that higher levels of education bring even more important benefits to the individual and society, such as improved health, longer life span, successful parenting, and increased civic participation. However, across the OECD nearly one in three adults only pass primary or lower secondary education. In some large countries, such as Germany, Italy, and the United States, reading or math skills rank at or below the OECD average.

Education is the most effective way to make long-lasting changes in inequality ratios. There is a premium for college and advanced education, and despite rising enrollment in tertiary education in many OECD countries over the past few decades, earnings differentials for college graduates remain substantial. In the United States, employees with college or advanced degrees earn more than twice the income of those holding no post-compulsory qualifications.

Spending more on education is essential not only to address inequality, but to improve economic strength and robustness. Unfortunately, fiscal realities, rendered considerably more acute by the financial crisis, mean that liberally allocating more funds across a wide range of educational institutions and methods is not feasible and prioritizing funding to where it will realize the most long-term benefits is more important than ever. Because the need is so great and costs will only rise, governments, and most particularly European governments, will need to look for new ways to involve the private sector and individuals to fund education. This is a contentious issue when for decades education was considered a state responsibility, but there is no reason the 21st century should apply pedagogical formulas that in many cases resemble methods practiced in the early 20th century.

Difficulties introducing new funding mechanisms, however useful or necessary they may be, should not distract us from how we can best apply available funds today. What practical measures will support and encourage children and young adults in the school and university years to make the most of their potential? How can we help those beyond the formal education years acquire the skills 21st century societies, businesses, and technologies require?

Two fields of education which have not attracted sufficient attention are early childhood education and vocational educational training. While these areas do not have the glamour and prestige of elite universities, nor draw notice through highly publicized league tables, both are highly cost-effective avenues to improve earnings and human capital. Children, who are at the start of their lives, have the longest life expectancy of any demographic group, which suggests that investing in early child education and support is not only fiscally prudent but vital for strengthening the skills of the next generation.

Early Childhood Education

Numerous studies confirm that early childhood education and care substantially improves an individual's chances in life. Governments have recognized the advantages of early educational programs. In 1998, on average across OECD countries, 40% of children four years and younger attended some type of educational program, and various efforts helped enrollment increase to 71% by 2007.[6] However, more resources should be allocated before the child enters compulsory schooling because these years offer much greater potential to instill good learning and social skills that lay a solid foundation for future success. Investing more in these early years, as well as the initial grade school, will also help lessen concerns about intergenerational inequality. In this regard, if fees for early childhood education and care are necessary, they should be minimal and refunded for poor families.

While the need for high-quality colleges and universities is incontestable, public funding for higher education tends to be regressive as most students come from a middle class background. It is much easier (though never easy) to attract additional private funding for higher education than preschools. High-quality, affordable, early childhood education and care offers substantial long-term benefits, especially for disadvantaged children and when budgets are limited, hence every effort should be made to prioritize and increase early childhood education for both equity and efficiency.

Vocational Education and Training

Greater competition, evolving markets, and rapidly changing technologies place a premium on education, but all too often life-long learning is just a slogan today. The need for the working population to acquire new skills and capabilities to meet the competitive demands of the "knowledge society" is more important than ever, yet most adults never attend any type of life learning course, and most of those who do, such as lawyers and doctors, are already well qualified. Fewer than 6% of the OECD's 30-39 year-old population participate in full- or part-time educational programs. While participation climbs to 10% in some Nordic countries, attendance drops below 3% in France, Germany, and the Netherlands, before plummeting

---

6 *Education at a Glance – Summary of Key Findings*, OECD, 2009, p. 4 (www.oecd.org/dataoecd/1/28/43654482.pdf).

below 1% for those over forty in most countries.[7] Clearly, if advanced economies are to rise to the challenge of adapting the working population to the new rules of global competition, greater efforts must be made to give adults better skills, and those skills desired by employers, which are essential to improve earnings.

Vocational education and training is gaining more attention because it can help workers adapt by improving their trade, technical, and professional skills. Some countries, such as Austria, have well-established programs where almost three-quarters of upper secondary school students participate in some type of apprenticeship program, while others, such as the United States, enroll few participants. While vocational and educational training attracts more attention across the OECD, there are concerns some countries do not have sufficient numbers of training establishments, trainers, and teachers to handle both younger and older trainees. Life-long learning programs can also suffer from a lack of relevance, perceived either by the employee or the employer. Recognizing the importance of vocational education and training, the OECD recently issued practical policy recommendations to improve the quality and reach of these programs, and these recommendations deserve widespread notice.[8]

An intriguing variant of traditional vocational education programs is the Danish model of flexicurity, which combines considerable educational resources and social support, to create a very flexible labor force. As a share of GDP, Denmark expends almost three times more than the EU average on active labor market policies and, for each unemployed individual, the country spends five to six times as much as a country like the U.K. on active labor market policies. Recent Danish statistics report that each year almost a third of employees change their job and a fifth experience unemployment, yet flexicurity has met with widespread workforce approval while also reducing unemployment.

The basic elements are a flexible labor market with low employment protection and high job mobility; generous welfare payments with high income security; an active labor market policy; collective agreements between the parties in the labor market; and a dynamic legislative process with regular review and revisions. Denmark is a small country exhibiting much higher trade union levels and a more cohesive culture than most

---

[7] *Education at a Glance 2009 – OECD Indicators*, OECD, 2009, p. 301.

[8] *Learning for Jobs, OECD Policy Review of Vocational Education and Training, Initial Report*, OECD, October 2009.

European countries, nonetheless some of the flexicurity program's elements may have wider applicability. In particular, as observed by a leading labor leader, "the most important thing is that the Danish model has been developed in a tripartite way, between workers, employers, and changing governments. Almost no legislation, but based on agreements between employers' organizations and trade unions. Very high level of trust as the foundation ... This trust and cooperation is what gives Denmark its main competitive advantage."[9]

Because a job offers the best opportunity for an individual to move out of poverty, the German government, as well as others, has introduced "combi-wage" programs to provide supplemental funding to top up low wages so the worker has sufficient income to meet basic needs. Recent experience suggests these programs help increase employment, especially when supplementary payments are paid directly to the employee rather than the employer.

Diversity

Lastly, companies should endeavor to move beyond observance of anti-discrimination equal opportunity laws to actively promote diversity in aspects such as sex, culture/nationality, age, and educational background. In a rapidly changing world with expanding cross-border trade and international markets, diversity in the workforce is a competitive advantage. Numerous studies confirm that diversity improves how a company can innovate and adapt competitively across all functions, from R&D and production through sales and marketing. In this regard, governments should work to ensure that immigration policies encourage the exchange of human capital, so necessary in today's globalized markets.

Improve Social Mobility

Social mobility is obviously extremely important, both for the individual and society. For the individual seeking to develop and apply his or her talents, the chance to succeed is certainly much greater without artificial social, cultural, or economic impediments. Social mobility helps a society economically because it encourages entrepreneurs, and a more generally active economy. A higher level of social mobility does much to engender a

---

9 Marie-Louise Knuppert, Confederal Secretary, Danish Confederation of Trade Unions, "Jobs and Growth," "Climate Change, Growth, Stability," *OECD Forum* 2008.

sense of fairness. Unfortunately, in some countries the likelihood a child will do better than his or her parents tends to decline over time, and at different rates, and the parents' economic and social position becomes a more accurate guide, on average, of how well or poorly, economically, the child will perform in life.

For example, the American Dream has and continues to attract millions to the United States for a chance to make a better life, while the United Kingdom suffers from a legacy as a "class-bound" country limiting upward mobility. While individuals, some quite prominent, have earned notable success, the reality is that average social mobility in both countries is very similar. Researchers have identified two clusters of countries sharing relatively similar levels of mobility: more fluid countries, for example Poland, Sweden, and Norway, and less fluid countries, such as Hungary, the United States, Britain, Italy, Germany, France, the Netherlands, and Ireland. They have also uncovered no statistically significant association between the party in power and relative rates of social mobility.[10] However, there is a statistical association (as well as exceptions) between relative rates of social mobility and income inequality, where countries with lower inequality exhibit relatively higher rates of social mobility. As the OECD reports, "In general, the countries with the most equal distributions of income at a given point in time exhibit the highest income mobility across generations."[11]

There is considerable academic debate about how multiple and complex factors, such as education, family, income, values and attitudes, social networks, childhood poverty, as well as various discriminatory practices, influence social mobility. While these factors undoubtedly play a role in the aggregate, we are all familiar, at least anecdotally, with individuals who have overcome daunting odds and others who have wasted opportunities. Furthermore, many researchers suggest that deep structural forces in the economy and society, largely beyond a government's immediate control, affect social mobility.

Potential difficulties in improving social mobility should nonetheless not prevent us from working to eliminate barriers to mobility, such as discrimination, equal access to infrastructure, services, financial capital, and participation in politics. As noted above, investing in education, expanding

---

10 Stephen Aldridge, "Social Mobility, A Discussion Paper," Performance and Innovation Unit, Admiralty Arch, Cabinet Office, April 2001.

11 *Growing Unequal?*, OECD, 2008, p. 213.

the reach of education, and improving educational standards is essential. Greater partnerships between government and business can improve the efficiency and effectiveness of training programs. Reducing and removing barriers to geographical and occupational mobility, such as improving the portability of pensions, can also help.

Lastly, we need to explore ways to incentivize mobility, and one of the major obstacles is a fear of failure, a reluctance to take risks. This is an area where governments can help, if only by reforming insolvency laws and procedures to reduce the stigma of bankruptcy. Programs, support networks, and funding to stimulate entrepreneurship can also play a very positive role to incentivize mobility. The media can also play a more constructive role by giving more exposure to responsible business practices and achievements. Social mobility can increase in a growing economy where individuals aspire to create and occupy new positions of authority and wealth. In this regard, government programs to support and supplement R&D investment and venture capital can stimulate new businesses to move advanced economies from old (industrial-based) jobs to new (knowledge-based) jobs.

Advocate Ethical Behavior

> *But I don't think that the basic situation can be changed unless we restore an ethical sense, a commitment of the human being toward a correct behavior that otherwise would be very difficult to promote strictly by regulation. (Gabriele Galateri)*

Liberalized markets and open trade helped lift half a billion people out of abject poverty in a matter of decades. Technological and service innovations, stimulated by competition, deliver more new products and services to more consumers at more affordable prices and at a faster rate than ever before. These economic achievements should not, however, excuse ethical failings in the search for profit, and as market-based transactions have increasingly replaced older relationship-based transactions, opportunities for unethical practices have increased. In earlier years, relationships and older traditions acted to restrain excessive behavior, but for diverse social and cultural reasons, these restraints have lessened in many countries.

The financial crisis, beyond its economic dimensions, has focused attention on the seeming absence of ethics as a partial explanation for the crisis. Ethical lapses played a role in some cases, but for the majority individuals followed common practices. These practices are now undergoing a salutary review. For example, major business schools are introducing new approaches to instruct students about ethics and corrections are under way. References to ethics receive more notice in the media (which has also contributed to changing mores). Professional societies and business associations are reviewing recommended standards and practices. Of course, ethics should be more than just good business practices and we should extend these efforts by considering other ways to reinforce ethical conduct. In this regard, leadership role models, both in the corporate and government sectors, are essential to help instill solid values, including a sense and respect for standards and discipline.

Ethics and civics, once standard elementary school courses in many countries, have disappeared from many curricula. Educators should review the merits of reintroducing ethics courses in elementary education because early instruction has greater potential to instill lasting values. Stricter enforcement of existing laws would demonstrate that no one is above the law, and compliance requires no new legislation, only greater commitment to uphold the law. Likewise, anti-corruption programs to deter ethical lapses should be rigorously enforced. Finally, ethical clouds have not only appeared in business. The political class also needs to assess its ethical standing, an effort which should reach beyond a review of lobbying rules. Social trust is a close relative of ethical behavior and improving trust could open new doors for management, labor, and government to explore mutually beneficial methods to improve economic performance.

Rethink Compensation in Terms of Corporate Governance

Over the past couple of decades, average CEO pay has risen considerably in many countries, but it took the financial crisis for the media to shine a bright spotlight on the trend. Unfortunately, the attention has more often generated heat than light. There have been excesses in compensation, which is not unexpected given the number of large companies working across multiple markets, and basic probability would predict some egregious examples. The press has been quite adept at using CEO profiles and lifestyle portraits to raise public anger during a recession, but the media target the wrong subject because they confuse the agent for the principal. The Board and the remuneration committee set executive compensation, and it is the much more complicated issue of corporate governance that deserves more public attention. The ultimate principals, of course, are the shareholders, but the complexities are such that it is much easier to broadcast segments about CEO paychecks than discuss corporate governance issues.

The principal-agent problem, where the agent acts as the principal rather than advancing the interests of the owner, is neither unique to CEOs and business, nor is it a contemporary issue. Ancient Roman legislators in various periods, avowedly voting in the interests of the people, craftily, and sometimes quite openly, promoted their own interests. With regard to CEO compensation, a conversation needs to evolve between shareholders, notably pension funds and other large institutions, and the boards of directors. Concerns about equitable pay, proportion, and appropriate incentives are the responsibility of the owners, the shareholders, to discuss with the directors. Recent proposals in several countries to introduce or strengthen "shareholder say on pay" is helpful in this regard, as are reviews underway in several U.S. states' courts to review corporate articles that can unreasonably restrict the ability of shareholders to change or remove Boards of Directors.

As a general observation, proportionate pay should be the guiding principle, based on a scale reasonable persons would consider appropriate for the circumstances. Higher-level compensation should derive from long-term performance supervised by the Board.

> *We must take a long-term perspective, remuneration must be based on real, bottom-line contributions to earnings, not on revenues, with vesting over several years. I think the more critical part is really to establish some sort of claw-back mechanism in the system such that if people make a lot of money in one year with very risky activities, they do not get the full pay-out if the company loses money on these activities in the following years. (Josef Ackermann)*

Government controls over how businesses compensate management and employees should be limited to preventing discrimination, tax evasion, and other irregularities. Governments already participate extensively in private contracts between corporations and their employees, for example through such measures as setting minimum wages, hiring and firing regulations, and pension plan obligations. Pay scales, which closely reflect market movements, corporate strategy, and priorities, are not a market economy government's responsibility.

Another aspect of compensation, however, deserves much more attention, which is the artificial divide between senior management and the rest of the company with respect to company share ownership and long-term performance incentives. Employees should have more opportunity to accumulate capital in their company, to enjoy similar incentives as senior management to align their interests with shareholders. These capital accumulation programs, however, should be designed to promote prudent portfolio management so that an employee's total financial assets are not overinvested in company shares. There is no convincing reason why a junior employee should not receive the same encouragement as the CEO to participate in and contribute to the company's future. Should the company prosper, increased employee participation will help address broader social inequality and the company could benefit from increased loyalty.

However, the number of companies offering employee capital sharing plans is quite low. The German Federal Ministry of Economics and Technology reports that a mere 4% of German companies offer employees capital sharing schemes. France has almost double the number, 7% of companies extending such options, while 23% of U.K. companies offer participation schemes. It should be noted that when only a fifth of less regulated Anglo-Saxon companies offer employees a chance to build capital through share ownership programs, this suggests a philosophic and execution inconsistency, because the number is too high to believe extending capital share ownership to employees is an eccentricity. As boards of directors and shareholders examine senior management compensation packages, they should at the same time give serious consideration to extending capital sharing and incentive plans to all employees.

Balance Taxation Intelligently

Market economies rely on the principle that millions of private individuals who make independent decisions to invest their capital in productive enterprises are more likely to make correct decisions than a few government agencies. Of course, human systems are not infallible, there are inconsistencies and failings, but despite the continual need to adjust and regulate markets, few would want to replace these obligations with the rigidity of centrally controlled economies. Entrepreneurial activity and business expansion occurs when there is access to more sources of private capital. The government should therefore give individuals as much opportunity as possible to apply capital to investment opportunities they choose by taxing income less during lifetime, but exacting a heavier inheritance tax. Historically, the United States has applied this approach much more than European countries.

Similarly, following the principle of using the tax system to encourage economic growth, advanced economies should consider collecting more revenue through indirect consumption taxes rather than direct individual or corporate tax levies. Reducing direct taxes, such as employer's social security contributions, can help make companies more competitive and encourage more employment. Excessively regressive features of indirect taxes that can harm disadvantaged individuals and families can be addressed through existing cash and benefits transfer programs. Indeed, over the past several years there has been a general trend in many OECD countries toward greater use of consumption taxes, and the trend should be encouraged. By contrast, in emerging countries, more direct taxation is preferred because a much higher percentage of the population is near or below the poverty line and the state does not have sufficient resources to compensate for the regressive nature of indirect taxes.

European welfare societies have brought undoubted benefits and support to wide swaths of the population, whose progenitors before the war were exposed to considerable economic disruption and dislocation. Charitable giving by wealthy families in the United States, which does not have as tight a social security net as Europe, extends back to the 19th century. European countries do not have this tradition, and the array of state-run services to support the disadvantaged tends to dampen the motivation to help the less fortunate. Today in the United States there are remarkable changes in philanthropic programs as younger, extremely wealthy individuals apply their business talents and demands for demonstrable, effective results to change both the missions and conduct of charities. Wealthy European families should consider exploring how they too can participate in novel approaches to improve social conditions because while we live in different houses, we travel the same streets.

Can Inequality Be Reduced by Building Better Markets?

David B. Grusky and Christopher Wimer,
Stanford Center for the Study of Poverty and Inequality

The growth in wage inequality within many late-industrial countries is one of the most spectacular and consequential developments of our time, spectacular because the turnaround was so sudden and undermined the conventional view that economic development would bring about widely diffused affluence, consequential because it is affecting the lives of so many people and in such profound ways. During the early stages of this takeoff in inequality, the dramatic changes in remuneration were happening largely under the radar, indeed the public was not just unconcerned by the changes but in fact largely unaware of them.[1] But that's no longer the case. We are now in the midst of a historic moment in which public debates about the legitimacy of extreme poverty and inequality have taken on a new prominence and urgency.

There are some scholars who regard this rise in inequality as entirely unproblematic.[2] However, the increasingly dominant view among scholars is that the the takeoff is problematic, and now is a rare moment in which the public is inclined to agree with such an assessment and may be poised to support reasonable anti-poverty and anti-inequality initiatives. It is striking that most of our contributors, themselves typically the beneficiaries of this takeoff, likewise tend to agree that inequality in its "excessive" form has become a major social problem. The question that then arises is that of how best to develop a winning strategy for reform.

We don't of course harbor any illusions that a major change in strategy can easily be achieved. In any late-industrial country, one will find a well-developed and deeply institutionalized apparatus for addressing poverty and inequality, and any changes in that apparatus will at this point likely be glacial. It is nonetheless important to continue revisiting and redefining

---

1 McCall, Leslie and Lane Kenworthy. 2008. "Inequality, Public Opinion, and Redistribution." *Socio-Economic Review* 8:35-68.

2 Henderson, David R. 2006. "Income Mobility: Alive and Well." *Hoover Digest* 2006 (1).

R. Berger et al., *The Inequality Puzzle: European and US Leaders Discuss Rising Income Inequality*, DOI 10.1007/978-3-642-15804-9_18, © Springer-Verlag Berlin Heidelberg 2010

the rationale behind such an apparatus and thereby ensure that any further changes and elaborations are consistent with that rationale. We will attempt in this chapter to lay out what we think is a promising rationale and how existing policies might then be elaborated to better serve it.

This type of exercise is only infrequently attempted. In many countries, perhaps especially the United States, there's a rather strong strand of pragmatism underlying poverty and inequality policy. If an anti-poverty program can be shown to work at low cost (i.e., reduce poverty), then that's enough for us and we're all for it and will embrace it. This pragmatist movement to identify "what works and what doesn't," which again is a movement that's especially prominent in the United States, thus elevates to center stage the very simple empirical question of whether a given program has its intended effects. We are of course all for program evaluation. But the usual evaluation exercises, almost by definition and certainly by convention, don't take into account the long-range effects of policy and, in particular, whether that policy is properly accumulating into a set of institutions that resonate well with our larger ideals.

We are therefore suggesting here that we would do well to have an ideology, a "constitution" of sorts, that underlies reform efforts, just as we have an ideology that underlies our attempts to fashion a more productive economy. We are of course continuously engaged in reforming our economic institutions: We have to decide whether to enter into proposed trade alliances, whether to reform tax law, whether to allow new types of corporate forms, and so forth. When such decisions are being made, we typically refer back to first principles by asking whether the proposed reform will be competition-enhancing, in effect whether it will allow the "invisible hand" to better operate. We call ourselves market economies precisely because of this a priori commitment. When, however, we turn to poverty and inequality reform, we seem rather less tethered to any a priori commitments. In the absence of principles, our interventions tend to grow and accumulate into a sprawling array, one without any obviously unifying rhyme or reason. The suggestions that we make in this chapter will, by contrast, be quite explicitly tethered to a simple guiding principle.

What might that principle be? We did not by happenstance alone choose to contrast our ideology-rich economic policy with our ideology-poor poverty and inequality policy. The contrast is especially instructive, we argue, because poverty and inequality policy is best founded on the same market principles that now inform our economic policy. We make this argument in particular for countries, such as the U.S., Germany, and the U.K., in which market principles are deeply written into the cultural DNA and hence have a special and abiding resonance. For other countries (e.g., Nordic countries), such principles are a less fundamental cultural commitment, and the rationale for building them into poverty and inequality policy is less compelling.

The reader may at this point be perplexed. How, it might be asked, could we possibly build our main anti-inequality interventions around market principles? Aren't profound poverty and inequality the main consequences of adopting market principles? Shouldn't we therefore expect yet more poverty and inequality insofar as we build labor market institutions that better adhere to market principles? These are good and important questions, and the rest of our chapter will be devoted principally to answering them, to showing that market principles, if we were to truly and fully commit to them, would yield far less poverty and inequality than we now have.

We well realize that this is a radical view. The conventional wisdom is indeed that poverty and inequality are (unfortunate?) consequences of market processes, that those with a pro-market commitment must therefore reconcile themselves to much market-generated inequality, and that insofar as less inequality is preferred the only recourse is then to engage in much corrective after-market redistribution. This conventional wisdom is so widely diffused and taken for granted that many people presume that progressive taxation and other redistributive after-market interventions are the *only* way to address poverty and inequality. The presumption, in other words, is that the market generates inequality and that after-market interventions are therefore the only way to undo inequality. We will argue that in fact nothing could be further from the truth.

We thus take the obverse position that *market failure* is a main source of poverty and inequality. Put simply: We'd have far less poverty and inequality if our labor market institutions were *more* competitive, if we committed in a *meaningful way* to a competitive market economy, if our commitment to competition wasn't of the lip-service variety but was an *authentic commitment* to which we held even when the rich and powerful might thereby lose out. If market failure is the cause of poverty and inequality, then the correct prescription is market repair. We argue that we can take on poverty and inequality by making our labor market institutions more competitive and thereby reducing the amount of illicit, non-competitive inequality generated within the market. This approach reduces the pressure to take on poverty and inequality via redistributive approaches that are typically viewed as ideologically suspect. We instead take on poverty and inequality by simply acting on our widely shared commitment to market principles, but now treating them as commitments to which we are *really* committed.

The test of any commitment is that we follow it no matter where it leads us. If the rich and wealthy, long the principal advocates of market principles, come to appreciate that they've been the principal beneficiaries of market failure and will in fact lose out under an authentically competitive market, then it's surely out of bounds if they then withdraw their commitment to the market. If they do, then their putative commitment is in the end merely convenient ideology. We are therefore asking the rich to bear the same harsh medicine of the market that has so long been doled out to the poor. The poor have, after all, long been lectured to the effect that the market's discipline must simply be borne, that the decline, for example, of manufacturing in the U.S. provides no justification for protectionism, that the 'losers' must instead take one for the team and get on with the market program. We will be arguing below that no less should be asked of the rich.

But so much for preliminaries. Let's get on now and make the case for two types of market repair. We begin by arguing that rising returns to schooling, well-appreciated as a main cause of rising inequality, are attributable to market failure in the form of barriers to free and open competition for higher education. We then argue that excessive executive compensation is likewise rooted in non-competitive practices and that a market wage would likely be inequality-reducing. Because of space limitations, we can't of course render the argument in any comprehensive way, and instead we refer the reader elsewhere[3] for a related and more comprehensive argument and supporting evidence. The two examples laid out here should be treated, then, as mere examples of the larger claim that market failure is a principal cause of inequality and that market repair is accordingly the correct prescription.

We will comment throughout this chapter on the matter of how this position is sometimes consistent and sometimes inconsistent with that of Roland Berger and our other contributors. In some cases, the reforms that we propose will be much the same as those proposed by Roland Berger (and some of the other contributors), but the rationale for carrying out those reforms will be different. Because the premise of our chapter is that principles matter, we'll take special care to lay out those instances in

---

[3] Weeden, Kim, and David B. Grusky. 2010. "Market Failure and Inequality," Center for the Study of Poverty and Inequality Working Paper, Stanford University.

which we agree with our contributors about the types of reforms that are desirable or necessary, yet even so disagree with them on why they're necessary.

Education and Market Failure

We begin by considering education policy. There may be nothing *less* controversial these days than issuing a call for increased investment in education. True to form, most of our contributors have indeed issued this call, although Fred Smith has additionally suggested that some workers might profit more from vocational training (or a community college experience) than a traditional four-year college experience. We agree that meaningful vocational training is undersupplied in many late-industrial countries (with the obvious exception of Germany). However, given that the rise in inequality is largely attributable to the growing earnings of the college educated, the undersupply of college education is arguably especially worth addressing insofar as the objective is to reduce inequality. The inequality-reducing mechanism is straightforward: Namely, if the supply of college-educated workers were increased, there would be more competition for the pool of jobs requiring a college education, such competition would in turn drive down the pay of college-educated workers, and inequality would accordingly decline. The implication is that, if we're really serious about reducing inequality, a simple but powerful way to proceed is to ratchet up the number of college-educated workers.

It might reasonably be asked why workers don't simply go ahead and pursue a college education when they well know that there's a high payoff to college. Are there, in other words, real structural impediments to raising rates of college attendance or are there just cognitive impediments? The "cognitive impediments" story, stated baldly, has it that workers are either stupid or lazy: That is, they may well understand that college yields a high payoff, but even so they just can't be bothered to pursue a college degree. The cognitive impediments theory strikes us, however, as rather less plausible than an account that recognizes that, while most workers appreciate that there's a payoff to college and are keenly interested in securing it, they are simply not in a position to do so. There are both supply-side and demand-side barriers that prevent enough workers from securing a college education: The *supply* of potential college students is artificially lowered because children born into poor families and neighborhoods don't have the training (in primary and secondary schools) that qualifies them for entry into college,[4] while the *demand* for college students is kept artificially low because, in at least some countries, elite private and public schools engage in explicit rationing of their available slots. It's not as if Oxford University, for example, is meeting the rising interest in its degrees by selling some profit-maximizing number of them. If top universities did meet the demand in this way, the excessive returns to a high-prestige education would disappear. But instead they've decided to ration.

When, by contrast, the demand for hybrid cars increased dramatically in the U.S., car manufacturers responded by ramping up production to a profit-maximizing level, not by setting up hybrid-car "admissions committees," not by carefully interviewing and testing prospective buyers, not by asking them to submit detailed resumes and statements about how the hybrid-owning experience will change their lives. The market for cars is therefore truly a competitive market, whereas the market for education is anything but. We have become so accommodated to the contemporary practice of rationing higher education that we don't any longer appreciate that practice for the profound form of market failure that it is.

These bottlenecks on the supply and demand sides mean that those lucky enough to have a college education are artificially protected from competition and reap excessive pay as a result. If all children, even those born into poor families, had fair and open access to higher education, these excessive returns would wither away under the force of competition. It's in this very important sense that market failure is generating inequality. The prescription is likewise clear: If market failure is the cause of inequality, the proper response is market repair. We can straightforwardly repair the market by addressing the supply-side and demand-side bottlenecks that now prevent workers from acquiring college degrees.

Who would win and who would lose under such market repair? We have already noted that the losers would be those who are now artificially protected from competition and are therefore reaping excessive returns. The winners, by contrast, are of course those who are currently locked out of higher education but would gain access once markets were repaired. But these are not the only winners. The other main winners would be the businesses that currently pay inflated prices for high-skill employees but will no longer have to do so once higher education is opened up fully to competition. It should come as no surprise that many of the business leaders interviewed in this volume expressed considerable frustration with educa-

---

4 Goldin, Claudia, and Lawrence Katz. 2008. *The Race Between Education and Technology*. Cambridge: Harvard University Press.

tional bottlenecks and noted that there just isn't a sufficient talent pool to maximize profit and growth. It's hardly in the interest of business to pay excessive returns to rationed secondary education, nor is it in the wider interest of any country to settle for the lower GDP that such restrictions on competition imply. The upshot is that market repair yields many winners and comparatively few losers.

If we are quite uncontroversial, then, in issuing a call for more educational opportunities, the rationale that we have proffered for such a policy is not the conventional one on offer. The main reason for ramping up educational opportunities is, we have argued, that it repairs market failure and corrects the excessive payoff to a college degree that such failure brings about. As noted above, the business leaders in this volume have made reference not to such excessive returns, but rather to the market inefficiencies that educational bottlenecks will necessarily generate. It's notable that our business leaders also stressed that opportunity-increasing interventions will lend legitimacy to the system and deflect any possible criticism of inequality by inducing workers to focus on the possibility of experiencing mobility themselves. The idea here, one that has a provenance extending back at least to the work of Werner Sombart,[5] is that extreme inequality becomes more palatable in the eyes of workers when they have an opportunity to rise to the top. For example, Josef Ackermann writes that "the government should invest as much as possible in education .... [because it] gives citizens the feeling they have opportunities in life" (p. 19, emphasis added), while Sir Mark notes that "what's extremely disruptive in inequality is not just inequality itself, it's when individuals feel that they are trapped in the unequal half of the equation" (p. 90). If workers feel they have a chance to get ahead and that their position in the "unequal half of the equation" is but a temporary one, then the presumption is that they will give their full blessing to a highly unequal system.

In Roland Berger's insightful chapter, it's additionally stressed that "early childhood education and care offers substantial long-term benefits" (p. 201), the point here being that educational opportunities not only make the labor market appear fairer but also reduce poverty by improving labor market outcomes for disadvantaged children. This rationale, which emphasizes that human capital investments (i.e., schooling) generate higher earnings, should again be distinguished from our market failure approach (see, for example, Gary Becker for the definitive statement of the human capital

---

[5] Sombart, Werner. 1906. *Warum gibt es in den Vereinigten Staaten keinen Sozialismus?* Tübingen: Mohr.

model).[6] That is, Roland Berger nicely emphasizes the returns to college for the poor, whereas we've made the obverse point that, just as the poor will earn more, so too those who have been profiting from protection against competition will now face that competition and will earn less as a result. Under the new non-rationing regime, the poor who were formerly excluded from education will now receive it and earn more, while the college-educated workers who were once protected from competition will now be exposed to competition and earn less. The total effect is therefore a reduction in inequality.

We've made a point of the excess returns that now accrue to lucky degree-holders because doing so reveals the inequality-increasing effects of market failure. This is not to deny the additional negative psychological effects of educational rationing that some of our business leaders have emphasized. We indeed agree with them that increasing educational access will make the system appear fairer and render existing inequality more palatable. But truth be told, we are more concerned with reducing inequality than with convincing workers that the current levels of inequality are unproblematic. Even more important, there is polemical value in a market failure account, as it focuses attention on how our current system is built on a form of rationing, a foundation that just can't be reconciled with a commitment to competitive markets. It's not just a matter of helping poor people, nor is it just a matter of making them think the system is fair. These objectives are all well and good, but for most people they are just side commitments, not nearly as important as our core commitment to a market economy. The need for educational reform becomes more urgent when it's grounded in this pro-market rationale as opposed to a more conventional and softer "do-gooder" commitment to helping the poor.

It is worth asking exactly *how* such education reform might be implemented. If the objective is to correct for market failure, we must undertake educational reforms that (a) allow low-income students to more freely compete, and (b) prevent high-income families from unduly shielding their children from competition. This agenda is more controversial than the usual calls for ramping up our investments in education. Consider, for example, the case of preschool in the U.S. Currently, high-income parents purchase high-quality early education, a purchase that involves scheming to purloin one of the carefully rationed slots in a premium childcare center. By contrast, low-income parents face a patchwork of state and federal ear-

---

6 Becker, Gary S. 1964. *Human Capital: A Theoretical and Empirical Analysis, with Special Reference to Education.* Chicago: University of Chicago Press.

ly education programs, many of which offer low-quality instruction and care that fail in the task of preparing children for school. If we are serious about correcting market failure, our publicly subsidized early education programs will have to look more like the high-quality environments purchased by high-income parents on the private market. Although we railed against the presumption that inequality-reduction can only proceed via ramped-up redistribution, ironically the road in this case to guaranteeing free and fair competition may well require just such redistribution.

We've all become inured to the severe bottlenecks in educational access and seemingly fail to appreciate them for the egregious form of market failure that they are. We should be able to say to ourselves that we're really committed to markets, that it's truly our signature commitment, and that we're prepared to engage in fundamental institutional reform to make that commitment real. It's high time, then, to move beyond the usual lip-service appeals to educational reform and appreciate that the current system makes a mockery of our market commitment and needs a massive overhaul.

Executive Pay and Market Failure

If one next considers CEO and executive pay, one again can't be all that impressed by our commitment to market principles. The main and well-known problem is that board members, sitting at the behest of the CEO, are making decisions about that CEO's pay.[7] This setup lends itself to board members favoring ample compensation packages because their own interests are best served by attending to the CEO. It should come as no surprise, for example, that CEO pay is higher when many of the outside directors have been appointed under the CEO.[8] It becomes difficult with such pay-setting practices to represent the resulting pay in market terms. It's rather like asking a professor's students to decide on the professor's pay in advance of receiving their grades. When the fox is guarding the henhouse, one has to believe the fox's interests are the principal interests being served.

---

7 Bebchuk, L. A., and J. Fried. 2004. *Pay without Performance*. Cambridge, MA: Harvard University Press.

8 For a review of relevant evidence, see Bebchuk, Lucian A., and Michael S. Wiesbach. 2009. "The State of Corporate Governance Research." Dice Center Working Paper 2009-21.

The board's particularism is, however, nicely camouflaged by the practice of hiring outside consultants to examine the pay of peer firms and make recommendations accordingly. The recommendation is of course represented as the pay level set by a competitive market. It's indeed the case that one can't expect CEOs to accept compensation below the prevailing compensation and that an individual firm may therefore have no reasonable alternative but to compensate at the prevailing level. It shouldn't, however, additionally be concluded that this package reflects the marginal product of the CEO. Rather, it's nothing more or less than the prevailing package, and the prevailing package simply reflects the prevailing practice of allowing CEOs to appoint board members who are then beholden to them. The resulting market pay is in fact simply the pay that's generated when non-market forces are allowed to affect the board's compensation decisions.

We don't of course mean to suggest that all economists see it this way. To the contrary, there's a large and powerful contingent of economists who instead view executive pay arrangements as the product of arm's length contracting between boards and executives, with the resulting compensation package indeed reflecting the marginal product of CEOs.[9] If existing corporate practices are delivering compensation that simply equals the value of the decisions the executive is making, then of course there's no market failure at all. The debate between economists who hold this view (i.e., the optimal contracting view) and those who reject it (i.e., the managerial power view) is long, acrimonious, and far from resolved.

Although we are deeply skeptical that existing governance practices can successfully deliver market pay, it goes well beyond our charge to review the relevant literature here and attempt to make that case. We will instead make the fallback point that one should at least avoid compensation practices that create the strong *appearance* of impropriety. It's possible that economists working within the optimal contracting view are entirely right that only the appearance of impropriety has been created and that at the end of the day compensation is efficient. But here's the rub: Even if this were true, the legitimacy of compensation practices are still everywhere doubted and called into question, and much corporate energy must accordingly be devoted to concealing, justifying, or explaining packages that the

---

9 Murphy, K. J., and J. Zabojnik. 2007. "Managerial Capital and the Market for CEOs." Working Paper, Queen's University; Gabaix, X., and A. Landier. 2008. "Why Has CEO Pay Increased so Much?" *Quarterly Journal of Economics* 123:49–100.

public and stockholders treat with much understandable suspicion. Because these packages are so public, the mere appearance of impropriety can lead to widespread cynicism about how fair our system is, with resulting costs in the form of increased disaffection and reduced initiative.

The upshot is that all of us, even those who hold to the optimal contracting view, should have an interest in setting up compensation practices that more plausibly generate the true market wage. We thus agree wholeheartedly with Roland Berger and Josef Ackermann that our remuneration systems need to be based on "real, bottom-line contributions to earnings, not on revenues, with vesting over several years." Although it's no easy task to develop such systems, Roland Berger and our contributors have advanced many sensible suggestions, including provisions for shareholder control (see Bertrand Collomb's and Gabriel Galateri's chapters) as well as "clawback mechanisms" to recoup bonuses due to transitory market events (see Josef Ackermann's chapter). We won't attempt to review such suggestions here. But the principle behind them should be clear: We must focus on compensating executives in ways that eliminate the appearance of impropriety and that plausibly approximate their marginal product.

This principle may seem obvious, but we were surprised that at least some of our business leaders don't wholly subscribe to it. It's useful in this regard to contrast two rather different approaches to reigning in compensation. The radical institutionalist approach, which we have been advocating here, entails recasting from the ground up the corporate institutions that generate pay packages, the objective being to eliminate the appearance of impropriety by developing practices that generate compensation rigorously in accord with product. We can, however, contrast our institutionalist approach with an alternative reformist approach that instead takes the existing corporate institutions as given and has us layering various pay-governing controls over those institutions. These additional controls may take the form, for example, of (a) internalized moral restraints on the amount of pay that executives should accept or be offered, (b) government regulations capping total compensation, (c) corporate pay scales constituting voluntary caps on compensation, or (d) government taxation of excessive compensation. Among the business leaders we interviewed, the preferred form of additional controls were not typically those emanating from government (i.e., government regulations or taxation), but instead were corporate-sponsored voluntary pay scales (see chapters by Poul Rasmussen and Maurice Lévy) or individualistic moral restraints (see chapters by Roland Berger, Gabriele Galateri, John Monks, Poul Rasmussen, and Jürgen Hambrecht).

These reformist approaches operate, it would seem, from the premise that two wrongs make a right. That is, they condition on deeply flawed institutions that are susceptible to non-market influence, yet instead of fixing those institutions they layer on top of them yet another non-market corrective (e.g., regulation). The evident premise is either that (a) two layers of non-market practices will, in conjunction, magically hit upon the true market wage, or (b) the main objective shouldn't be to capture that elusive competitive market wage but instead just to reign in compensation any way possible.

We think such cynicism underestimates the public and, in particular, their commitment to competitive markets. As we see it, the informed public wants nothing more or less than competitive market wages, and high levels of compensation are quite unproblematic in market-focused societies (e.g., U.S., U.K., Germany) when they're justifiable in market terms. There's much empirical evidence suggesting, for example, that the U.S. population is prepared to accept quite extreme inequality insofar as it's fairly generated under competitive market rules.[10] As Jürgen Hambrecht puts it, "people are more willing to tolerate differences in wealth if they can see a correlation between what a person earns and what they contribute to society." It's accordingly wrong to interpret the current public outrage about CEO pay as some mass protest against high compensation. It's rather a mass protest against corruption, against sweetheart deals, against foxes guarding the henhouse. If we're right on this point, the institutionalist approach is clearly preferred, and we should accordingly turn to developing corporate practices that will plausibly yield market pay.

Conclusion

We've argued here that there is much market failure in late-industrial societies, that such failure generates high inequality, and that market repair is our best bet for reducing inequality in a way that resonates well with our core commitments. The conventional wisdom is of course that competitive markets are inequality-generating machines and that perhaps the worst possible principle around which to build a commitment to equality is the market principle. This conventional formula confuses markets as they are with markets as they should be. In their current form, markets are indeed

---

[10] Hochschild, Jennifer. 1995. *Facing Up to the American Dream: Race, Class, and the Soul of the Nation.* Princeton: Princeton University Press.

inequality-generating machines, but that's mainly because they encompass various forms of closure, corruption, and supply bottlenecks that are inconsistent with a purely competitive market. If such market failure could be purged from the system, and we think it can, we would end up with strikingly less inequality. We have focused here on two especially important examples of this argument: (a) we first suggested that rising returns to schooling, well-appreciated as a main cause of rising inequality, arise because schooling is rationed in non-competitive ways; and (b) we next showed that excessive executive compensation is likewise rooted in non-competitive practices and that a market wage would likely be inequality-reducing.

We don't mean to suggest that inequality should exclusively be addressed via market repair. Although after-market redistribution is also an important tool for inequality reduction, it's too often assumed to be the only tool. The obvious problem with focusing exclusively on after-market intervention is that in some countries it's ideologically suspect and won't likely garner enough support to reduce inequality to palatable levels. The market principle is, by contrast, one of the core commitments of most late-industrial countries and hence a more promising base upon which to build anti-inequality initiatives.

About the Authors

Roland Berger, founder and Chairman of the international strategy consulting firm Roland Berger Strategy Consultants, also the founder of the Roland Berger Foundation.

David B. Grusky, Director, Stanford Center for the Study of Poverty and Inequality, and Professor, Department of Sociology, Stanford University.

Tobias Raffel, member of the Executive Board of the Roland Berger Foundation, graduated from London School of Economics (LSE), holds a Ph.D. from Potsdam University, Germany.

Geoffrey Samuels, business writer, graduated from Stanford University and the John F. Kennedy School of Government, Harvard University.

Christopher Wimer, Associate Director, Collaboration for Poverty Research, Stanford Center for the Study of Poverty and Inequality.

Partnering Institutions

Roland Berger Foundation

The Roland Berger Foundation, an independent public foundation under German civil law, was established in 2008 by Prof. Dr. h.c. Roland Berger. It is headquartered in Munich, Germany. The charitable goals of the Roland Berger Foundation are two-fold:

- Global preservation of human dignity: The Foundation is committed to respecting, supporting and protecting human dignity and human rights throughout the world. It promotes international understanding and tolerance, in order to foster a free and peaceful society in which all people can achieve their full potential. The Roland Berger Human Dignity Award recognizes individuals and organizations whose exemplary and successful endeavors promote human dignity, international understanding and tolerance. The annual EUR 1 million award endowment supports efforts in these areas.
- Educational advancement: The Roland Berger Foundation sponsors gifted youths from socially disadvantaged families. A scholarship program enables them to obtain a high-quality education and thereby achieve self-determination in their lives.

Stanford Center for the Study of Poverty and Inequality

The Center for the Study of Poverty and Inequality supports research and training on issues of social, economic, and political inequality. As a unit of the Institute for Research in the Social Sciences, the Center has approximately 125 Stanford faculty affiliates, over 400 national and international fellows, and an active program of visiting scholars. With funding from the Elfenworks Foundation, the Center brings scholars of poverty and inequality to Stanford University to teach classes, deliver public lectures, and develop new policy. The Center has partnered with the Kennedy School at Harvard University to form the Collaboration for Poverty Research, an initiative dedicated to taking on pressing domestic problems of poverty and inequality through research, policy analysis, and innovative dissemination. The Center sponsors the *Controversies in Inequality* book series with Stanford University Press and has launched a new magazine, *Pathways*, devoted to presenting trends in poverty and inequality and publicizing promising interventions and policies. The Center's web site, www.inequality.com, serves as a clearing house for research, videos, podcasts, and trend data on poverty and inequality. These and other activities are generously funded by the Elfenworks Foundation and Stanford University.

The manufacturer's authorised representative in the EU is Springer Nature Customer Service Centre GmbH, Europaplatz 3, 69115 Heidelberg, Germany. If you have any concerns regarding our products, please contact ProductSafety@springernature.com

Printed and bound by CPI Group (UK) Ltd, Croydon, CR0 4YY
30/09/2026
02225601-0008